LAURA SCHWARTZ is Career Development Fellow in History at St Hugh's College, University of Oxford. Her research interests are gender and radicalism in modern Britain, and she is currently working on her second book, 'Infidel Feminism: Secularism, Religion and Women's Emancipation, England, 1830–1914', to be published by Manchester University Press.

A SERIOUS ENDEAVOUR

Gender, Education and Community at St Hugh's,
1886–2011

LAURA SCHWARTZ

P

PROFILE BOOKS

To my sisters,
Bianca and Antonia

First published in Great Britain in 2011 by
Profile Books Ltd
3A Exmouth House
Pine Street
London EC1R 0JH

www.profilebooks.com

A CIP catalogue record for this book is available from the British Library.

ISBN 978 1 84668 515 6
eISBN 978 1 84765 780 0

Text design by Sue Lamble
sue@lambledesign.demon.co.uk
Typeset in Bembo by MacGuru Ltd
info@macguru.org.uk

Printed and bound in Britain by Clays, Bungay, Suffolk

FSC
Mixed Sources
Product group from well-managed
forests and other controlled sources
Cert no. SGS-COC-2061
www.fsc.org
© 1996 Forest Stewardship Council

The paper this book is printed on is certified by the © 1996 Forest Stewardship Council A.C. (FSC). It is ancient-forest friendly. The printer holds FSC chain of custody SGS-COC-2061

CONTENTS

ILLUSTRATIONS

A NOTE ON ARCHIVE SOURCES

The research for this book was undertaken while the St Hugh's College Archive was being re-catalogued. All material has been recorded under the old cataloguing system. Material for which the new cataloguing system was already in place has a second reference in parenthesis.

ACKNOWLEDGEMENTS

This book, perhaps more than most, was a collective endeavour to which an entire community contributed. It benefited from many conversations over college lunches, from the support of my colleagues, and from staff in every department of St Hugh's whose work made it possible for me to write its history. I hope that they will all recognise themselves somewhere in its pages.

Special thanks must go to Mary Clapinson for sharing her knowledge of the college with me; Amanda Ingram for her expertise in the archive; Rachel Rawlings for her support from the Development Office; and St Hugh's historians George Garnett, Patrick Healy, Gregg McClymont, Senia Paseta and John Robertson. Senia and John were kind enough to endure early versions of the manuscript, while draft chapters were also read by Julia Bush, Lucy Delap, Carol Dyhouse, Brian Harrison, Janet Howarth, Alison Light and Pat Thane. Their insightful comments were greatly appreciated, whether or not they were followed, and any errors remain my own.

Past and present students of St Hugh's were, of course, crucial to this project, particularly in guiding me towards unknown sources or under-explored corners of the college's history. Especially helpful were Penelope Rundle, Ann Soutter and Hannah Boston; as well as the Senior Students who completed the questionnaire and sent me their reminiscences. All those who agreed to become the subjects of oral history deserve special thanks, not only for giving me their time and their stories, but also for reminding me that history is populated by real people and that writing it can be complicated, dangerous and wonderful.

St Hugh's first students and Principal, 1887: Back row, left to right – Jessie Emmerson, Charlotte Jourdain, Wilhelmina de Lona Mitchell. Front row, left to right – Annie Moberly, Constance Ashburner, Grace Parsons. Wilhelmina de Lona Mitchell joined slightly after the four original students. (St Hugh's College Archive)

INTRODUCTION

St Hugh's College and the movement for women's education

AT FIRST GLANCE they are just another group of stiff and dully respectable Victorian ladies, dutifully posing to record the moment for institutional posterity. A closer look at this portrait of St Hugh's first students and Principal is, however, slightly more unsettling. Charlotte Jourdain has evidently been asked to demurely lower her eyes, but is she, in fact, frowning? And what are we to make of Grace Parsons's challenge to the camera as she stares directly back at us?

Whatever we might imagine to be the story behind this photograph, we are left in no doubt that it depicts a group of extremely serious young women. And rightly so, for, as pioneers of one of the first women's colleges, they had a hard task ahead of them. Buttoned up they may have been, but they were also on the front line of women's struggle to acquire knowledge and, with it, some kind of freedom. They were part of a wider movement for women's education, driven by women's rights advocates, university reformers and some sections of the Protestant churches, out of which St Hugh's came to be founded in 1886.

It is hard for us today to fully grasp what an immensely important symbol the right to education (especially the right to attend university) was for women in the nineteenth century. How, for instance, are we to interpret the 1869 pamphlet written on the apparently prosaic subject of girls' secondary schools, which suddenly ends with a call to:

Set free the women who sigh in the dark prison-houses, the captives of ignorance and folly. Cruel tyrants are these; slay them![1]

And why were so many so violently opposed to the idea of four young women gathering together in a house in North Oxford with the intention of studying for a few exams?

Answers to some of these puzzles only emerge once we begin to understand the extent to which St Hugh's was born into the grip of fierce debate on the very question of what it meant to be a woman. Calls for the improvement of female education arose out of a rapidly changing society, marked by recent industrialisation, the rise of a professional middle class, and the emergence of an organised women's movement. During the first half of the nineteenth century, the position of women was transformed as the majority of the population moved from the countryside into the cities and as work (that is, productive waged labour) moved out of the household, where a wife would have helped her husband in his trade, into the factory or office, from which she was, in theory, excluded. Changing patterns of labour and production were accompanied by changing ideas about what constituted manhood and womanhood, and femininity came to be increasingly identified with the home, family, emotional life and morality.

The emergence of a 'public' sphere of work and politics and a 'private' domestic sphere was an uneven, partial, and continually contested process. As the women pictured above testify, the Victorian woman cannot be reduced to the cliché of the 'Angel in the House' concerned only with bearing children and creating a domestic haven for her husband to return to after a hard day's work. Many, even middle-class, women continued to have to work to support themselves while others actively contributed to the world outside the home as writers, journalists, philanthropists, missionaries and church workers. Yet the ideological relegation of women to the domestic sphere did have important material implications – most particularly, for middle-class women, their exclusion from almost all paid professions and institutions of higher education.

From 1850 onwards, some women began to collectively organise against their exclusion from and lack of recognition within the public sphere, marking the beginning of a 'first wave' of British feminism. Education was one of the earliest and most enduring demands of the Victorian women's movement, for it represented the first hurdle in their struggle to participate on an equal basis with men as economically and politically active citizens. Without adequate education, women would not be able to find financially and intellectually rewarding work, nor would they be able to make responsible and reasoned decisions about how their country ought to be governed. Feminist thinkers earlier in the century had directly equated women's oppression with their enforced ignorance, and this theme was taken up by post-1850 activists such as Josephine Butler, who declared that, '[w]orse than bodily privations or pains … are these *aches and pangs of ignorance*'.[2] The early feminist periodical the *English Woman's Journal* (est. 1858) made education one of its central campaigning issues, decrying the extremely low standard of girls' secondary schools and the almost complete lack of higher education for women. One of its editors, Barbara Leigh Smith Bodichon, lamented that female talent was going to waste when it could be engaged in useful work for the betterment of society. 'We hear cries that the world is going wrong for want of women,' she wrote, 'that moral progress cannot be made without their help', and yet how were women to carry out their moral mission if they remained barred from the universities and prevented from taking up meaningful professions?[3]

Feminist arguments were also strongly moralistic and highly critical of the enforced idleness of the idealised vision of the middle-class wife engaged in neither household labour (performed by servants) nor professional occupation.[4] Such idleness robbed women not only of their independence, but also their dignity: 'It is to the last degree indecent,' protested Elizabeth Wolstenholme, member of the North of England Council for the Education of Women, 'that women should be dependent upon marriage for a professional maintenance.'[5] Yet demand for women's education was not merely an abstract principle but also a question of pressing necessity, for it was becoming increasingly clear that many women were not able to rely upon a husband or father to support them financially. The 1851 census recorded 876,920 'surplus' women, and in 1861 Josephine Butler estimated that at least two fifths of women were unmarried, and one quarter of married women were compelled to perform some labour to maintain themselves and their families.[6] Without adequate training or employment, middle-class women were forced into low-paid positions of genteel drudgery, most commonly as teachers or governesses. Their lack of education was widely perceived to be an 'evil' not only for the women who entered these professions, but also for the children they were so ill-equipped to teach.[7] As well as better training for teachers, feminists wanted women to be educated to enter a variety of professions – the more radical among them arguing that women could work as medical doctors, as managers of hospitals, workhouses, prisons and charitable institutions, and also go into farming or business.[8]

The women's movement may have been the most vocal and forceful advocate of the need to improve female education, but the institutional developments that occurred during this period were driven by a variety of agendas. Many of the first professionally run girls' schools were often led by women with connections to women's rights networks, such as the North London Collegiate School, established in 1850 by Frances Buss, and Cheltenham Ladies' College, established in 1854 and presided over by Dorothea Beale from 1858.[9] Their high academic standards and ethos of public service marked an important shift away from the more 'domestic' model of privately run girls' schools which had proliferated in the first half of the century.[10] After 1870, however, the government also played an important role in establishing secondary schools for girls, reflecting a desire to rationalise and reform Britain's education system generally.[11] A more competitive and meritocratic form of education was also championed by some of the 'leading lights of liberalism' at Oxford and Cambridge, whose support for the founding of women's colleges was only one element of their drive to modernise the ancient universities and ensure that they were not superseded by the more professionally-orientated colleges growing up in London, Manchester and other provincial towns.[12] The Church of England also helped to establish a number of girls' schools and women's colleges during this period, for it was keen to retain some influence in an area of education in which non-denominationalism was rapidly gaining a foothold.[13]

The first higher education establishment for women was founded by Christian Socialists Frederick Denison Maurice and Charles Kingsley in London in 1848. Queen's College was initially set up to provide training for governesses, though they soon found that many 'ladies' of a slightly higher social standing were also keen to attend their lecture series. This was followed by the Unitarian Elizabeth Jesser Reid's Bedford College London in 1849, which, like Queen's, was not residential but simply provided a base for lectures and classes often delivered by male academics from the University of London.[14] Throughout the 1860s and 70s, Ladies' Educational Associations were set up in most large

English towns, attracting a mixture of prominent local residents and church members, wives and daughters of university men, women's rights advocates, and other reform-minded members of the community. Along with helping to organise 'lectures for ladies', they also pushed for girls to be allowed to sit for Local Examinations and lobbied their nearby universities for access and facilities.[15] Such associations played a key role in eventually persuading universities to open first their classes, and then their degrees, to women. The University of London was the first to do so in 1878 (admitting women to all degrees except medicine), and by 1897 the university at Manchester also accepted women students in all subjects bar medicine and engineering.

Yet the journey thus far had not been an easy one, and by the end of the nineteenth century women were still a long way from being fully accepted into the universities. Many continued to question the wisdom of educating women outside the home, and support for women's right to higher education was still a minority position.[16] Wholesale opposition remained both within and outside the universities. Women's intellects, it was claimed, were insightful, sensitive and ill-suited to the rational, evidence-based judgements that academic scholarship required. It was also feared that women were not physiologically equipped to deal with the rigours of university education, which would threaten their capacity to bear children. And because their vocation in life was supposed to be different from men's, it was seen as pointless and cruel to educate them beyond their sphere as wives and mothers. Those who did manage to acquire an education were abhorred as aberrations – unwomanly women for whom the acquisition of reason had destroyed their natural femininity.[17] Resistance to women's higher education was perhaps strongest at the formerly monastic universities of Oxford and Cambridge, where women were not admitted to degrees until 1920 and 1947 respectively.

The first women's college to consciously model itself on the ancient universities was founded in 1869 by the *English Woman's Journal* editor, Emily Davies. Davies's Girton College was joined at Cambridge in 1871 by Newnham College, founded by Anne Jemima Clough and university reformer Henry Sidgwick, with the support of the North of England Council for the Higher Education of Women (est. 1867).[18] The women's colleges at Oxford were not established until slightly later, although the ground began to be prepared in 1867 when the Delegacy of Local Examinations asked Oxford University's Hebdomadal Council for the power to examine girls as well as boys. In 1873, a future member of St Hugh's Council, the seventeen-year-old Annie Rogers, came top in the 'Senior Locals', winning Exhibitions to Worcester and Balliol College which were quickly withdrawn once college officials discovered she was a girl. Two years later women began to be allowed to sit for University exams, corresponding to Oxford's Responsions, Moderations and Final Schools.[19]

The women's colleges at Oxford grew up in a somewhat haphazard fashion. Certainly they could not have been established except in a more general atmosphere of university reform, prompted by the Royal Commissions set up to investigate the ancient universities and the subsequent Acts of Parliament in 1854 and 1877. These ended the Church of England's monopoly and finally permitted dons to marry. Yet women's education was not a central concern of either the Commissioners or the reformers who championed them, and no systematic plan was laid down to extend Oxford's privileges to women.[20] It has been suggested that the lack of central planning may have made things easier, for, unlike suffrage campaigners, supporters of women's education did not have to wait for an Act of Parliament or require the support of political parties. Instead, women's education was pursued in a localised manner, looking to personal initiative and friendly individuals within already existing institutions. In theory, anyone who wished to establish a women's college simply did so, and at Oxford they were set up without any official recognition from the University. The collegiate system, which allowed individual colleges a large degree of autonomy, was also a helpful precedent, especially the tradition of Private Halls whose main purpose was simply to provide accommodation. Anyone could set up a Private Hall, and the 1854 Oxford Act had especially encouraged their establishment as a speedy and convenient way of bringing about reform without having to confront the University head-on.[21]

In 1878 a committee was formed which included the Principal of Keble and future Bishop of Winchester, Edward Talbot; the university reformer Mark Pattison; the leading liberal thinker T. H. Green; the well-known preacher Dr Liddon of Christ Church; and the author and women's educationalist Mary Ward. By 1879 the committee had divided into two camps: those who wished to open a non-denominational Hall went on to set up Somerville while those who believed that women needed to be educated on a definite Anglican basis founded Lady Margaret Hall (LMH). These colleges soon began to flourish under the governance of Councils made up of both men and women.[22] St Hugh's, by contrast, began as Elizabeth Wordsworth's personal project after she received an unexpected windfall. Wordsworth (1840–1932), who was already Principal of LMH, used the money to rent a house in Norham Road where the first four students took up residence in 1886. This small venture was rather grandly named St Hugh's Hall after St Hugh of Avalon, as a tribute to Wordsworth's father who, like St Hugh, had been Bishop of Lincoln. Wordsworth may have been seeking to free herself from the bureaucracy of a college Council (with which she co-governed LMH) while also intending that St Hugh's should only ever exist as a satellite to the older college.

Wordsworth retained complete authority over St Hugh's until 1891, when a governing committee was first formed, consisting of Annie Moberly (1846–1937, St Hugh's first Principal) and men and women otherwise unconnected to the college. Yet Wordsworth continued to see herself as the head of St Hugh's, and in 1893–4 she attempted to amalgamate it with LMH, without even consulting St Hugh's committee. LMH, however, rejected the offer and St Hugh's went on to flourish as an independent institution thanks to the hard work of Annie Moberly, who, from the very beginning, asserted herself as the Principal of a third women's hall rather than simply the 'housekeeper' that Wordsworth envisaged. In 1894–5 St Hugh's acquired its first constitution, an important step which transferred the property of the Hall over to four Trustees, of which Wordsworth was one. A governing Council was formed which included St Hugh's tutors Annie Rogers and Edith Wardale, and marked the first step towards the self-governance enjoyed at many, though not all, of the men's colleges.[23] Although the Principal had considerable authority in the day-to-day running of the college, the Council met monthly and made binding decisions on issues such as employment, fees and scholarships. St Hugh's independent status was assured in 1897 when Clara Mordan visited the college and announced her intention of becoming its patron: she immediately pledged £1,000 for a scholarship with the promise of further support.

Eleanor Jourdain, whose sister Charlotte had been one of the college's first four students, joined St Hugh's as Vice-Principal in 1902. Student numbers had increased year on year, and by 1891 fifty students had 'graduated' from St Hugh's, though the University still refused to grant them degrees.[24] Wordsworth rented successive properties in Norham Road, Norham Gardens and Fyfield Road to cater for the expanding college, but having students spread out over a number of houses was far from ideal and in 1913 the Council purchased the leasehold of a site on St Margaret's Road with the hope of constructing permanent college buildings. Plans threatened to stall with the outbreak of war in 1914, but the work continued thanks to Jourdain and Moberly's perseverance and a timely legacy from Clara Mordan the following year. Headed by its new Principal Eleanor Jourdain (appointed 1915), St Hugh's moved into Main Building in January 1916. The original plans were eventually completed in 1928, with the erection of the Mary Gray Allen wing, named after Clara Mordan's companion, who bequeathed the rest of Mordan's estate to the college. Moberly and Jourdain had correctly predicted that the war would increase the number of women applying to university. In 1916 they had 64 resident students, 81 in 1917, 107 in 1919, and in 1920 women were finally made members of Oxford University and permitted to read for degrees.[25]

By 1923 St Hugh's had become the largest women's college with 151 undergraduates. Yet its future survival was seriously threatened the following year by the constitutional crisis arising from 'The Row' between Eleanor Jourdain and history tutor Cecilia Ady. Ady's unfair dismissal led to a walkout by the other tutors and a boycott of St Hugh's by the rest of the University, amounting to a scandal that culminated in Jourdain's sudden death from a heart attack in April 1924. St Hugh's, however, was experienced in battling on in the face of adversity, and the college managed to survive this painful period under the guardianship of Principal Barbara Gwyer. Gwyer also held St Hugh's together during the Second World War, when it was evacuated to Holywell Manor on St Cross Road while its buildings were used as a military hospital. Evelyn Procter took over in 1946, and in 1959 she became the first St Hugh's Principal to be granted equal status with the male heads of colleges, when what had been previously known as the five women's 'societies' were finally recognised as colleges. St Hugh's continued to grow under the Principalship of Kathleen Kenyon in the 1960s when more and more female students competed for the very limited number of places available to women at Oxford. The unfair exclusion of female applicants from the vast majority of colleges was one of the arguments put forward in support of co-residency from 1972 onwards. St Hugh's, however, only began to admit men in 1986, after a number of years' soul-searching and serious discussion of the college's founding mission and future identity.

The last history of St Hugh's was published on the cusp of this definitive moment, and it both celebrated the achievement of one hundred years of women's education and mourned the end of its life as a college exclusively for women.[26] Men have now been at St Hugh's for almost a quarter of a century, and both Principals since Rachel Trickett (1973–91) have been male (Derek Wood, 1991–2003; and Andrew Dilnot, 2003–). Its time as an all-female community is a more and more distant memory while, throughout Oxford, the notion of a single-sex college is fast becoming something of an anathema.[27] Gender, whether we are discussing individual women, social relations between the sexes, or ideals of masculinity and femininity, nevertheless remains crucial to understanding the development of St Hugh's. An analysis which pays attention to how women's role has been continually redefined over the course of the period, and what meanings are given to the categories of 'male' and 'female' in an educational context, is therefore central to this book.

St Hugh's institutional identity – how its members understood it and how others perceived it – was inextricably bound up with ideas about who women were, how they should behave, and what role the college ought to have in producing them. Supporters of women's education varied in their willingness to challenge those who opposed women's entry into the universities on the

grounds that they were inherently different from men and therefore unsuited to a masculine form of education. Emily Davies
argued that 'there is between the sexes a deep and broad basis
of likeness' and she felt that only good would come of enabling
women to take a greater part in the intellectual and public life
of men. She preferred a method of training that sought to culti-
vate the 'common human element', rather than one that began
by 'dividing mankind into two great sections and forcing each
into a mould'. Although Davies claimed not to question the existence of 'distinctive manhood and womanhood', she asserted
that while women continued to be denied the opportunity to
develop their intellectual powers, it was not possible to say what
was 'naturally' feminine and what was merely the result of 'convention'. At Girton, Davies insisted that her young women study
the same curriculum as male students, sit for all the examinations, and complete the degree in the same time allowed to other
undergraduates. Davies believed that if women did not strive to
achieve the same standards as men, their qualifications would be
disregarded.[28] Those at Newnham, however, argued that it was
pointless for women to 'slavishly' follow the outdated curriculum which so many reform-minded Cambridge dons were fighting to change. Newnham students were therefore permitted to
follow a self-guided course of study, and instead of Greek and
Latin for the degree examinations, they studied new subjects such
as history and English literature.[29]

Newnham's decision reflected a different approach to
women's education, which, while entirely compatible with
strong support for women's rights, emphasised the importance
and value of distinctively 'womanly' characteristics. Newnham's
supporter Josephine Butler complained of certain (unnamed)
advocates of women's education who 'speak of women as if it
were a compliment to them, or in any way true, to say that they

are like men'. The best kind of education would, in Butler's view, actively encourage 'every good quality, every virtue which we regard as feminine' to 'develop more freely'.[30] This did not mean that Newnham wanted to feminise its curriculum, but more that, without Davies's preoccupation with meeting male standards, Clough could open her doors to a much more diverse body of students who had not necessarily had the training to pass the entrance examinations required at Girton.[31] The question of women following an identical curriculum to men was never as sharply posed in Oxford as in Cambridge. The original statute which permitted women to be examined for equivalent exams to men did not make Greek or Latin obligatory (many female students lacked their brothers' classical training), though women were permitted to attend most lectures and classes alongside male undergraduates.[32] St Hugh's followed Newnham's more flexible approach and did not require its students to sit for examinations until after the First World War, though many of them chose to do so long before it became compulsory. Elizabeth Wordsworth and Annie Moberly also promoted a vision of women's education rooted in ideas of sexual difference and women's distinctive contribution to doing God's work in the world. Chapter 1 discusses this religious tradition that permeated St Hugh's throughout its early years, particularly the High Anglican vision of women, faith and knowledge promoted by bishops' daughters Wordsworth and Moberly. It looks at how these ideas related to both more explicitly feminist currents within the women's movement and those sections of the Church of England hostile to women's rights.[33]

Many of St Hugh's Victorian values, especially the investment in its all-female identity, remained important into the interwar period, in spite of the significant changes that this era ushered in. Chapter 2 explores St Hugh's as a 'women's community', looking at how this shaped the college and the relationships that formed within it. The newly emerging professionalism of female academics and the changes to women's role precipitated by the Great War all contributed to the tensions which led up to 'The Row' in 1924. St Hugh's foundation was bound up with sexually specific attitudes to education and segregated social practices. Adapting to the post-1945 University, in which most of the formal barriers separating men and women had been removed, thus posed serious challenges. Chapter 3 looks at the ambivalent attitude of the postwar generation of dons to St Hugh's older tradition of feminism, and at their struggle to compete as equals within a male-dominated university. Should women be treated exactly the same as men, or ought there to be fuller acknowledgement of the difficulties they faced on account of their sex? We encounter this question at every stage in the history of St Hugh's, and it was returned to with renewed passion in the 1970s and 80s when Oxford colleges gradually began to go mixed.

History was frequently invoked in the co-residency debates, for this was also a period during which a new movement for women's liberation inspired many historians to re-examine the development of the women's colleges from an explicitly feminist perspective. The new histories questioned some of the more triumphalist versions of the struggle for women's education, and pointed to the incipient inequalities that lingered on after women had received formal recognition.[34] The supposed benefits of the cautious and assimilationist approach of the early women educationalists were also more closely scrutinised, leading one historian to conclude that the reformers 'bought intellectual freedom at the price of political timidity, a frequent fear of change and a dislike of innovation … they might have gained more by daring more'.[35] The question of whether the struggle for education ought to be read as part of a general narrative of women's emancipation is addressed in Chapter 4, which looks at the history of

St Hugh's domestic workers. The movement for higher education was unquestioningly geared towards the interests of middle-class women, and the class tensions inherent within their
vision of freedom clearly emerge when we turn our attention to
those women who cooked, cleaned and cared for the rest of the
college.[36] Yet the story of class at St Hugh's is not a straightforward
one, for, despite being part of a highly elite institution, the college
was always something of an outsider. All the women's colleges
were seen as rather déclassé compared to the ancient grandeur
of the men's colleges, while their limited endowments subjected
them to relative poverty. St Hugh's was, furthermore, known as
the place for girls who couldn't afford to go to Lady Margaret
Hall. Chapter 5 explores the legacy of St Hugh's commitment
to lower fees, and situates it within a wider history of higher-
education funding in the twentieth century. From the struggles
of grammar school girls in the 1930s, to the student radicals of
the 1970s, to the free education activists after 1998, asking 'who'
education should be for also leads us to consider 'what' it is for.
The final chapter returns us to some of the questions asked by the
college's founders: what kind of educational experience should St
Hugh's offer and to what ends should its students be educated?

Writing this new history of St Hugh's posed the difficult question of how one tells a story which is at once your own yet also
that of so many others – all of whom have experienced it in their
own distinctive ways. This author is a member of the community
of which she writes, an 'insider historian' with privileged access
to sources which include not only the archive but also oral tradition, the physical environment, and the living memories of those
around me. The danger, however, of such insider status is that it
will lead to a 'cosy' anecdotal account, with too great a focus on
past achievements.[37] The pressure to write an optimistic history is
especially present in the case of the women's colleges, for there are

good reasons why one might wish to portray women's struggle for education as a story with a happy ending. We must, therefore, be even more wary of narratives of progress which obscure problematic aspects of an institution's development. This history of St Hugh's strives to go beyond an insider's perspective, and position the college within the broader history of education, feminism and changing gender roles in nineteenth- and twentieth-century Britain. It seeks an unbiased assessment of St Hugh's contribution to the provision of university education for women: how it managed new generations of students and negotiated changing social mores; how it responded to wider political upheavals; and how it secured its position within the higher education establishment.

Yet this 'scholarly' approach does not claim to be more 'objective', for I am acutely aware of the extent to which it is imprinted with my own experiences as a student and then a Fellow at St Hugh's. Understanding subjectivity and memory have been crucial to writing this history. Not only have I had to examine my own assumptions about which aspects of college life warrant historical exploration, but I have also worked with the reminiscences of hundreds of others, all of which tell a different and sometimes contradictory story. Far from being safely locked away in the past, many of my historical subjects are very much part of the present, capable of answering back and providing alternative versions of events. Rather than avoid the institutional nature of St Hugh's history, this book uses it as a framework for understanding the interrelationship between personal experiences and collective accounts. It asks how St Hugh's developed its institutional identity, how this changed over time, how it both reproduced and resisted dominant social norms, and how it shaped the values and aspirations of its members. An institutional perspective allows us to go beyond looking simply at the relationship between women's colleges and the male university, to highlight internal hierarchies and power dynamics *within* St Hugh's. Rather than conceptualise the college as a staging post in the life of a single type of St Hugh's member, this book approaches it as a place in which various groups of women (and later men) worked and interacted to create a unique community.

1

FOUNDING IMPULSES

Women, faith and knowledge, 1886–1914

W HEN ELIZABETH WORDSWORTH founded St Hugh's in 1886, the new Hall possessed two defining features. The first of these was that it was intended for students who could not afford the fees charged at Lady Margaret Hall, where Wordsworth was already Principal. This pledge was quickly found to be impractical and St Hugh's soon did away with its more modest prices, though the early intention to provide for less wealthy students continued to shape St Hugh's identity well into the twentieth century. The commitment to lower fees was, however, closely connected to a second feature which did remain at the heart of St Hugh's constitution: that it should be an explicitly Church of England establishment. In fact, the main reason that Wordsworth proposed St Hugh's ought to welcome students of lesser financial means was to provide for the daughters of impoverished Anglican clergymen who might otherwise be compelled to send them to non-sectarian places of education.[1] St Hugh's was intended to be not only a Christian college, but, most specifically, an institution infused with a form of High Church Anglicanism inspired by the Tractarianism that had swept through Oxford in the 1840s, 50s and 60s. Such religion also determined the social and intellectual milieu of both Elizabeth Wordsworth and Annie Moberly, and it was their shared heritage that prompted Wordsworth to employ Moberly as St Hugh's first Principal.

The contribution of the Church of England to women's education has been the subject of much historical debate, with the outspoken opposition of many leading clergy hard to reconcile with the fact that three out of four women's colleges at Oxford were Anglican institutions. Mapping the intellectual and social networks of Wordsworth, Moberly and other key figures in the founding of St Hugh's, and looking more closely at the kind of education they promoted, reveals a distinctive Church of England vision of women's education which incorporated ideas propounded by both Anglican opponents and supporters of the women's colleges. Historians have also argued over how to position the movement for women's education in relation to the first wave of activism around women's rights during this period, asking if figures such as Wordsworth and Moberly ought to be described as 'feminist'. They have struggled to understand the paradox of a group of women who preached caution while facing down considerable opposition in their efforts to establish places of female learning. Oxford women, especially those around Lady Margaret Hall and St Hugh's, were even more conservative than their Cambridge counterparts, and some of them opposed female suffrage. Their ambiguous position can better be understood, however, if it is framed in terms of a distinctive form of High Anglican feminism. Although St Hugh's was considered to be one of the more conservative of the women's colleges, by the early decades of the twentieth century it combined a continued commitment to Church values with an explicit, though sometimes contradictory, feminist identity.

The Anglican inheritance

The importance of religion to the establishment of St Hugh's reflected the central place it occupied in the lives of its founders Elizabeth Wordsworth and Annie Moberly. For Moberly's appointment as Principal of the new women's college was based upon her Anglican credentials rather than her academic qualifications. Charlotte Anne Elizabeth (always known as Annie) was close to the well-known High Church novelist Charlotte Yonge, and a family friend of the leading Tractarian Churchman John Keble.[2] Keble and Yonge preached a form of Anglo-Catholicism that remained loyal to the Church of England after many leading figures in the Oxford Movement, such as John Henry Newman, had gone over to Rome. The Anglo-Catholics upheld the Oxford Movement's belief in 'High Church principles' (the Catholicity of the Church of England, the Apostolic Succession, the centrality of the Sacraments, the importance of prayer and the beauty of holiness), seeking to position themselves against both the liberal theologians and the 'Protestantism' of the Evangelicals.[3] In defending the state monopoly of the Church of England and the privileges conferred on it over the Dissenting churches, the Tractarians emphasised the central role that the Church played in uniting the nation across the social classes. Far from promoting a complacent form of Anglicanism, however, the Oxford Movement had emerged at a crucial juncture in the history of the Church when each party sought in its own way to recreate a form of spirituality that would meet the needs of a rapidly changing society.

Annie Moberly later described the religious feeling with which she grew up as 'the self-controlled vivacity of high spiritual existence …' Theology was not a set of abstract principles or dry doctrines, but 'a thrilling interest' whereby one's every movement, speech and thought was imbued with the sense of 'unseen presences'.[4] The religious teachings of her elders remained with Moberly all her life. Her father, George, was a more moderate Anglo-Catholic than Keble, and politically more liberal – though he voted for the Conservatives because of their position on Church questions. The fierce party rivalry that characterised the Church during the middle decades of the century compelled George to ally himself more definitely with the Tractarians, alliances which also impacted upon the women in his family. For George Moberly's teaching of the catechism and Churchmanship at Winchester attracted the wrath of his Low Church opponents, and while he, as a result, was excluded from preaching anywhere in the diocese, his wife and daughters were barred from taking part in any parochial or district work that would normally have formed a central part of their duties.[5] Annie Moberly's fierce loyalty to her family and their religious principles never abated, and in 1911 she wrote *Dulce Domum*, which was not so much a biography of her father as a memorial to a lost world of cathedral cities, earnest theological discussion and a Christian morality that, while intensely spiritual, was never emotional or ostentatious.

Elizabeth Wordsworth's family occupied a very similar social and intellectual milieu. Wordsworth had also been strongly influenced by Charlotte Yonge, whom she met in Oxford in 1870.[6] Her brother John had succeeded George Moberly as Bishop of Salisbury, and it was here that Elizabeth first met Annie in 1885. Moberly went to stay with Wordsworth at Lady Margaret Hall during Lent the following year. Intending to visit for only a few days, she ended up remaining at the college for six weeks. Wordsworth must have reassured herself that Moberly was a woman from a world that she knew and trusted, for during the Easter vacation she invited Annie to become the first Principal of the not-yet-founded St Hugh's. In the months leading up to the opening of the college in the autumn of that year, Annie went back and forth between Salisbury and Oxford. At LMH she also met Eleanor Jourdain, then one of Wordsworth's students, and they soon struck up a friendship. Jourdain helped Moberly to prepare the residence in Norham Road, and together they measured walls and floors and discussed the furnishing and decoration of the new college. In the evenings, Eleanor Jourdain would sit in Moberly's room 'on the top floor at LMH, looking out on the trees of the Parks bathed in moonlight, and discuss Buddhism, which was much in vogue just then, the Jews, and much besides'.[7]

Annie Moberly was chosen by Wordsworth 'as someone to whose care anxious Church of England parents would be happy to entrust their adventurous daughters'.[8] That her academic record (or lack of it) had little bearing upon her appointment was nothing out of the ordinary, for the Oxford women's colleges were at this time primarily residential establishments rather than academic institutions. Tutorials and lectures took place under the aegis of an external body, the Association for the Education of Women, to which separate tuition fees were paid. Moberly may have been respectable, but she was not wealthy. In fact, she was in many ways typical of the Victorian women's movement's main constituency: those from middle-class backgrounds whose families were nevertheless unable to financially support their daughters should they fail to find a husband. Though the Moberly family had enjoyed a large degree of social prestige and Episcopal grandeur while George Moberly was alive, after his death his widow and unmarried daughters found themselves banished from the Bishop's Palace to a poky house in the town. For Annie, faced with the daunting question of how to earn a living, Wordsworth's offer came at just the right moment.[9]

Grateful as she was for the opportunity to head up St Hugh's, Moberly had to wrestle with a permanent sense that both the

college and its Principal were overshadowed by their counterparts across the road at Lady Margaret Hall.[10] Elizabeth Wordsworth was widely renowned as a charming and entertaining
woman, a popular figure on the Oxford academic social scene.
Annie Moberly was shy; and she was also aware that just as she
lacked Wordsworth's social confidence, St Hugh's lacked the prestige of LMH. Helena Deneke, who came up in 1900 to study at
St Hugh's and stayed on as one of its first tutors, remembered well
Miss Moberly's sensitivity about the college's supposedly inferior
status:

> Miss Wordsworth was sailing the crest of the wave while Miss
> Moberly felt she must struggle to swim. There had been no
> Bishop Talbot (then Warden of Keble) to invite her to be head
> of a budding college [Talbot had invited Wordsworth to take on
> LMH], no established Council of men and women to support
> her.[11]

Although, on the surface, relations between the two colleges
were more than amicable, Deneke remembered Moberly sometimes muttering under her breath that Wordsworth had created
St Hugh's as 'a rubbish heap' for LMH. Such a suspicion might
have been confirmed had Moberly seen the minutes of LMH
Council, which rejected Wordsworth's proposal that St Hugh's
be amalgamated into the larger college on the grounds that if
this were to happen, 'the tone and average standard would not be
quite so select and high'.[12] Furthermore, not only were the fees
at St Hugh's initially far lower than at LMH − £45 per annum
compared with £75 − but Annie Moberly's salary was a pitiful
£40 compared with the £100 Wordsworth received.[13]

Rather than dwell upon her difficult situation, however,
Moberly set her heart on seeing that 'her student body emerge
from the "rubbish heap" by virtue of moral and mental quality'.[14]

If Moberly could not depend upon well-known supporters or well-born students, she could look to her religious upbringing to provide her with the confidence necessary to undertake this task. A newspaper article advertising St Hugh's in its early years thus proudly declared that:

> The religious teaching is on the same lines as that at Lady Margaret Hall, and the name of Miss Moberly, the present Principal, is the more suggestive from the fact that she is avowedly in sympathy with the teaching of her father, who was thirty-one years the headmaster of Winchester.[15]

Joan Evans, another longstanding member of St Hugh's College who arrived as a student in 1914, found such constant reminders of Moberly's impressive family connections somewhat tiresome. 'We were never allowed to forget,' she recalled in her autobiography, that Moberly 'was the daughter of a man who had been successively Head-master of Winchester and Bishop of Salisbury'. Even she had to admit, however, that Moberly's upbringing had brought her into contact with a standard of scholarship that secured the credentials of the new Hall.[16]

Moberly never went to school but she was sometimes permitted to sit in on her brothers' tutorials, and otherwise picked up bits and pieces of learning from listening to the conversations that took place around her at Winchester and Salisbury. She remembered how 'books lined every room in the house ... and others were perpetually pouring in, and the Yonges kept us supplied with any number ...'[17] As a girl she had taught herself to read Hebrew and Greek, 'because she could not imagine anyone really caring for the Bible without wishing to read it in the original'.[18] Moberly's foremost task as Principal was to provide religious instruction, in keeping with Wordsworth's vision of St Hugh's as an avowedly Church of England institution. In a lecture to the Church Congress on women's education in 1894 Wordsworth insisted on 'the absolute necessity of a religious element – if possible a chapel, certainly daily prayers, and some religious training …' This had been her condition for accepting her own Principalship, and she later wrote that 'I should not have cared to go near LMH, if it had not been for the *definite* Church basis'. Wordsworth had not wanted any non-Anglican students to attend LMH, though she was persuaded to include a conscience clause in its constitution.[19] St Hugh's followed the same pattern: prospective students did not have to pass a religious test but the college was advertised as being for Church of England students.[20] St Hugh's Council was entirely made up of Anglican members, though in 1910, after a long argument, it was agreed that only a majority of members need be, so that no distinguished educationalists would be ruled out.[21] The first scholarships at St Hugh's were open only to Church of England women,[22] and in 1889 Wordsworth offered a scholarship specifically for religious knowledge, though this was not renewed.[23] The religious constitution was adhered to in the face of some disadvantages. An appeal for funds made in 1913 reminded readers that because St Hugh's was 'a Church of England College' it was not therefore eligible for assistance from any public bodies.[24]

Sunday evening Bible classes and lectures were compulsory at St Hugh's, and also offered Annie Moberly her main opportunity to shine – showing herself to be a Churchwoman and scholar worthy of her father. Moberly subsequently published her lectures on the faith of the Prophets and the Book of Revelation,[25] though her former student Edith Olivier believed that 'the printed page completely fails to reproduce the impression given during those evenings in the sitting room' when Moberly was 'carried away by the wonders of these visions'.[26] The centrality of religion to the lives of women such as Wordsworth and

Moberly is not easily translated into twenty-first-century sensi-
bilities. Moberly's religious publications prove especially frustrating: their subject is strictly, one might say drily, theological, and
the detailed biblical exegesis initially appears to be of little interest to the cultural historian. Yet if we can make the leap of imagination required to grasp the importance and intensity of these
religious questions to Moberly, Wordsworth, and their students,
we gain enormously in our understanding of what drove these
women and how the early identity of St Hugh's was formed. At
a time when women were barred not only from any position of
authority in the Church of England, but also from parliament
and the majority of professions, interpreting the Holy Book for
public audiences offered a rare opportunity to exert cultural and
intellectual authority. Lucille Iremonger, a graduate and rather
unsympathetic chronicler of St Hugh's, provided an insightful
account of the transformative effect that the assumption of such
authority had upon Miss Moberly:

> This short, stout woman in her forties, so shy and tongue-tied in
> social conversation, so cold and austere in the habits of her daily
> life, became another person on these weekly occasions. The dark,
> short-sighted eyes would flash beneath the heavy eyebrows that
> almost met, and the plain face would light up as she poured forth
> a flood of fantastic imagery ... She became a different person.[27]

Religion, for these women, was bound up with a powerful sense of moral purpose and social duty. Such seriousness can
again appear trying or alienating to the modern reader – certainly
Elizabeth Wordsworth's continual emphasis on disciplining one's
desires in order to practise acts of self-sacrifice hardly strikes a
chord with a more modern form of feminism.[28] And yet serious
moral intention was central to the nineteenth-century women's
movement. To renounce the superficial values of middle-class

womanhood in favour of embarking upon a course of moral or religious struggle was itself a form of rebellion. And it is this aspect of Moberly and Wordsworth's religious inheritance that provides a way into understanding their commitment to women's education.

Visions of women's education

The contribution of the Church of England, or rather the kind of High Anglicanism promoted at St Hugh's, has only recently been attended to in histories of the movement for women's education. Anglicanism is more frequently remembered for its opposition than for the inspiration it also provided.[29] Annie Rogers (1856–1937), a longstanding member of the St Hugh's Council, recalled the hostile response of sections of the clergy when women were for the first time permitted to sit for University examinations in 1884. She remembered especially Dean John William Burgon's sermon to the University of Oxford entitled 'To Educate Young Women Like Young Men, and with Young Men – A Thing Inexpedient and Immodest'. Burgon condemned the members of Convocation who had voted to allow women into examinations, and warned them that they would soon come to regret their actions when Oxford was overrun with 'strong minded women of advanced opinions'. He based his arguments on the Book of Genesis, which, he maintained, taught that God had created man and woman differently and intended them to perform separate roles. Women had no need to cram their heads in preparation for competitive examinations, nor should they have classical learning 'defile that lovely spirit with the filth of old world civilisation'. Instead, Burgon claimed, 'Woman's strength lies in her essential weakness'; she was intended to be man's helpmate, not his rival, and although she might excel in many areas of 'knowledge', she had no need of the professionalised form of 'instruction' offered at the University.[30]

Burgon's misogynistic sermon has been pointed to by subsequent historians as typical of clerical hostility to women's education.[31] The Dean's position was couched in distinctively High Church theological terms, and he defended his literal interpretation of Genesis against those liberal Anglicans who preferred to read Scripture as a collection of historical accounts that could be reconsidered in light of modern values.[32] Yet Annie Rogers did not believe that Burgon represented the voice of Oxford's Anglican majority. In fact, when he unleashed his vitriol, she claimed, the congregation simply burst out laughing.[33] The historian Janet Howarth has recently argued for a more nuanced account of the influence of the Church of England on women's education. Pointing out that LMH, St Hugh's and St Hilda's were all Church institutions, she maintained that the Anglican contribution to women's education was 'cumulatively very significant'. This was in part due to its decentralised and pluralised structure, allowing a variety of initiatives to grow up, so that the Church should not be characterised as having a uniformly conservative impact. Howarth also began to identify a distinctively High Church vision of the higher education of women, which saw education as desirable if directed towards religious ends. In practice this could lead to an ambiguous attitude towards the wider movement for women's education on the part of those who helped to found LMH and St Hugh's.[34]

Many of Wordsworth's and Moberly's religious friends were initially unsure of their support for the women's colleges. Charlotte Yonge and Christopher Wordsworth (Elizabeth's father) followed Dean Burgon in advocating a traditional interpretation of Scripture, believing that God had created woman to serve man.[35] Charlotte Yonge wrote unenthusiastically to Elizabeth when she heard that she was taking up the Principalship of LMH, and warned her against creating 'merely a boarding house run on good principles where young ladies may be sent to prepare for examinations'.[36] Likewise, Elizabeth's brother John, who by this point had replaced Annie Moberly's father as Bishop of Salisbury, seemed to think that Elizabeth's main task was one of damage limitation. '[I]f I thought your not going would put an end to the whole thing,' he wrote to his sister, 'I should say, Don't go; but as I don't suppose it will, I think you had better accept.'[37] In 1884, Christopher Wordsworth published a sermon on 'Christian Womanhood', dedicated to 'his dear daughter … Principal of Lady Margaret Hall'. This sermon could easily be read as a conservative warning against the movement for women's education, and Dean Burgon quoted from it extensively to support his pronouncements against the entry of women to University examinations. Christopher Wordsworth spoke on the Book of Genesis and St Paul's writings on women, both of which affirmed that woman was subordinate to man and that her glory lay in deriving her authority from him. Wordsworth also condemned the competitive and ambitious 'self-display' that he believed the newly professionalised girls' schools encouraged when they entered their students into public examinations.[38]

Yet Wordsworth's sermon was prefixed with a prayer that God might give His blessing to his daughter's project at Oxford, and he by no means ruled out the possibility of higher education colleges for women. What mattered was the *kind* of education they provided. Christopher Wordsworth concluded by declaring that 'the only true "Higher Education of Woman" is that which trains her to look upward to God'. By this he did not mean that women should be restricted solely to religious study; science was important to comprehend God's workings in the 'natural world', while women would also benefit from the poetry of Classical civilisation. What *was* crucial, insisted Christopher, was that intellectual endeavours be directed towards spiritual ends. There was nothing worse than a woman who pursued academic achievement for her own glory, in order to assert her independence from men by earning her own livelihood. But a woman who gained a greater knowledge of the world so as to better illuminate her understanding of God working within it could only contribute to His glory. Furthermore, as the guardians of true religion, women had a vital role to play in the Church's battle against the forces of secularisation. 'If they receive "higher education" in the true sense of the word,' wrote Christopher Wordsworth, 'they might do much to check the poison of Unbelief in modern society.'[39]

Ten years later, Elizabeth Wordsworth delivered an Address to the Church Congress at Exeter in which she elaborated upon this view of the *First Principles in Women's Education*. She too used the Book of Genesis as her starting point, agreeing that God had intended woman to be the helpmate of man. Yet for Elizabeth, this was to be interpreted as 'Not merely one woman for one man; but all women for all men'. In other words, God had bestowed upon women a special duty to society, which was to be achieved through the right kind of higher education.[40] She also made this point in her Sunday evening sermons to her students at Oxford: '[D]o let me remind you dear girls that the future of the country is very largely in the hands of yourselves.' Far from being restricted to their lives in the home, to the needs only of their husbands and children, her students were trained to shape the whole of society through individual acts of self-sacrifice, religious devotion and pure moral conduct.[41] Wordsworth believed that one of the most important reasons for women to educate themselves was to enable them to become religious teachers, and this applied equally whether they intended to marry, teach, or to take on more professional roles within the Church. Women should have the requisite knowledge to read and interpret the Bible accurately, and to defend the writings of the Church Fathers and Anglican Divines against secularising forces that sought to oust the Church of England from its position at the heart of the nation.[42]

Elizabeth Wordsworth was therefore operating within the same religious framework as her father and other Anglican critics of the women's colleges, while at the same time supporting an expanded public role for women. Rather than reject the claims of the wider women's movement for improved educational opportunities, Wordsworth argued that these needed to be met with a specifically Anglican vision. The Church thus had a duty to provide for women's education, to 'keep pace' with the rest of the women's movement. It was up to the Church to ensure that 'advanced women' were not lured away by irreligious institutions that promised them intellectual enlightenment.[43] Elizabeth was also, like Burgon and her father, concerned that educated women might be introduced to an 'irreligious system of philosophy' that threatened their true role as guardians of the faith. But she turned around the conservative logic of her male peers to argue for greater action on the part of the Church to ensure that women received the proper kind of higher education: one that was firmly rooted in Church principles. Wordsworth and Moberly believed that women's intellectual development ought only to occur as part of their spiritual development – their education must therefore be about far more than simply passing examinations. Rather than have 'facts … ruthlessly and unremittingly shovelled into her brain', a girl's poetic and spiritual imagination ought to be nourished and attended to at all times.[44]

This essentially religious perspective on the principles of women's education was clearly incompatible with the approach of Emily Davies and her supporters at Girton, who insisted that female students strictly follow the existing University curriculum and take the same examinations as male undergraduates. LMH and St Hugh's favoured greater flexibility for female students and did not require them to take the full degree course. Practical reasons for this decision were bound up with a belief in feminine difference, grounded in Scriptural accounts of the Creation. Wordsworth believed that, rather than deny the differences between the sexes, women should celebrate them.[45] While sermonising to her students she declared, 'Put women into whatever circumstances you will, they (happily for the world) will always remain women.'[46]

While this emphasis on essential womanly qualities was in many ways conservative, it also countered the arguments of those who warned that women who attended university would be shorn of their femininity. Such a position was not in conflict with the views of many in the wider women's movement who also valued what they believed to be the distinctive characteristics of their sex, but it did have ambiguous implications for the development of women's education. As the Girtonians had argued, for women's qualifications to be taken seriously they needed to conform to established male standards. Female students therefore needed to take the degree examinations for their university education to be properly recognised. Annie Rogers also believed that although '[i]ndividual students have no doubt received considerable advantage by the liberty granted them to vary the degree course ... the claims of students as a body to full and direct recognition by the University have been thereby weakened.'[47]

Rogers thus pressed St Hugh's Council to require students to at least work towards some kind of examinations, even if they did not pursue the official University curriculum. In 1895 she successfully passed a motion that introduced this as general practice, though the Council still reserved the right to make exemptions in individual cases. It is not clear, however, if this motion was ever put into practice. In 1909, the St Hugh's Club for Old Students of the college debated whether the money they had raised for a scholarship should specify that its holder take the full degree course. The previous year it had been agreed that such a criterion was too restrictive because many girls who were otherwise excellent scholars had not the requisite education in Greek to take the examinations for the BA. The Vice-Principal, Miss Jourdain, however, was, like Rogers, keen to push for a more professional culture. It was therefore agreed that scholars should take the full degree course unless 'otherwise recommended by the Awarding Committee'.[48] Nonetheless, Joan Evans recalled how as late as 1914 St Hugh's, '[l]ike a Methodist Chapel', might as well have had a notice outside the door stating 'All are Welcome.' 'By no means all students were reading for a degree, and admission was easily obtained.'[49] Eventually, the views of Annie Rogers and Eleanor Jourdain won out, and by 1917 an advertisement for St Hugh's clearly stated that 'All students are expected to read for a University Examination, a research certificate or diploma. No one is accepted who intends to follow the degree course unless they have passed responsions or stated subjects, or some other examinations which the University will take as an equivalent.'[50]

Those who had been encouraged to take the full degree course in 1917 were no doubt thankful, for by the end of their three years, in 1920, women at Oxford were finally granted degrees. This concluded forty years of struggle. Since 1884 women had been permitted to take the BA examinations, and the fact that some of them scored more highly than male undergraduates highlighted the unfairness of a system which refused them the right to graduate. The women's colleges and the Association for the Education of Women thus began to discuss whether they ought to take a formal position in favour of degrees for women.

The years 1894–6 saw a serious push by reformers to force the University to vote on the question, though not everyone agreed that this was the right moment to make the move. Elizabeth Wordsworth had, for most of the 1880s, felt the issue of degrees to be of little importance, and in 1894 her close friends Bertha Johnson (President of the AEW) and Lucy Soulsby (Headmistress of Oxford High School, 1879–89) came out firmly against the call for women's degrees.[51] They, like Wordsworth, favoured the more flexible curriculum for female students and thus believed that the admission of women to BAs was not in their best interests. In 1894, however, Elizabeth Wordsworth decided that it was worthwhile to support the move for degrees, though she was persuaded by the more conservative Church elements on the LMH council to prevent her views from becoming known.[52] When the AEW Council came to vote on the question in December 1894, Wordsworth was (perhaps conveniently) absent due to illness and LMH voted against pressing the University at this stage for women to be granted BAs.[53]

The previous year, St Hugh's Council had also passed a motion concluding that 'it is unnecessary at present to raise the difficult question of the BA degree for women'.[54] In 1894, however, St Hugh's representative on the AEW Council voted in favour of women's admission to degrees. In 1895, Annie Rogers and tutor Edith Wardale proposed another motion to St Hugh's Council, affirming its support for women's BAs, and this was carried by six votes to three (another three members abstained).[55] Pressure from the AEW, St Hugh's and Somerville led Convocation to vote on the question in 1896, but their proposals were rejected. Annie Rogers nevertheless felt that this defeat did not represent much of a setback in the long term. In 1907 Lord Curzon was elected Chancellor of the University and began to introduce a series of reforms with the hope of heading off more drastic changes threatened by the newly elected Liberal government. High on his agenda was the wish to rationalise the position of women at Oxford and to bring them under University control. Although women's admission to the privileges of full membership of the University was not his priority, he was not against their being granted degrees. The result was the formation of the Delegacy for Women in 1911, which for the first time formally recognised the existence of the five women's 'societies' (including the Society of Home Students, later to become St Anne's), and ruled that only female students registered at one of these were permitted to sit for examinations. In Rogers's view, this marked a watershed in the position of women at Oxford, for it formalised their presence in the University and implicitly accepted that they were there to stay. With the ground prepared in 1911 women were relatively swiftly granted full membership of the University following the upheavals of the First World War.[56]

St Hugh's and the feminists

It is often asked if the early campaigners for women's education should be understood as part of the feminist movement. The first historians to pay the women's colleges serious scholarly attention tended to take it as read that their establishment was part of this 'first wave' of agitation for the extension of women's rights and opportunities.[57] Over the last few decades, however, historians have begun to question whether the relationship between feminism and women's education was so straightforward. For a start, many of the pioneers of women's education saw themselves as part of a more general move for university reform, motivated less by concern for women's rights and more by the need to modernise Oxford and Cambridge.[58] Furthermore, the founders of some of the women's colleges supported an extremely conservative vision of women's social role. For while they challenged entrenched ideas about women's inferior intellectual capacities, their colleges nevertheless reinforced much conventional thinking on femininity.[59]

The early educational reformers pursued an extremely cautious strategy, summed up in the title of Annie Rogers's history *Degrees by Degrees*. It was premised on the belief that acceptance into male establishments was more likely to come as a reward for good behaviour than in response to confrontational demands. By the beginning of the twentieth century this approach was often at odds with the increasingly militant tone of large sections of the women's movement fighting for the suffrage. Emily Davies was the most straightforwardly 'feminist' of the early heads of the women's colleges. Prior to establishing Girton, she had been active in the Langham Place Group and its various projects to promote the interests of women, which are often seen as marking the beginning of an organised women's movement in Britain.[60] Yet even Davies was careful not to tarnish her project at Girton with the less respectable suffrage cause, let alone the campaigns around prostitution to which many Victorian feminists devoted themselves.[61] Historians have characterised such conservatism as exceptional, contradictory and paradoxical. For the assumption is that anyone who seeks to educate women, and who fights against the odds in order to do so, must in some sense be defined as a feminist. Wordsworth's biographer believed this contradiction to be central to understanding St Hugh's founder, declaring that: 'Elizabeth Wordsworth is one of the great figures in the women's movement, a cause in which she took not the faintest interest.'[62] Historians have posited a variety of arguments to explain away such a paradox. It has been suggested that Oxford women did not push for more formal recognition by the University because they enjoyed their institutional autonomy; that restrictive ruling

on acceptable feminine behaviour was a canny strategy for infil-
trating male institutions unheeded; and that the position of the
women's colleges in Oxford was shaped less by abstract principles
and more by the reality of their relationship with a male institution and their desire to be accepted into it.[63]

Most recently, however, the historian Julia Bush probed further
the caution and pragmatism of Oxford campaigners for women's
education and concluded that what emerges is a distinctly conservative picture. Bush's argument was not to deny the existence of an
important feminist current within the campaign for women's education, but to identify also an alternative vision which was compatible with more conservative views on women's role in society and
with opposition to the suffrage. Advocates of these two different
approaches shared enough common ground to work together pro-
ductively, but the latter should not be viewed as simply a watered
down or a confused version of the former but as a conservative
model for reform consistent within its own terms.[64] Some key
figures in the early history of St Hugh's College were used by Bush
to illustrate this approach to women's education. Elizabeth Wordsworth was 'a tacit anti-suffragist for many years', believing, along
with many other female anti-suffragists, that although women had
an important contribution to make to society, their role was distinct from that of men and would be tainted by participation in the
public political sphere. Wordsworth, however, was never involved
in organised anti-suffrage activity, and by 1913 she had come to
accept that the female vote would gradually be granted – though
she remained appalled by the attitudes of many in the campaign.[65]
Miss Alice Ottley, who ran a school in Worcester which funded
one of St Hugh's main scholarships, was a signatory to 'An Appeal
against Female Suffrage' (1889), one of the first nationally organised moves by *women* to oppose their suffragist sisters.[66] Other
prominent women connected to St Hugh's through religious and

university networks also opposed the extension of the franchise, including Charlotte Yonge, Louise Creighton, Mary Ward and Lucy Soulsby. Yet they all supported women's education and saw it as a way for their sex to achieve their pre-ordained role in society – a role that they defined in a conventional manner, unconnected to dangerous notions of gender equality.[67]

Without using too restrictive a definition of the term, I think it *is* useful to describe the woman-centred thinking that lay behind the founding of St Hugh's as in some sense 'feminist'. In schooling their students in the Bible, Wordsworth and Moberly drew upon a longstanding tradition of Christian feminism, which sought to demonstrate that women's rights could be reconciled with Church principles. Wordsworth's sermons frequently referred to the women of the Old Testament as role models for present-day womanhood, and Annie Moberly also lectured on 'the woman's [*sic*] movement of the present day in connection with Scripture'.[68] Historians, however, have tended to characterise this tradition of Christian feminism as 'Evangelical', while Tractarians, or High Churchmen, are more commonly typified as anti-feminists. Yet by the beginning of the twentieth century there was a significant number of High Church Anglicans who began to actively identify themselves with the moderate wing of the women's movement. As this Church of England women's movement developed into the new century it came to encompass a variety of views on the woman question, but it nevertheless provided an important context for the kinds of feminism found at St Hugh's.[69] Church of England feminists deliberately set about carving out a middle path between opponents of women's rights and more radical versions of feminism. Elizabeth Wordsworth, for example, began her address on *The First Principles of Women's Education* by arguing for the importance of avoiding 'blunders on the side of over restriction [of women's activities] on the one hand, or excessive and mischievous concession on the other ...'[70]

In 1912, various Churchmen delivered a series of addresses on the theme of 'the religious aspect of the women's movement' to an audience at Queen's Hall, London. One contributor was the leading High Anglican Charles Gore who, like Wordsworth, began his speech by distinguishing himself from the 'revolutionaries' in the women's movement, and insisted that he remained the enemy of anyone who sought to 'derogate the supreme dignity of motherhood or to alter ... the law of indissoluble marriage'. Yet, having established his true Christian credentials, Gore went on to praise many of the feminists' achievements.[71] As a member of the *Lux Mundi* group, Gore took a much more liberal approach to Scripture than the older generation of Anglo-Catholics who had so influenced Annie Moberly and Elizabeth Wordsworth.[72] He nevertheless identified with the Tractarian tradition and was part of the same Oxford-based circles as the ladies of St Hugh's.[73] Another member of the *Lux Mundi* group, Canon Scott Holland, had even closer ties with the college – an old friend of the Moberly family and godfather to St Hugh's history don Cecilia Ady.[74] In 1912 he became president of the Oxford branch of the Church League for Women's Suffrage (CLWS), an Anglican organisation committed to securing the parliamentary vote for women in order to 'establish equality of rights and opportunities between the sexes'. The CLWS had been founded in 1909 and by 1912 had sixty-five branches and approximately 3,600 members.[75] Annie Rogers was an active member of the Oxford branch and it is possible that other St Hugh's members may have attended meetings or at least kept up to date with their activities via Miss Rogers.[76] In 1915 the League even considered using St Hugh's as the venue for one of its conferences.[77] St Hugh's was also affiliated to and attended conferences of the National Union of Women Workers, one of the largest women's organisations of the period, which in

1912–13 pledged its public support for women's suffrage.[78]

By the start of the twentieth century, St Hugh's was home to a considerable amount of suffrage activity. The question was already a subject for 'sharp practice' (the college debating society), though student Edith Olivier considered it 'rather rot'.[79] In 1907, however, Cecilia Ady took the side of the suffragists in a debate that many found 'most stirring'.[80] Eleanor Jourdain, in many ways a deeply conservative woman, was nevertheless an active supporter of female enfranchisement, advertising London suffrage marches on the college notice board and marching in a special St Hugh's contingent with a number of undergraduates and Old Students on Suffrage Sunday in 1908.[81] The *St Hugh's Club Paper* for these years contains frequent letters from past and present students expressing their support for the women's franchise and reporting on their latest efforts for the cause.[82] By 1910 the college had acquired its own banner to take on national suffrage marches, with some members discussing the need for St Hugh's to form its own suffrage society.[83] Only peaceful methods of campaigning were promoted in college and in 1913 St Hugh's allowed the non-militant National Union of Women's Suffrage Societies to rent their buildings in Norham Gardens only on condition that they did not publicly associate themselves with St Hugh's in their advertising.[84] The college did, however, have unofficial links with the more radical Women's Social and Political Union, which advocated civil disobedience in the struggle for the vote. St Hugh's most important patron and Council member, Clara Mordan, was a committed feminist and supporter of the WSPU, and one wonders how she got on with Elizabeth Wordsworth, who famously abhorred the militants' tactics and lamented 'the modern spirit of the younger generation' of women activists.[85] Nor do we know how St Hugh's responded in 1913 when former student Emily Wilding Davison threw herself in front of the King's horse at the Royal Derby to become the suffrage movement's most famous martyr.[86]

By the eve of the First World War, support for women's suffrage and the more overt commitment to feminism that it entailed was an established part of St Hugh's culture. Former students used the correspondence pages of the *Club Paper* to discuss the discrimination they encountered after graduation and the unequal status of female professionals. One woman had acquired a post teaching in a co-educational school, but, she wrote, she continued to support single-sex education because of the manner in which at her present place of employment 'the male element, from the Staff throughout the School, have all the privileges'. Later, in 1917, an Old Student engaged in war work commented wryly on how, once a certain area of industry had been deemed suitable for women, 'the pay is lowered accordingly!'[87] The almost intoxicating sense of freedom made possible by education and subsequent employment is beautifully expressed in a postcard sent by a Miss M. J. Tew to the *Club Paper* in 1912:

> For the last three years I have been very busy discovering of inexhaustible delights of London life. These seem to range from the supreme joy of a flat of one's own, to the surprise of meeting St Hugh's friends in the most unexpected places. I have not yet got used to sitting down in a bus next to someone whom I last saw seven years ago, or to 'lining-up' in a Suffrage procession with one of my own year. Another joy of London seems to be that of finding oneself doing the most unnatural things in the most natural way, such as spending the night on a friend's drawing-room floor in order to 'resist the Census', or crowded into a very stuffy gallery at the Old Bailey. In the summer holidays I went for a bicycling tour in Normandy, and had the most glorious time ... Incidentally, I teach history at Graham Street High School, manage the games and edit the magazine ...[88]

Many paradoxes are thrown up by this picture of the intellectual and religious life of St Hugh's in its founding years. On the one hand we encounter a world of the utmost respectability, closely connected to the upper echelons of the Anglican clergy and Oxford's most orthodox and conservative circles. Viewed from another perspective, St Hugh's becomes the home of suffrage marches and political debates – funded by a committed feminist militant. The religious impulses that lay behind the founding of St Hugh's have been examined here as a possible way into understanding such paradoxes, even suggesting that the picture may not have been as contradictory as it first appears. The somewhat narrow Anglican basis upon which St Hugh's was established also provided the moral impetus required to overcome the college's lack of financial support and social prestige and to ensure its success as the third of the Oxford women's foundations. The St Hugh's High Church vision of women's education was premised on an assertion of sexual difference which meant that the college did not take a leading role in pushing for its students to receive an identical education to male undergraduates. But although Elizabeth Wordsworth adopted the same religious framework as her father and other Anglican critics of the women's colleges, she simultaneously supported an expanded role for women in society and argued that the Church was responsible for educating women to perform such a role. The founding of St Hugh's thus needs to be situated within a broader context of Church of England feminism: a tradition that accommodated both pro- and anti-suffrage, and conservative and more radical positions.

2

'A WOMEN'S COMMUNITY'

Continuity and transformation, 1914–39

THE GREAT WAR, the move into permanent college buildings, the admission of women to the University, and the
constitutional crisis of 1923–4, all brought with them fundamental changes. Yet what is distinctive about St Hugh's during this
period is the way it combined rapid development with loyalty
to the Victorian way of doing things. Many aspects of college
life in the interwar period continued to be organised just as they
had been in the late nineteenth century. St Hugh's remained a
women's community – a sexually segregated institution in which
daily life was modelled not on a workplace but on a large family
home. Students and staff mixed in a relatively informal manner,
helping to develop a distinctive college tradition, one made necessary by their ongoing exclusion from many aspects of male
University activity. Female students became more integrated into
the rest of Oxford after the First World War, yet homosocial-
ity continued to shape life at St Hugh's well into the 1920s. All
variety of relationships grew up within this all-female community, where love, friendship and desire were strongly influenced
by institutional structures. The all-female identity of the college,

though valued by many, had also to be enforced by strict disciplinary codes which not only restricted interaction between men and women but also imposed ideas of correct 'feminine' behaviour upon St Hugh's undergraduates.

The disciplining of female students' bodies and minds, and the careful regulation of physical space in both the college and the city of Oxford, reflected concerns about women's rapidly expanding role in the first few decades of the twentieth century. Affected by the enormous upheavals of the Great War, the admission of women to degrees, and the postwar backlash against their presence in Oxford, the role of the 'undergraduette' had to be constantly reinvented. Both students and an increasingly professionalised body of academic staff became ever more critical of Victorian approaches to running St Hugh's. The constitutional crisis of 1923–4 (commonly known as 'The Row' because of the conflict between Eleanor Jourdain and Cecilia Ady) needs to be understood in the context of these wider changes. St Hugh's historians have argued that 'The Row' should not be reduced to a tale of personality clashes and petty rivalries between female academics, but approached as an important stage in the constitutional development of the college. Yet this moment of crisis was also fundamentally determined by the gendered identity of St Hugh's: the outcome of a variety of circumstances, tensions and intergenerational conflicts distinctive to an all-female community.

Everyday life in a women's community

Putting together a picture of daily life at St Hugh's helps us to understand how the college managed to survive as an institution during times of difficulty as well as expansion. St Hugh's followed its predecessor, Lady Margaret Hall, in modelling itself on the life of a 'Christian family'.[1] This reflected, and hoped to assuage, the popular belief that educating women would defeminise them, bringing them into dangerous proximity with men and making them unsuited to family life.[2] Colleges thus reproduced the rituals of the middle-class home: Annie Moberly, for example, insisted that her room in college be treated not as a study (where one would knock before entering) but as a drawing room which students had to walk into without knocking and then stand around awkwardly waiting to be noticed.[3] In 1916 St Hugh's moved out of the houses in Park Town into its new buildings, becoming the first purpose-built women's college in Oxford. The new site on St Margaret's Road nevertheless tried to emulate a domestic dwelling, situated a safe distance from the city centre. The buildings resemble a large country house or boarding school rather than a public building or traditional Oxbridge college.[4]

Many students, away from home for the first time, found this familial environment comforting and enjoyed a degree of maternal attention which might strike today's students as somewhat overbearing. In the early 1920s the domestic Bursar, Miss Salt, kept a careful eye on the health of her students. When Esther M. Power, for example, first arrived at St Hugh's, showing the beginnings of a cold, Miss Salt ordered her hot milk and rubbed her chest with oil![5] Eating, praying, working and even sleeping were collective activities, carried out at set times, just as they would have been at boarding school or in an especially strict family home. Students were expected to work in the morning, use the afternoon for exercise, return to College for tea and then work again until dinner time. The start of each activity was indicated by bells, and the early 1920s students could expect to be interrupted by their ringing nine times in the course of their day.

The Principal was often seen as the mother of the family – eating with her students, entertaining in her private rooms, and even kissing them goodnight. Like any family home, however, the college

Trinity Term 1924.
ST HUGH'S COLLEGE.

OXFORD.

BELLS.

	Week-days.	Sundays.
Calling	7 a.m.	8 a.m.
"	7.30	8.30
Chapel	7.55	8.55
Lunch	1.15 p.m.	1 p.m
Tea	3.45	3.45
Dressing bell	7.15	7.15
Chapel	After dinner.	7.25
Dinner	7.25	
Last Bell	10.10	10.10

N.B. A warning bell will be rung at
10 p.m. When the bell rings at 10.10
students living in houses outside the
College, and all visitors, must leave
the main buildings at once.
Students are expected to be in their
own houses or rooms at 10.15 p.m.
unless late leave has been given.

M. E. Robertson

Acting Principal.

St Hugh's daily timetable, Trinity Term 1924. (St Hugh's College Archive) was a place of surveillance as well as comfort, and the Principal also assumed a disciplinary role.[6] There were few activities students could undertake without her knowledge, and the style of the new St Hugh's buildings facilitated this, for, like other women's colleges, it was organised around corridors rather than staircases. Prior to the establishment of the women's colleges, the Oxbridge college had always been built around staircases, with students' rooms clustered vertically rather than horizontally. Emily Davies is said to have opposed this model for Girton on the grounds that it would make it too difficult for her to keep an eye on the students.[7] At St Hugh's, corridors enabled Principal Jourdain to stroll up and down and quickly take in any activities that caught her interest – something she was reported to do frequently and often at strange hours of the day.[8]

Most tutors lived in college during term time, and their relations with students were far freer and more intimate than in the men's colleges. It was customary to invite one's tutor to tea at least once during one's time in college and Molly McNeill, a student at St Hugh's during the First World War, greatly enjoyed putting on a fine spread for Miss Ady. '[W]e got on magnificently in the way of conversation,' she reported to her mother. 'We talked about everything.'[9] The following year, when Molly's close friend was killed on the battlefield and she felt unable to speak to any of her peers about how she felt, it was Miss Ady that Molly eventually turned to for much-needed comfort.[10] Tutors were, like their students, excluded from University societies and a social scene centred on the all-male colleges, and so they had little choice but to participate in the women-only entertainments that took place at St Hugh's. Cecilia Ady, for example, attended the students' debating society on Sunday nights, while Eleanor Jourdain was often the central attraction at meetings of the Philosophical and Literary Societies where she gave papers on subjects ranging from Plato to Futurist Art.[11] This feminine subculture offered a supportive and nurturing environment for young women to develop their expertise in areas otherwise dominated by men.[12] St Hugh's own sports teams, academic societies and debating chambers proclaimed their right to engage in similar pursuits to male undergraduates, even if they had to do so separately. St Hugh's also participated in the Oxford Students Debating Society which constituted itself as a female counterpart to the famous Oxford Union. The Society (which some members wanted to name the Oxford Women's Union) was so proud of its exclusively female atmosphere that it sometimes voted against inviting even very famous male speakers.[13]

This celebration of female self-sufficiency also applied to student journalists who rejected the offer of a small women's column in the *Cherwell* and the *Isis* in favour of setting up *The Fritillary* in 1913. This independent women's publication was staffed by members of all five women's societies and in 1927 was edited by St Hugh's Renée Haynes and Margaret Lane, providing them with an important preparation for their subsequent careers as professional writers.[14] St Hugh's students also produced *The Imp* from 1918 to 1929, followed by *The Cygnet* in 1931. These magazines were intended as literary publications, offering prizes for the best poems and short stories, but they soon found that it was necessary to supplement such entries with college notices and opinion pieces that often made reference to St Hugh's 'characters', gossip, and in-jokes. When too few people sent contributions to *The Imp*, its editors rebuked their fellow students for losing sight of the importance of retaining their own college publication. 'Does St Hugh's wish for a magazine of its own, or does it not?' they demanded to know. 'Personally, we are convinced that a right thinking community of this size should have a paper of its own, and should make that paper a sign and expression of its acknowledged vigour and progress.'[15]

The all-female identity of St Hugh's may well have been a source of pride, but it had also to be enforced by rules which strictly policed interaction between male and female undergraduates. Disciplinary codes dominated life at St Hugh's during this period, determining where women students could walk, how they ought to dress, and what political, intellectual and social activities they should take part in. 'Chaperonage' had been a key concern for the women's colleges from the very beginning. One of the main objections to their foundation had been that Oxford and Cambridge – populated exclusively by men except for the servants and prostitutes – were not suitable places for young middle-class women. Chaperone rules were therefore deemed necessary by the early women Principals to protect the reputation of their colleges and to reassure families that their daughters would be properly protected. Students were told that good behaviour was a small price to pay for admittance and perhaps future acceptance into the University. Late nights, socialising alone with men, and living independently outside college were strictly prohibited. Students were expected to pay a chaperone (an older woman not herself a college student) to accompany them to most University-related activities, including lectures and tutorials. It was not until 1915 that the women's college Principals decided, on a motion put forward by Eleanor Jourdain, that third-year students should be allowed to attend lectures without chaperones. First- and second-year students, however, still had to be decided upon on a case-by-case basis. Even in wartime, the women's colleges 'felt that as a rule it is undesirable for a student to … [be taught] alone in a man's college, and that such an arrangement should be avoided if possible, even for two students together.'[16]

At first such rules were enforced at the discretion of the college Principal, rather than by any central or external University body. In 1909, however, with the prospect of women's admittance into the University becoming more likely under Chancellor Lord Curzon, disciplinary procedures were codified. Annie Rogers and Emily Penrose, Principal of Somerville College, were commissioned by the Association for the Education of Women to compile a more formal and uniform regime. The heads of the various women's colleges met regularly from then on to discuss discipline and the correct interpretation of the finer points of this code.[17] At St Hugh's the Principal still had overall responsibility for discipline, and Eleanor Jourdain took a personal interest in ensuring that the proper codes of conduct were enforced. Her obituary, written by Annie Moberly, recalled how: 'In order to maintain the honour of the College, she looked after such apparently small matters as the correct dress and general bearing of students ...'[18] In 1919, for example, a student appeared at the beginning of the year sporting one of the newly fashionable bobs, only to be told by her Principal that she had to grow it out again. Students' political activity was also regulated. In 1911 and 1912, all four women's colleges refused permission for their students to attend the London suffrage procession, despite the fact that many college heads – including Miss Jourdain – supported the suffrage cause.[19] The following year, when the Oxford Men's Political Union for Women's Suffrage (a University organisation) invited the Oxford Women Students' Debating Society to debate militant tactics in the suffrage movement, the topic was deemed distasteful and forbidden.[20] It was, however, agreed by the Principals that they could not interfere in the private conversations of their students, and so anyone wishing to pursue political activity in this fashion was permitted to do so.[21]

When women were admitted to the University in 1920, some students hoped that this would also signal a relaxation in the chaperone laws. Ina Brooksbank, for example, heard a rumour that men would finally be allowed to attend St Hugh's dances. Yet such hopes were soon to be disappointed: now that women were officially under the authority of the University they became subject to a new and no less draconian disciplinary code.[22]

Inter-collegiate rules for women undergraduates (c. 1920)

1. A woman undergraduate may not reside in Oxford out of Full Term except by permission of her Principal, and under the conditions laid down by the Delegates of Lodgings.

2. A woman undergraduate may not enter men's rooms either in College or in lodgings without obtaining leave from her Principal. She must have a chaperone approved by her Principal. It is understood that conversation between men and women undergraduates before and after lectures is not encouraged.

3. A woman undergraduate must obtain leave from her Principal before accepting invitations for the evening, or for mixed parties. She may not go out after dinner without permission, and must always be back by 11 o'clock and must report her return.

4. A woman undergraduate may invite men friends to tea in the public rooms or grounds of the College or Hall to which she belongs, after obtaining permission from her Principal, provided that there are at least two women in the party. A woman undergraduate may receive her brother in her room, but not other men.

5. A woman undergraduate may go to matinees with men friends if leave is obtained from her Principal, provided that there are two women in the party.

6. Mixed parties may not be held in cafes, restaurants, or hotels without a chaperone approved by the Principal.

7. A woman undergraduate may not attend a subscription dance.

8. All Joint Societies must be approved by the Principals and such approval must be renewed annually. Meetings of such societies must not be held in undergraduates' rooms, and may only be held in men's colleges with written permission from the Dean of College, provided that a woman senior member is present.

9. A woman undergraduate may not go for walks, bicycle or motor rides alone with a man undergraduate other than her brother. Permission for mixed parties may be given at the discretion of the Principal.

10. A woman undergraduate may not boat with men (other than her brother) without a chaperone approved by the Principal.

11. A woman undergraduate may only be present at football or cricket matches or boat races under conditions approved by her Principal.

12. Women undergraduates are not allowed to play mixed hockey.

Mixed or joint societies, attended by both men and women, grew in number after the First World War but the rule that a senior female member had to attend every meeting could cause considerable difficulties for the more unconventional societies. From 1916 onwards the Socialist committee struggled to find a senior female member, so that women students were often prevented from attending their meetings. Miss Bullen, the Bursar at St Hugh's, was sometimes able to attend as chaperone but the society encountered new problems after 1920 when Bullen defected to the Labour Club.[23] Curfews became ever more of an issue in the 1920s, and at St Hugh's students continued to have to request permission to stay out after 10.15 p.m. and to return to College at 11 p.m., even when this meant leaving the theatre early.[24] Those students staying in lodging houses outside college (due to the postwar shortage of accommodation) were subject to similar controls, and their landladies were given strict instructions to lock their charges in at night and never to issue them with their own key.[25]

Changing times and new women

In 1920, Oxford University finally permitted women to hold degrees as part of their admission as full members of the University. Even those who had been involved in the campaign for degrees for many years were surprised by the scope of the new decrees, which admitted women to MAs as well as BAs, and made them members of Convocation. The changing role of women in the University corresponded to broader socio-economic upheavals following the end of the First World War, and was accompanied by the Representation of the People Act (1918) and the Sex Disqualification Act (1919) – both of which appeared to finally remove the last obstacles to women's full participation in professional and political life.[26] An advertisement in *The Imp* for a women's employment bureau, if overly optimistic about the job opportunities on offer to women in 1925, certainly encapsulated this sense of rapidly expanding horizons.

> Twenty years ago what could the average University Woman contemplate as her life's career? In nine cases out of ten there was no choice but to spend the rest of her working life in a Girl's School as an Assistant Mistress … To-day, what a different situation presents itself! … To-day, medicine, law, politics, journalism, commerce, all have opened their doors to women. What boundless opportunities lie before the woman who is keen and who understands her work![27]

The students who began to arrive at the women's colleges after 1918 were in many ways markedly different to their pre-war predecessors.

The war had done away with much obsessive etiquette surrounding the conduct of middle-class girls. When the novelist Vera Brittain came up to Somerville in 1914 she had to be escorted to the railway station and then immediately telegraph home to confirm her safe arrival. Only a year or so later, working as a nurse in a military hospital in Camberwell, South London, she was able to walk the streets of this working-class area at night, completely alone, with no one to give a thought to her whereabouts.[28] Although this degree of freedom was never permitted in Oxford during wartime, war work in kitchens and on local farms must still have brought new and unusual experiences for St Hugh's students.[29] Ina Brooksbank contemplated working in the Ministry of Pensions during the summer vac, though she feared that her mother would not like her living alone in London.[30] Although this state of exception was not to last, the postwar generation of students brought with them a different view of 'appropriate' feminine behaviour. In 1919, for example, Ina Brooksbank counted three women students who rode motorcycles round Oxford. One wore 'Leggings, wide skirts, [a] small hat and one yard of veil floating behind', another 'patronises a trench coat and a flappy hat which she holds on with one hand', while 'the third trench coat and gloves, leggings and brogues and concussion helmet'.[31] The postwar craze for dancing also hit Oxford, and although the University authorities stuck to their previous policy of prohibiting women from attending most dances, students often tried to ignore the ban.[32] Mixed-sex or 'joint' societies proliferated in spite of the disapproval of the women Principals, who even failed to prevent their female students from smoking at such meetings.[33]

Matriculation c. 1912–14. (St Hugh's College Archive)

Did the close of the First World War also mark the end of a 'women's community' at St Hugh's? Earlier histories of the women's colleges tended to identify both admission of women into the University, and women's changing role in society more generally, as marking the beginning of a period in which Oxford women came more and more to mix with men.[34] Most recently, however, Kathryn Eccles has convincingly argued that women's colleges in the interwar period found themselves 'locked in' to the separatist culture that had been so important to them in establishing themselves before they were officially part of Oxford.[35] The admission of women into the University, although formally comprehensive, was hardly wholeheartedly practised and a high degree of hostility to women's presence lingered on after the war. Although it was women students who kept it going during the

Matriculation c. 1917–18. (St Hugh's College Archive)

war years, the University showed more resentment than gratitude once the fighting was finally over.[36] 'There are now half the
number of men back,' wrote Ina Brooksbank in February 1919,
'1,500 and they are still coming.'

> The history lectures are crowded out. They have now 100 men,
> where they used to have about 5 and twenty women ... Lots
> of the men coaches have refused to coach women any longer,
> and next they will turn us out of lectures if they get any more
> crowded ... They were glad enough to have us when they had no
> one else.[37]

Such hostility, coupled with the new disciplinary codes which
continued to exclude women from many areas of University
life, meant that many women-only societies and social practices
continued.

Students themselves also had mixed feelings about some of the new 'modern' roles on offer to them. In 1917, Molly McNeill met a very unusual young woman at a lecture. She had initially been rather impressed by this woman's glamorous and unusual clothes ('rather freakish with a lovely silver bag'), her free and open manner, and her 'foreign' looks. However, after visiting her new friend for tea the following week, McNeill was put off on finding that the student was not only married, but also had an eight-month-old baby, and was combining motherhood with life as a Home Student. The whereabouts of the husband was not mentioned, and Molly proved unable to cope with such a lack of convention. 'Did you ever hear the like of that?', she wrote to her mother on her return. 'Altogether she gave me a rather miserable feeling ... I hope I won't have to see any more of her. I wish I hadn't gone to tea.'[38] Ina Brooksbank displayed a similar combination of fascination and repulsion in her account of the dashing women who sped around Oxford on their motorcycles. Although she spent some time describing their outfits in a letter to her mother, she finally concluded that they were the worst 'freaks' she had ever seen in her life.[39] The prospect of women taking advantage of new opportunities and adopting modern habits remained a source of concern well into the 1920s. In 1927 *The Fritillary* reviewed a book which warned of a 'growing misogyny' to be found in England, especially in the universities, resentful of 'a post war tendency among women to intrude into the spheres of men' instead of keeping within their proper roles as wives and mothers. The reviewer was thus reminded that '[t]o the public ... the woman student is the arch type [*sic*] of feminist, a forbidding and unnatural phenomenon'; anxious to distance herself from such a stereotype, she concluded that women should be recalled to their 'normal status as mothers'.[40]

Educational institutions are always contradictory spaces, on the one hand designed to reproduce dominant social values and to serve the economy through the production of efficient and well-socialised members of society; on the other, offering individuals the possibility of transcending the confines of their own lives and redefining their identities. The women's colleges during this period were full of such conflicts. They retained their Victorian routines and traditions, while also educating a modern female workforce – not simply enabling the 'modern girl' to achieve all she could but also to a large extent creating her. The cultural theorist Maria Tamboukou has described women's colleges in the late nineteenth century as 'crisis heterotopias' – spaces of transition in which women crossing into previously uncharted terrain and in the process of creating new roles for themselves could act out the tensions created by this state of flux.[41] By the 1920s, women's colleges, though no longer transitional in Tamboukou's sense, continued to be contested spaces, zones of tension where old and new gender roles coexisted and were tested out. Chaperone rules played a crucial role in this process, *containing* many of the effects of social change, while also providing a point of reference against which students could define themselves as 'modern women'.

The chaperone rules themselves might not have changed much after the First World War, but what had changed was the students' willingness to put up with them. In 1919, Ina Brooksbank complained to her mother of the unfairness of these rules, when the college authorities refused to allow the end-of-term dance to continue past 11 p.m. 'The girls said that it was not long enough and they weren't going to be treated like babies,' she recorded, and some claimed that they would rather have no dance at all than under such conditions, although in the end the student body voted against cancelling it.[42] This vote was probably taken by the Junior Common Room (JCR), the formal democratic organisation of St Hugh's students formed during these years. In 1924 the JCR presented a number of formal requests to Eleanor Jourdain to amend the chaperone rules, including asking that regulations for mixed river parties be relaxed, and for permission to return from the theatre later than 11 p.m.[43] Over the course of the decade opposition to the chaperone rules increased. St Hugh's student Renée Haynes wrote an editorial for *The Fritillary* condemning the lack of faith in women's moral judgement and ability to manage their own lives which such rules implied.[44] Even more forthright was an interview in *The Imp*, in which a progressively minded student (probably Barbara Betts, later Barbara Castle) was asked what she thought of the chaperone rules. 'I should say they were B******', she declared, 'and the people who invented them have minds like D****** S******.'[45]

The heads of the women's colleges resisted these calls for change as much as they could. The minutes of their meetings for the early 1920s reveal an overwhelming preoccupation with disciplinary matters. Very seldom is any serious breach of the rules recorded, and yet the women Principals spent large amounts of their time discussing and clarifying 'points of etiquette' on questions such as whether women could play golf with men unchaperoned.[46] Concessions were sometimes made in response to petitions by students, and perhaps the women Principals privately found the enforcement of these rules as tedious as the undergraduates. Yet we need to ask why such time and energy was devoted to these outdated codes of feminine conduct. Chaperone rules were not simply imposed by external University authorities, but also strongly endorsed and upheld within these women's communities. To the women's college authorities, attempting to negotiate the new position of women at Oxford and the new kinds of women they were expected to train up, the chaperone rules became a helpful focus for a much broader set of uncertainties and anxieties. They acted as a reminder of the authority of the women Principals over the new and disturbingly different generation of students; they symbolised the institutional continuity of the college; and they offered, even if it was notional, the prospect of controlling and containing the potentially explosive effects of the gendered upheavals taking place in the world at large.[47]

The professionalisation of St Hugh's

It has been said of the Oxbridge women's colleges that 'the 1890s saw a shift away from graciousness and bad food toward professionalism and bad food'.[48] At St Hugh's, the shift towards professionalism occurred when Annie Moberly handed over the Principalship to Eleanor Jourdain after 1915. Jourdain was one of the first generation of women to attend university; she had read for the degree course at LMH and held a doctorate from the University of Paris. Before coming to St Hugh's she had a successful career as headmistress of two girls' schools and was an experienced administrator and teacher.[49] Perhaps because these were not skills of which she herself could boast, Moberly was deeply impressed by Jourdain's 'clear brain for finance and gifts of organisation'.[50] Jourdain also possessed the necessary powers of leadership to ensure the college's survival during the difficult war years. Early in 1918, for example, the war office had mooted plans to turn St Hugh's into a military hospital, subjecting it to the same fate as Somerville, whose buildings were taken over and severely damaged. Jourdain immediately wrote a strongly worded letter insisting on the impossibility of such a move and rallied her supporters in the men's colleges, forcing the war office to back down.[51]

The role of Principal may have been one of relatively high status for professional women during this period, but it also entailed the gruelling hard work recalled here by Joan Evans:

Between 1915 and 1920 ... [Jourdain] moved the entire College twice, dealt with the endless difficulties of food, heating, and discipline that the war and post war years produced, nursed us all through the 1918 influenza epidemic and minor visitations, faced a serious crisis in the College finances, and worked with her colleagues at the other four Colleges in the slow and anxious task of preparing the regulations for women students when they were to become members of the University. Besides all this she was first Tutor in French in the College and then Lecturer in French at the Taylorian Institute, and made time not merely for writing the necessary lectures but also for working them up into a book on French eighteenth-century drama. Moreover she preached a sermon to us in Chapel on six Sundays of term.[52]

Unlike many other heads of women's colleges, Jourdain also managed to continue her research and to publish a number of books on French literature and philosophy.[53] She was also reported to be an excellent teacher.[54] Despite such impressive scholarly achievements it took a long time for posts at the women's colleges to be considered fully academic roles. Even as late as 1923 St Hugh's Council debated whether to require candidates for the position of Vice-Principal to have a degree.[55]

Nonetheless, by the 1920s the days of women such as Bertha Johnson refusing remuneration for their work were long gone, and University women began to demand salaries that reflected their professional status.[56] Although still below the amount recommended by the Association of University Teachers, St Hugh's Principal's salary doubled from £300 in 1919 to £600 by 1923. This was significantly more than the tutors were paid: for the first two decades of the century they still had to piece together an income from hourly-paid teaching provided by the Association for the Education of Women. Towards the end of the war, St Hugh's benefactor Mary Gray Allen wrote to Jourdain expressing concern at the tutors' low salaries and proposing to donate £25 towards improving them on condition that the college match her contribution.[57] Over the next few years St Hugh's did make increased efforts to provide some kind of guaranteed income for their resident tutors and by 1923 it offered a minimum salary of £275. Tutors were also of an increasingly high academic calibre. In 1918, forty-one candidates applied for the post of English tutor, ten of them having First Class degrees.[58] Cecilia Ady (1881–1958) was one of the first of St Hugh's senior members to achieve serious scholarly recognition. She had read history at the college from 1900 to 1903, and returned as tutor in 1909 having already published a book on Renaissance Italy. Ady had acquired her passion for Italian history from her mother, Julia Cartwright, who was also a respected scholar in this field. Yet she consciously rejected her mother's literary approach in favour of professional academia, eventually becoming a Doctor of Letters at the University of Oxford.[59]

The women's colleges were slow to employ their own tutors, having previously used those supplied by the Association for the Education of Women (AEW). When St Hugh's did begin to appoint resident tutors at the turn of the century, they were not offered permanent full-time positions, but combined in-college tutoring with AEW teaching elsewhere. Helena Deneke, employed in 1903, was given free room and board but did not receive a salary.[60] This situation only began to be rectified when the college started to guarantee its tutors a minimum salary so that they did not have to take on external AEW teaching, and in 1919 it determined that anyone providing tuition for St Hugh's students should be paid directly rather than through the AEW. Their position changed rapidly after 1920, when they were admitted as full members of the University. The AEW was dissolved, and tutors became solely responsible for organising their students' work. The following year the Delegacy for Women was abolished and tutors also took responsibility for entering their students into exams. They were now eligible, by special status passed in 1921, for membership of Faculties, Faculty Boards, Examining Boards and University Committees.[61]

With a more clearly defined role within the college, St Hugh's tutors began to meet regularly to discuss students' assignments and academic progress. Their relationship to college governance, however, remained uncertain. Individual tutors had sat on the Council at different times since 1895, but there was nothing in the constitution that ensured that they were represented. After 1915, the number of tutors on the Council declined significantly and in 1921 a committee was set up to look into securing them more permanent representation. Two years later this committee recommended that St Hugh's should end its status as a company and apply for a Royal Charter, making tutors into Fellows and members of Council by virtue of their office. This process was finally completed in 1926 and gave St Hugh's a mixed constitution governed by a Council consisting of both college staff and external members.[62]

Relations between women

St Hugh's nurtured many different kinds of relationships between women: from friendship, to student 'raves', to affection between staff and students, to 'female marriages' between colleagues. Annie Moberly and Eleanor Jourdain's relationship was particularly important to the early development of the college. They had become friends during Moberly's very first visit to Oxford, while Jourdain was still a student at LMH. It is not known if they remained in touch after Jourdain left Oxford to work as a teacher and then headmistress in various girls' schools, but in

1901 Moberly suggested that her old friend be appointed Vice-Principal of St Hugh's. She also proposed they visit Paris together, partly to see if they would get along well enough to form the close working relationship required of a Principal and her second in command.[63] Their subsequent 'Adventure' at Versailles, where they believed they had travelled back to the time of the French Revolution, formed a unique basis to their lasting and intense friendship. Although there were suggestions that Jourdain exerted an unhealthy degree of control over Moberly, the two women undoubtedly cared a great deal for each other. They worked closely during term-time and also chose to vacation together, sometimes with Moberly's family, sometimes escaping just the two of them from family ties and professional commitments.[64] After Moberly retired in 1915, she continued to live nearby and Jourdain would speak to her every night on the telephone and stay with her during vacations. Jourdain's death in 1924 left Moberly so devastated that she never forgave the people involved in 'The Row', which she believed had caused Eleanor's heart attack.[65]

Moberly and Jourdain's intimate relationship, combining the roles of colleague and companion, was not unusual in the late nineteenth and early twentieth century when a small but significant minority of single women chose to live together in what historians have termed 'female marriages'. This was particularly common among the heads of women's colleges, and the first Principals and Vice-Principals of both Westfield College, London, and Homerton College, Cambridge, forged similar relationships.[66] Between 1909 and 1919 Jourdain was also extremely close to Cecilia Ady. For the first ten years of her appointment, Ady's friendship provided Jourdain with a crucial source of emotional support during her time as Vice-Principal under Moberly who, in spite of Eleanor's affection for her, she often found very difficult to work for. Jourdain and Ady exchanged many passionate letters, in which Jourdain spoke of her immense gratitude to her 'Cara Cecilia' and 'Baby Don'.[67] 'If it wasn't for you,' she wrote, 'I don't quite think it would be bearable', and during Ady's research trips abroad Jourdain longed for her return in the knowledge that 'when you are at home things won't hurt so much ...'[68] Ady's sweet nature also helped Molly McNeill settle into college life and McNeill's letters to her mother made no secret of her crush on her history tutor. On returning to St Hugh's at the beginning of her second year McNeill was overjoyed to meet again with Cecilia, informing her mother that night that 'if it wasn't for Miss Ady I don't know what I'd do'.[69] Over the next few months Molly regaled her mother with affectionate observations on Miss Ady, never failing to report on even the briefest of encounters with her. 'She has got a rather sweet navy blue shirt and blouse, a sort of dress almost which suits her tremendously well', she noted one week, while on another occasion McNeill blushed to be caught staring at Ady during dinner, in return for which Ady 'gave me one of her sweet smiles'.[70] McNeill described conversations with Ady as 'glorious', attempted to arrange one-to-one tutorials with her, and believed Ady to be 'one of the dearest souls living'.[71]

Relationships between younger girls and older women were a not uncommon feature of female institutions, and St Hugh's students might already have encountered them at school.[72] They were also a popular theme of 'college girl' novels, a variant on the boarding school story, some of which provided convincing enough accounts of life in a women's college to appeal to their 'real-life' subjects. L. T. Meade's *The Chesterton Girl Graduates* (1913), for example, received a glowing review in *The Fritillary* which approved of its account of Chesterton College for women in the fictional city of 'Oxenholme'.[73] In the early 1920s St Hugh's students adapted Meade's book for the college play, in which they mischievously portrayed the character of the Principal as a caricature of Miss Jourdain, on the basis that Jourdain, like her fictional counterpart, was rather fond of kissing her students.[74] *The Chesterton Girl Graduates* also depicted passionate love between female undergraduates, and Meade's writing did not shy away from conveying the passion and physicality of such relationships. One passage, for example, described the heroine, Tara, falling 'on her knees by Beechey's side. She took one of her soft white hands and kissed it with her passionate red lips.' A few minutes later:

> Beechy gently pushed back a lock of Tara's lovely raven-black hair. 'I like you,' she said. 'Just at present it so happens that I have no special friend in the College. Will you become my friend, Tara?'[75]

Renée Haynes, a student at St Hugh's in the early 1920s, went on to write another college girl novel, naturally taking St Hugh's as inspiration. At one point the heroine, Sylvia, attracts the attention of the glamorous Ira, who was 'the sort of girl who had been the subject of innumerable "raves" at school – and she always liked to have some adorer about, and thought Sylvia might possibly become one'.[76]

How are we to interpret such friendship, affection, love and desire when expressed in language which today we would readily define as sexual? For the last few decades historians have wrestled with the question of how to understand relationships between women in a period before the modern identity of 'lesbian' had emerged. It is generally agreed that in the nineteenth century women were able to have 'romantic friendships' with other women, sometimes living together in 'female marriages' without necessarily being defined as deviant. Such women often spoke of each other in highly passionate terms, and their relationships may well have included a physical element. Although there has been much disagreement as to whether these relationships can be termed 'lesbian', or 'sexual' and to what extent they really were acceptable to mainstream Victorian society, it is clear that an important shift occurred in the late nineteenth and early twentieth century.[77] The rise of sexology during this period led to the first public 'scientific' discussions of female-to-female sexual passion, and to the emergence of a distinctive 'lesbian' identity or label. While such developments may have enabled some women to better understand and express their sexual desires, they also increased the likelihood of any relationship between women being suspected of deviance. Lucille Iremonger's history of St Hugh's, written in the 1950s, is an example of the more knowing and condemnatory attitudes that came about during the twentieth century. Without making any outright 'accusations' of lesbianism, Iremonger recounted how Jourdain and Moberly were said to be 'like husband and wife', how 'an awful lot of kissing' was said to go on, and how Jourdain's popularity among the students 'was such as to engender an atmosphere in the college which must to us today seem unhealthy ...'[78]

It has been suggested, however, that in the early decades of the twentieth century, women's colleges remained one of the places, fewer and fewer in number, where women continued to be able to practise female marriages and retain a more positive sense of the meaning of their connection with other women.[79] At St Hugh's, at least until the 1920s, women might develop intense feelings for each other without attracting too much adverse attention or fearing that they were abnormal. The question of whether these women actually 'had sex' is not something that is possible for the historian to answer. Moreover, historians of sexuality have argued that we need to move away from such a narrow focus on this particular aspect, and to ask instead questions regarding the meanings of these relationships – how they did or didn't challenge gender power relations and ideals of femininity and heterosexuality.[80] Martha Vicinus's groundbreaking work on homoerotic relationships between college women showed how they were shaped by the institutional context and expressed the wider aspirations of the women involved in them. Romantic friendships in this context were often 'seen as completing life's work, as validating the decision not to marry, to have a career'. Such relationships were part of 'the struggle to build a new kind of family, to develop a new kind of homoerotic friendship that met the different needs of public life ...'[81] Relationships between women at St Hugh's are better understood by such an approach, which takes into account the interconnections between women's love for each other and the institutional context during a period in which women's role in society was undergoing significant change. Jourdain and Moberly's female marriage could well be described in Vicinus's terms as embodying their sense of themselves as professional single women, carving out a new role, and achieving emotional fulfilment outside traditional family structures.

Similarly, McNeill's crush on Miss Ady provides a glimpse into the needs and aspirations of young college women during this period. Molly did not discuss intellectual questions with her mother, though her letters reveal her to have been deeply committed to her studies. Her passion for history continued after she left St Hugh's and she was to publish a number of books on the history of Ireland. Vera Brittain, who came up to Somerville only a year before McNeill arrived at St Hugh's, recalled in her autobiography the deep frustration she felt at the refusal of her middle-class family and friends to take her thirst for knowledge seriously.[82] We do not know if Molly McNeill suffered a similar fate, which was no doubt common to many young women of her class and generation, but perhaps part of the excitement Molly felt during her encounters with Cecilia Ady can be attributed to the thrill of finding an older woman who showed an interest in her intellectual ambitions. 'She really does expect you to be in earnest about whatever you do,' Molly recorded of Ady. 'That's why it's frightfully nice to be praised by her because you feel she really means it.'[83] Not only did Cecilia Ady provide a role model for academic womanhood, she also offered a different kind of academic style – an alternative to the masculine tone of the rest of the University that many female students found so intimidating. In 1917, Molly wrote to her mother complaining of a tutorial she had just had with the All Souls historian Mr Stampa. 'He gave me the impression he spent the whole time trying to find out exactly how much I didn't know instead of how much I did,' she despaired. Although Mr Stampa was 'a perfect mine of information, he seems to know the date of every possible event that took place in English history, but all the same he seems entirely bereft of originality, and never attempts to discuss anything'. By contrast, Molly enjoyed tutorials with Miss Ady so much because 'she is always eager to argue about ideals and things like that, which appeal to me far more than facts. I don't know how it is when I'm with her she always makes me feel quite clever but Mr Stampa leaves me with a sense of utter ignorance.'[84]

To focus on the institutional context of relationships between St Hugh's women is not to define them as purely platonic. The intensity with which these women felt for each other must have been fuelled by erotic energy, however we conceive of it. And as the obsession with chaperone rules reminds us, the spectre of sexuality loomed large within the women's colleges – whether or not it was acted upon. Yet desire does not exist in a vacuum, and an exploration of how relationships were woven into the college setting only reflects the extent to which love, life and work often became inseparable from one another. No relationship illustrates this better than that between Eleanor Jourdain and Cecilia Ady.

Jourdain's expressions of love were often couched in terms of the contrast between the emotionally and physically draining nature of her job and the sustenance provided by Ady's companionship. St Hugh's women had to live and work together in what often became an unbearably claustrophobic environment. Intimacy between one woman and another was therefore often expressed through confession of a secret dislike for a third party. Jourdain frequently apologised to Ady for being indiscreet, before giving an account of her most recent argument with other tutors. At the same time she would declare that she knew that Ady's goodness, sweetness and honesty meant that she would be immune from any of the unpleasant effects of sharing such information. St Hugh's College, then, provided an explosive emotional terrain, encouraging intense alliances which might easily transform themselves into equally powerful enmity.

'The Row'

It is only since the 1980s that 'The Row' has been written or even spoken about openly at St Hugh's – such was the trauma of this series of events upon the college.[85] It began in November 1923, when Principal Jourdain called Cecilia Ady into her office and announced her decision not to renew Ady's appointment on account of her 'disloyalty'. As it turned out, Ady's post had technically expired in the spring of that year, though she, like everyone else, had failed to notice this and so had not renewed it. This left her in an even more vulnerable position with regard to Jourdain's decision to dismiss her, though the college's constitution already placed Jourdain in a position of supreme authority over the academic staff. St Hugh's Council, the governing body that Jourdain was a member of and answerable to, next met on 24 November. There A. J. Jenkinson of Brasenose proposed

Ady's reappointment, and when his motion fell by one vote six members of the Council and five tutors (the vast majority of St Hugh's academic staff) resigned in protest. This led to the boycott of St Hugh's by the tutors of the other women's colleges, leaving the students with very few teachers. With the college in disarray, the students, parents and Old Students expressed their dismay by calling for the University Chancellor, Lord Curzon, to act as Visitor and carry out an independent inquiry into the situation. This was finally agreed to in March 1924 by the rump of the Council, who had until that point remained stubbornly defensive. On 4 April 1924, Curzon ruled that Miss Ady had been without fault, and he strongly hinted that St Hugh's tutors needed to have a more formalised constitutional role in order to prevent the situation recurring. Horrified by this outcome which, though diplomatically expressed, clearly found her in the wrong, Eleanor Jourdain died of a heart attack on 6 April 1924, giving rise to rumours that Ady's supporters had hounded her to death.

The drama of these events and the complex and powerful personalities of the women at the centre of them partly account for the unwillingness of subsequent St Hugh's authorities to have them discussed or written about, for the pain of the personal betrayals lingered on for many years. This has also led more recent historians to argue that 'The Row' needs to be 'related dispassionately' in order to properly assess the significance of the constitutional changes it brought about.[86] After Lord Curzon's verdict, the *Oxford Magazine* declared that St Hugh's was not a proper college but a girls' school subject to the tyranny of former headmistress Eleanor Jourdain. St Hugh's historian Colin Matthew argued that this focus on the gendered nature of 'The Row' was misleading, for St Hugh's was not so much like a girls' school as a Private Hall – a particular constitutional variation on the Oxford college – where the Principal had full authority and the tutors were denied any say in college governance. Matthew opposed a 'gender-slanting' analysis of 'The Row' and stressed that men's Private Halls had also to undergo constitutional reforms in order that they might resemble other self-governing Oxford colleges. It is, however, necessary here to depart from previous accounts to argue that, while 'The Row' should not, of course, be reduced to a 'feminine' spat, it is nevertheless important to understand it in its gendered context, for it arose out of circumstances distinctive to St Hugh's as an all-female institution.[87]

The problems between Principal and tutors which 'The Row' brought to a head were structural as well as personal, and reflected the unique difficulties faced by female academic staff. Lacking financial support, full access to University resources and (prior to 1920) any formally recognised position at Oxford, the job of Principal was an extremely difficult one. Heavy workloads inevitably led to stress and exhaustion. In 1911, when Jourdain was still Vice-Principal, she confessed to Cecilia Ady that:

> I *am* very weary. I am beginning to feel that what is the matter is the nine years accumulated weariness at St Hugh's, and to wonder how many more I can safely add to it. You see I cannot do the work here without taking it to heart, and in the past taking the difficulties rather bitterly to heart – but I have a rather dangerous feeling of being ready to go to pieces at the least excuse. I don't think a term or a year off would do any good: it is just the conditions which are straining …[88]

As Eleanor's letter shows, an enormous emotional investment was demanded of women academics. Not only did they work in far more challenging conditions than their male counterparts, but they were also expected to do so out of a sense of personal commitment to the project of women's education. Jourdain herself proclaimed that the college would fall apart if staff did not put St Hugh's before everything else.[89] At times the emotional and physical strain became unbearable, and while Jourdain only *worried* that she might 'go to pieces', her colleague Edith Wardale did in fact have a breakdown and was off work for a full term in 1920.[90]

Lacking the support or relief that their male colleagues received from wives and families, these women instead sought emotional sustenance from within the college. The deliberately cultivated familial atmosphere encouraged professional disagreements to be played out in personalised terms. When Jourdain and Moberly argued over administrative arrangements in 1914, they were finally reconciled not, for example, at a formal meeting, but by Annie visiting Eleanor in her room at night 'to try to make amends'.[91] Jourdain once rebelled against this blurring of her personal and professional lives, declaring that 'if only we could be private persons with no St Hugh's' she and Annie Moberly could have had a far less tempestuous relationship – though interestingly it was the intrusion of work into personal matters rather than the reverse that Jourdain complained about. The affectionate support provided by a close friendship among colleagues was crucial to the smooth running of St Hugh's. Though this also meant that the effects on the college could be disastrous should such a relationship break down.

Jourdain and Ady fell out at some point between 1915 (when Jourdain appointed Ady as her Vice-Principal) and 1919 (when Ady resigned from this post). Their subsequent estrangement must have been extremely painful for both of them, given the amount of affection and support which they had previously shared. Against such a background it becomes easier to comprehend the accusations of disloyalty and betrayal that Jourdain levelled at Ady, claiming that she undermined her authority and goaded students and fellow staff into insubordination.[92] Seemingly outlandish delusions on the part of Miss Jourdain in fact spoke of the loss of a once true friend. Her belief that the tutors were plotting to usurp her authority also expressed Jourdain's deeper discomfort with their growing professionalism. 'The Row' occurred at an important moment of transition for St Hugh's. Jourdain liked to deal with individuals, and she was considerably skilled at either charming or threatening them into doing her bidding. This was becoming increasingly difficult with the tutorial staff now meeting regularly as a separate professional body and Jourdain was understandably anxious that she was beginning to lose overall control of the college.

During 'The Row' the tutors asserted their professional status and organised themselves as workers. They opposed Jourdain's right to dismiss them on a whim and protested that those she employed to replace them during the boycott were not adequately qualified.[93] The women tutors had, in effect, organised a solidarity strike, and although this is something that has been passed over in the histories of 'The Row' it was abundantly clear to contemporaries. Eileen Stopford, one of the tutors employed by Miss Jourdain during the boycott, referred to the other tutors' actions as a 'strike', and those like herself as 'strike breakers'.[94] Miss Ady and her supporters were aware that the withdrawal of their labour was the only real leverage they had, and were conscious that the outcome of their actions would determine the position of female academics in the University as a whole.[95] As one of Ady's supporters informed her, 'I am sure that you have greatly strengthened the position of women in the University by demonstrating their capacity for acting in defence of our dearest heritage, freedom of thought and action without which scholarship and teaching are a mockery and a sham …'[96] C. M. Coate, Cecilia Ady's colleague from Lady Margaret Hall, forwarded her a protest signed by all the history tutors across the women's colleges and informed Ady that a meeting would be held the following day to plan for the proposed boycott:'St Hugh's will learn,' she reassured her colleague, 'that you have *all* the tutors behind you.'[97] Older ideas of duty to the college and personal commitment to the students had not, however, disappeared overnight. Cecilia Ady was deeply devoted to her students and invested a large amount of time and energy, which might well have been spent on her own research, in nurturing the intellects of under-confident young women such as Molly McNeill.[98] She, like many other tutors, found it extremely difficult to refuse to teach them, particularly as exams began to loom, and it was claimed some of them did indeed try to coach their third years in secret.[99] It was surely this Victorian notion of duty to the college over any professional interests that led Cecilia Ady, after Jourdain's death, to quietly take up a position as tutor for the Society of Home Students rather than push for her reinstatement at St Hugh's.

This struggle between the old and the new is powerfully conveyed in the account of 'The Row' by Mary Hopkirk (née Perkins), who was JCR President at the time. The problem as she and the other students saw it was that Miss Jourdain was 'a leftover from the nineteenth century', unable to relate to either her staff or her students. Hopkirk believed that Jourdain lived in fear lest any foul move on the part of a student jeopardise the future of the women's colleges, yet it appears that, after 1920, Jourdain was not so much afraid of the wrath of the University authorities, as she was of the 'modern' young woman – a fear that could sometimes lead to tyrannical behaviour. Cicely McCall, for example, was sent down in 1921 because she returned to her room five minutes after the 9 p.m. deadline on Sunday evening.[100] Retaining her disciplinary authority became increasingly important to Jourdain, and one of the main accusations levelled at Miss Ady during 'The Row' was that she had not properly supported

Jourdain on this question and instead had taken an overly liberal approach to student welfare.[101] St Hugh's undergraduates, meanwhile, were clear that Jourdain's manner of governing was no longer acceptable to them. Mary Hopkirk attempted to explain to the Principal 'as tactfully as possible, how the students resented the old-fashioned, school-mistressy attitude of the authorities towards them ...'[102] Jourdain was totally bewildered by such a revelation. She had lived side by side with students at St Hugh's for more than twenty years. Once they had appreciated her maternal attentions. Could it really be that they had changed so much?

It appeared that they had, for students were now confident enough to organise politically against the actions of their Principal. When undergraduates found themselves not only without tutors, but also subject to constant harassment from Jourdain and her supporters (as well as a few from Miss Ady's camp), they decided to meet as a JCR every Sunday to determine collectively what action should be taken. Under the leadership of Mary Hopkirk they wrote letters to the press and the Chancellor, and played a key role in persuading the parent body to push for an independent inquiry. Marjorie Reeves, a student who later became a history tutor at St Hugh's, remembers them as 'very revolutionary, very radical kinds of meetings. We all got up and made terrific speeches about how awful things were and how badly we were served and everything ... we were almost like the 1968 protesters and revolutionaries.'[103] Indeed, the students seem to have imbibed some of the political spirit of the times. One of them penned a humorous song about 'The Row', which made an analogy between the JCR and the Russian Bolsheviks, while a letter from a recently graduated student to Cecilia Ady suggested that the only way to deal with Miss Jourdain was for all the students to follow the 'syndicalist' approach and go on general strike![104] Students subsequently attributed their intransigence

during 'The Row' to the fact of their having been the first properly 'postwar' generation: too young to have direct experience of
the devastating impact of the war, and the first group of female
students to arrive at St Hugh's as full members of the University.
'[I]t was ... a most exciting time,' one student later recalled, 'we
were almost the first year to come up in a normal way; *everything*,
almost, was new.' [105]

Towards another war

'The Row' led to the establishment of a mixed constitution in
1926, and therefore marks an important stage in the development
of the college. Yet it needs to be understood not as the cause, but
as one of the effects of a number of key transitions occurring at St
· Hugh's during this time. These modernising forces accelerated in
the 1930s, when undergraduates, especially, became increasingly
confident in finding ways around the Victorian rule book. 'My
policy was to ask permission when I knew it would be granted,'
remembered Phyllis Wallbank, 'but to refrain when the result was
uncertain.' [106] The rise in the number of students owning cars
also helped, making it possible for St Hugh's women and their
male friends to easily and speedily escape the watchful eyes of the
Proctors. [107] It was still forbidden to keep alcohol in one's room
but some undergraduates ordered it nonetheless, asking Oxford
wine-merchants to disguise their goods before delivering them
to the college lodge. [108] Many students from this era recall that
college authorities were less and less likely to require that they
be chaperoned at university lectures and events, though their
participation in mixed societies continued to be restricted by
college hours. This was particularly frustrating for the ever-grow-
ing number of undergraduates who became heavily involved in
politics during this period – particularly left-wing and anti-fascist

societies such as the Left Book Club, the Peace Pledge Union and the (Communist) October Club.

The Labour Club was one of the most active societies in the University, dominated by St Hugh's Barbara Betts (who as Barbara Castle would later be a Labour cabinet minister) and Edna Edmunds (who subsequently married the Labour politician Denis Healey). The political atmosphere of St Hugh's seems to have shifted quite radically to the left during this decade – the JCR welcomed the Jarrow hunger marchers; ate bread-and-cheese lunches to raise money for the Republicans during the Spanish Civil War; and listened to the Domestic Bursar Gertrude Thorneycroft recount with enthusiasm her visit to Communist Russia.[109] The majority of the college authorities, however, remained conservative in outlook and continued to implement harsh disciplinary action if a student should get caught breaking the rules. One young woman was sent down for getting engaged to a Balliol undergraduate, though it was suspected that her left-wing political activity was the real source of disapproval.[110]

By the time St Hugh's came to celebrate its Jubilee in 1936 it was able to boast of a number of successful 'modern women' among its graduates: 'barristers, doctors, civil servants, missionaries, teachers, researchers, novelists, journalists, actresses, business-women, besides wives and mothers and voluntary workers of many kinds'.[111] Returning to college to celebrate fifty years of women's education, Old Students were able to prove to the undergraduates of the 1930s that it *was* possible to succeed in a male-dominated profession. Women academics were also slowly gaining more of a foothold within the University. Even before the onset of the Second World War, then, the question was already being asked: what future did a women's community like St Hugh's have in an increasingly 'mixed' University?

3

DIFFERENT OR EQUAL?

Women in a men's university, 1939–87

I N 1986, AFTER ONE HUNDRED YEARS as an all-women community, St Hugh's Governing Body voted to admit male undergraduates. Many former students felt this to be a betrayal of St Hugh's founding values, and even today some claim that they find it difficult to think of it as *their* college now that men occupy its buildings. Others, however, felt that 'going mixed' was a positive development: either because they had disliked attending a single-sex institution or, having only known St Hugh's as a co-educational college, they found it impossible to imagine it any other way.[1] In many ways, St Hugh's tradition of all-female education was too much the product of a Victorian mentality to survive into the latter half of the twentieth century. The culture of the women's community had grown up in the face of enforced separatism and made little sense in an Oxford where women were increasingly free to mix with men outside their colleges. The Second World War, in spite of the tragedies and disruption that came with it, accelerated the process by which women moved from the margins to the centre of the University. St Hugh's students were relocated to Balliol's extension buildings at Holywell

Manor when Main Building and the Mary Gray Allen wing were requisitioned for use as a military hospital. Although the dispersal of the college created many difficulties, there were also benefits to living closer to the heart of the University. St Hugh's undergraduates undertook fire-watching as part of their war work, and so found themselves responsible for some of Oxford's most important sites, including the Bodleian Library and the University Museum.[2] With so many male academics joining the armed forces, women dons acquired a far greater role in university administration, taking charge of examinations and supervisions, and began to be appointed chairmen of Faculty Boards.[3]

By 1946 Barbara Gwyer was thus able to declare, in a speech to mark her retirement, that:

> [W]e are moving out of the adolescent stage of Women's College. life in Oxford. We produce among our Heads and Fellows women whose achievements place them on a level with the men … I don't think that even the most conservative of our male colleagues now feel they can do without the women.

Such optimism was embraced by a younger generation of postwar dons, who had little time for the older traditions and allegiances of the 'women's community' which appeared to mark them out from their male colleagues. Their decision to combine academic careers with marriage and motherhood represented a serious challenge to the idea that the college *was* one's family. This left them juggling their multiple responsibilities with little college support and their anomalous position encapsulated many of the difficulties faced by 'women in a man's world' – caught between the desire to be judged according to one's academic abilities rather than one's sex, and the realisation of the need for more 'women-friendly' institutions.

The tension arising from the wish for equality of status, on the

St Hugh's women participate in mixed-sex societies: St John's Madrigal Society, 1947. (St Hugh's College Archive)

one hand, and recognition of difference, on the other, affected St Hugh's women throughout this period. The question of equality vs. separatism returned to the fore in the 1970s and 1980s when Oxford began to introduce co-residency, first with the admission of small numbers of female students to five of the men's colleges, followed by their admission to most of the men's colleges, and finally with the women's colleges accepting male undergraduates. At St Hugh's, the question of whether to admit men divided the college for eight years before the decision was finally made in 1985–6. Both sides at times claimed some form of feminist argument while also sometimes appearing to work on the assumption that female institutions were irredeemably low-status. The JCR, however, went much further in reviving the tradition of pride in an all-female community – retelling the history of St Hugh's feminist origins to influence decisions about its future.

Women in a man's world: mid-century backlash?

By the 1950s many Oxford women were beginning to feel that they had finally achieved equality in the University. The ardent feminist Vera Brittain believed that by the beginning of that decade 'very few old rules were now left which had applied to women only and made them a separate society'. She described the postwar era as 'a human society', in which women could finally escape from being defined by their sex. Gender itself, Brittain implied, was no longer relevant or even visible. Women at Oxford had certainly achieved formal equality with men by the end of the 1950s. In 1946 the women's appointments committee, which provided careers advice specially tailored for women, was amalgamated with its male counterpart – implying that finally women might compete alongside men in any one of the professions. In 1952 the University stopped listing women's exam results separately, and by 1957 the quota on the number of women undergraduates allowed into Oxford (prevented from rising above ¼ of resident students) was finally removed.[4] The first two female Oxford professors were both from St Hugh's: Agnes Headlam Morley (Montague Burton Professor of International Relations 1948) and Ida Mann (Titular Professor 1945).[5] Yet there were still very few female dons in the top University posts: in the late 1950s only one of Oxford's ninety-seven professors was a woman and there were only three among its 595 members of boards of electors to chairs. Nevertheless, women at Oxford constituted a slightly larger proportion (13 per cent) of academic post holders than the national average of 10 per cent.[6]

They might even have been slightly better off than at the civic universities where there were no academic posts reserved exclusively for women.[7] It has also been suggested that the position of women academics at Oxford was marginally better than at Cambridge because of the introduction of the Common University Fund, available to women's colleges to pay for Fellowships which their small endowments would not otherwise have stretched to.[8]

The privileges enjoyed by Oxford women compared with their counterparts nationwide were, however, only relative in a situation in which female academics were paid far less and tended to occupy lower-grade positions than men. The Oxford women's colleges could offer only low-paid Fellowships compared with the wealthier men's colleges: in 1945 the St Hugh's mathematician Ida Busbridge earned only £300 per annum despite directing the teaching of all female maths undergraduates. As late as the 1970s St Hugh's tutors still had to bear the brunt of their college's relative poverty by accepting lower salaries.[9] Located a long way from the city centre, female academics were also excluded from informal networks crucial to both intellectual stimulus and career progression. Mary Warnock was appointed Lecturer in Philosophy at St Hugh's in 1949 and made a Fellow three years later. Through her husband and fellow philosopher Geoffrey Warnock, Mary possibly had greater access than other women dons to the male-dominated world of Oxford philosophy. Her memoirs recall the early 1950s as an extremely exciting time for her area of research at the University, dominated by the leading thinkers Gilbert Ryle and J. L. Austin. Ryle and Austin held informal meetings on Saturday mornings where discussions took place that were to lead to some of the most important developments in British philosophy of the postwar era. Yet Warnock also remembered how 'it was some time before women were admitted to this meeting'.[10]

Mary Warnock was the first married don to be appointed at

St Hugh's.[11] Susan Wood was also appointed lecturer (in history) in 1949, and became engaged within a few months. Before the Second World War universities tended to employ only single women, while some women's colleges required their employees to resign on marriage.[12] Although St Hugh's does not appear to have operated a formal marriage bar, those small numbers of tutors who did marry always resigned on announcing their engagement.[13] Warnock and Wood's position as married female dons was therefore considered rather novel, even more so when they decided to start families without giving up their posts. St Hugh's gave Mary Warnock four weeks' maternity leave, after which she employed a live-in nanny to help look after the baby. It appears that, provided one could employ someone to care for one's children, an academic career was easier than most to combine with raising a young family. Both Warnock and Wood stressed the job's flexibility as an immense advantage. Susan Wood recalled being able to ask students at the last minute to come to tutorials at her house, should she need to stay home with one of the children; while one student remembered how Mary Warnock 'seemed to us to be constantly pregnant or involved with very small children ... billowing up St Giles on her bicycle, exasperated at the beginning of my tutorial because Kit [and Felix] ... had, to be helpful, just put into the bath all the clean clothes that had been put out for them to wear ...'[14]

Warnock and Wood, joined soon after by another young married don, Betty Bleaney, nevertheless found their pioneering position a challenging one. Warnock spoke of how, during the years in which her first two children were born, she felt under enormous pressure to maintain a high standard of housekeeping, constantly cleaning and cooking elaborate meals. Living in Summertown, to the north of the college, she remembers how 'I seldom went further south than St Hugh's ... I took magazines

like the then popular *Housewife*, and felt totally submerged.'[15]
Susan Wood similarly recalled the multiple pressures and conflict-
ing demands on her time and energy:

> I spent a lot of time thinking I wasn't doing anything properly.
> I wasn't as good a tutor as I might be, I certainly wasn't as good
> a wife and parent as I might be, and … for a time I really wasn't
> doing very much in the way of research, so it was a matter of sort
> of scrambling through for many years.[16]

'Although our senior colleagues were very kind,' wrote Wood,
in having children 'we were made to feel we had done something slightly frivolous; and, in my case, disappointing … Later,
to appear in college pregnant required some resolution.'[17] Mary
Warnock's account of the attitude of the other dons at St Hugh's
towards her and her friend's anomalous position is rather more
explicit. According to Warnock,

> Poor Susan had to go and see Miss Procter, the Principal, after
> she had been in the college for a few weeks, and confess that she
> had become engaged. This was especially dreadful because the
> Principal, herself a medievalist, and a most formidable woman,
> pale and reserved, but capable of deep passions, had plainly set her
> heart on Susan's following her as a dedicated scholar. Susan came
> out of the Principal's office shaken to the core.[18]

Such unsympathetic attitudes resulted less from personal
hostility than from the fact that the institutional structures of St
Hugh's were not yet adapted to postwar patterns of gender and
work. In the first half of the twentieth century, tutors and Fellows
were expected to provide not just academic expertise but also a
significant amount of affective labour. The college was structured
according to the expectation that a Fellow would live in college
and be available to provide undergraduates with emotional

support and even friendship.[19] Warnock remembered how 'it was thought impossible that we should give our minds properly to our jobs' and Susan Wood agreed that their not living-in was a problem. According to Wood, the college hesitated over whether to make her and Warnock Fellows following their probationary period as lecturers, because Governing Body doubted 'whether married Fellows would give as much time and heart to the college, or indeed stay (at the time it was generally assumed that a Fellow should be happy to stay for her working life)'.[20] But the anxiety surrounding the appointment of the first married dons at St Hugh's was indicative of more than just concern that such women would not be able to meet the responsibilities of the job. The tradition of residential academic posts was key to the 'family home' model of the college community and central to its identity. The idea of having emotional ties and time commitments outside college was perceived by many of the older generation of dons not just as a problem for the day-to-day running of St Hugh's, but also as a threat to women's education as they knew it.

In turn, the younger dons found the atmosphere of the Senior Common Room unbearably claustrophobic. Susan Wood wrote of how:

> The first impression for both of us was of an almost suffocating cosiness. Conversation was ladylike: concerned at its most intellectual with Jane Austen or the best detective fiction, otherwise largely with gardening or ornithology. My heart sank at being asked ... at lunch on my first day, 'will you belong to the Bird faction or the Flower faction?'[21]

The accounts of only two individuals cannot, of course, be taken as the definitive version of life at St Hugh's during this period. Mary Warnock's description of the atmosphere in the college at the time, though rich in detail and extremely entertaining, is particularly idiosyncratic. She eventually gave up her Fellowship in 1966, glad to embark upon a new career path and leave an institution where she had not been entirely happy. Susan Wood, on the other hand, remained at St Hugh's until 1986, and became an important figure on Governing Body, suggesting that the college cannot have been so resistant to the new generation of scholars as Warnock's account implies. What such reminiscences can tell us more about, however, is the sense of a breach in mentalities that occurred at St Hugh's around this time and how this shifted attitudes towards women's sense of their position within the male university. Wood and Warnock described the stuffy atmosphere of the 1950s Senior Common Room in decidedly gendered terms, associating intellectual and social conservatism with a cloying femininity. Warnock was repelled by a Common Room dominated, she felt, by 'jealousy, spite, [and] passionate suppressed love' – a place tainted by emotional incontinence, so different to the robust atmosphere of Magdalen where her husband was a Fellow.[22] Susan Wood recognises in retrospect that a few older dons wished to strike up 'a sort of heightened emotional one-to-one relationship', and some of the younger Fellows felt that the reason their seniors needed such emotional sustenance from other members of the college was because they could not receive it from husbands or children.[23] The problems with St Hugh's SCR could be summed up in a word that crops up again and again in their accounts – the college was too 'spinsterish'.

For some of these young postwar academics femininity was associated with a lack of status, and in seeking to succeed as men's equals they preferred to ignore their sex altogether. Mary Warnock described the progress of women's position at Oxford up until the 1950s thus:

In the early years of the century, it was practically impossible for
women undergraduates to forget that that was what they were
… Later, between the wars and for what seems like a long time
afterwards, it became possible for women in the university to
simply get on with their lives. Though greatly outnumbered, they
were able to take a rest from reflecting constantly on themselves
and their role.[24]

The desire to 'forget what they were' certainly prevailed among
this new generation of Oxford women, the first to enjoy a degree
of formal equality with men.[25] They did not feel themselves in
need of the female solidarity that the women's colleges had provided in the earlier part of the century. To the contrary, working
in a particularly male-dominated subject, Mary Warnock claimed
that she 'loved being the only woman, the successful one … I did
not want all women in competition with me.'[26] Rachel Trickett
also insisted that, as an undergraduate at LMH during the Second
World War, and then later as a Fellow at St Hugh's in the 1950s,
'there was certainly no feeling of discrimination against women'.
Most exclusionary practices towards female academics had been
swept away by the war, so that the 'inward-looking and defensive
attitude among women' that such marginalisation had created
was disappearing by the 1950s. Although Trickett acknowledged
that there continued to be some areas of 'neglect' in terms of
women's access to University positions, she implied that over-
sensitivity to one's sexual identity was now considered to be a
rather unattractive trait.[27] When asked, in 2009, about experiences of discrimination during the early years of her career, Susan
Wood conceded that it did exist. She remembered, for example,
not even being considered for the post as chair of examiners
alongside the three male candidates, and yet this was a 'rather
sort of passing resentment, it wasn't something that coloured my
whole attitude'.[28] Like Warnock, Trickett and Wood appear to

have preferred to avoid dwelling on discriminatory attitudes they might have encountered and instead decided to 'simply get on with their lives'.[29]

Unsurprisingly then, feminism was viewed with some trepidation – sometimes even rejected as obstructive to the individual's claim to equality in a man's world. An undergraduate at St Hugh's in the 1950s was repelled by what she saw as the aggressive and man-hating attitudes of some of the older female dons, and blamed them for intensifying hostility to women's education within the University at large.[30] Susan Wood, rather more diplomatically, remembers feeling 'impatient' with the older style of feminism, or rather feminine pride, left over from the late nineteenth and early twentieth century.[31] Such feelings were not unusual among female academics in Britain at this time. Feminism as a political principle had already been explicitly rejected by the National Union of Teachers and the Association of University Teachers. As the historian Carol Dyhouse has pointed out, even before the Second World War too partisan an endorsement of feminism was seen as at odds with professionalism while the high status of university teaching was not easily reconciled with conventionally feminine attributes.[32]

Mary Warnock consistently affirmed that 'I had never been, and have never been a theoretical feminist' – a claim important enough to warrant such repetition. When assessing her position as a woman at Oxford after the Second World War, Warnock is at times sharply averse to the possibility of any kind of feminist analysis or action. For example, her memoirs recall the constant sexual harassment that she and many other female students were subjected to by their Classics tutor Eduard Fraenkel. Warnock told of how she was so naïve at this age that it did not occur to her that there was anything she could do to stop it, and so week after week she simply endured Fraenkel's unwelcome 'kissing' and 'tussling' with her underclothes. Sixty years on, Warnock's friend and fellow victim still felt traumatised by this experience, which she believed had left her with long-term sexual problems. Yet Warnock maintains that 'the impropriety of his sexual behaviour seemed utterly trivial' compared with the 'intellectual riches he offered us'; and she remained firm in her belief that 'I cannot think that anything would have been improved if I ... had indulged in displays of self-important feminism ...'[33] Again, we are confronted with a powerful sense that sex — both sexuality and sexual difference — was better put aside by women seeking to make their way in postwar Oxford.

Warnock's views on feminism are interesting because in spite of insisting upon her preference for a gender-blind approach, she nevertheless devoted a significant amount of her memoir to discussing her views on this issue, while her conclusion to St Hugh's centenary publication also takes feminism as its topic. Warnock expressed the uneasy relationship women academics of her generation had with feminism. Despite their desire to avoid 'constantly reflecting' on their position as women, they found themselves unable to escape the intensely gendered identity of the women's college. At certain points in writing about her experiences at St Hugh's, Warnock appears to change her position and declare that she does support feminism, but only feminism of a certain type. In her conclusion to the St Hugh's centenary history she strongly condemned 'radical feminism', which she defined as the belief that women are different from men and the desire to create newly feminised standards of truth and knowledge. Such separatism, she believed, was 'in danger of putting the clock back', for by accentuating sexual difference it threatened to return women's education to the days of segregation when they had separate lectures, curriculums and facilities imposed upon them. Instead, Warnock championed 'conservative' feminism, which could be summed up by the statement that 'women are human', and should receive identical treatment with and compete on the same grounds as men.[34]

While Warnock's definitions of radical and conservative feminism might be questioned by scholars of the movement, they nevertheless reflect two important currents of feminism found at St Hugh's throughout the twentieth century. Such different ways of understanding women's position in the University generated tensions which dominated debates about co-residency at Oxford and the St Hugh's decision to go mixed. Such views did not always exist as polar opposites, and could be expressed by the same individual at different moments. The position of the postwar generation of St Hugh's Fellows during the co-residency debates thirty years later is indicative of the fluidity of these competing feminist viewpoints. Rachel Trickett, Mary Warnock and Susan Wood were all strongly opposed to the admission of men to St Hugh's in the 1980s, with only Wood changing her mind in the final stage of this debate. Recalling these events, Susan Wood felt that perhaps in championing the single-sex college, she and her generation were 'regressing a bit to an old-fashioned feminism'.[35] Certainly this older form of pride in an all-women's community returned with a vengeance in the 1980s, particularly among the undergraduate body at St Hugh's, who, Susan Wood was able to comment, were not 'remotely spinsterish'.

Co-residence, 1972–7

The 1960s and 1970s were a time of expansion for the Oxford women's colleges, building on the formal equality of status established in the 1950s. Yet rather than continue to champion a politics of 'gender-blind' equality, many young women of this period began to advocate renewed attention to the effects of sexual

difference via their involvement in the emerging Women's Liberation Movement (WLM). The first conference of the WLM
was held at Ruskin College in 1970, only ten minutes' walk from
St Margaret's Road, making it likely that at least a few St Hugh's
students attended. Certainly there was a core of undergraduates
in college who were interested in feminism from the beginning
of the 'second wave'. In 1968 St Hugh's JCR subscribed to the
newspaper *Women Unite*, and in 1972 another student requested
that they also receive *Spare Rib*, one of the most influential magazine publications of the WLM.[36] The minutes of JCR meetings
throughout this period show that there was always at least a handful
of St Hugh's women actively engaged in feminist activism such as
the National Abortion Campaign and the International Women's
Day rallies.[37] Although the return to gender-based politics might
have surprised those postwar dons who had wished to throw off
the distinction of sex, second-wave feminism was in many ways
the product of the greater formal equality that emerged after
the Second World War. The WLM received much of its impetus
from a new demographic of young, university-educated women,
able to take advantage of more egalitarian state-funded secondary
education and the introduction of relatively generous government
grants. Better integrated into the University than any preceding
generation, many young women students of the 1960s and early
70s participated in left-wing student politics, and their experience of being treated differently from male activists – despite the
lip service paid to formal equality – was an important factor in
the re-emergence of feminism in the early 1970s.

Of course there must have been many women at St Hugh's who
took little interest in the WLM and who wished to disassociate
themselves from militant feminism.[38] Yet even the less politicised
among them had their experience as women at Oxford shaped by
the social change that marked this era. By the late 1960s college

regulations had relaxed somewhat, reflecting shifting social mores and the emergence of the 'permissive society'. Students became increasingly confident and vocal in their petitioning for greater freedom within St Hugh's, and especially for the abolition of gate rules and extension of visiting hours for men. Although the views of the St Hugh's authorities were far behind those of the students in such matters, by 1968 undergraduates were allowed to stay out as late as they pleased providing they checked in with the lodge on their return. Men's visiting hours were gradually extended in response to continual protests from the students, and, perhaps as an accompanying measure, the college doctor began providing contraceptive advice in 1966.[39] Although the women's colleges can hardly be said to have embraced the sexual revolution of the 1960s, they were certainly not immune to its effects.

Against this backdrop of increased social mixing between men and women in the University and a resurgence of feminism within society at large, Oxford began to discuss ending sexual segregation once and for all through the introduction of co-residency. The possibility of allowing women undergraduates to attend men's colleges was first voiced at New College in 1964, and by 1970 a group of men's colleges had formed quietly to discuss the question. This committee was not made public until 1972, by which time it had consulted with the women's colleges, and put in a request to the University to change their college statutes so that women could become members. On 24 April 1972, Hebdomadal Council announced its intention of granting permission to Balliol, Brasenose, Corpus Christi, Hertford, Jesus, New College, St Catherine's and Wadham to admit women. (Corpus wished to accept women only at postgraduate level, Balliol only as Fellows.) The following month this decision was fiercely debated by college representatives at University Congregation. It was eventually agreed to permit the five named colleges to introduce co-residency, though no other college would be allowed to go mixed until 1977, when Council would carry out a review assessing the impact of allowing young men and women to live and study side by side.[40]

The strict regulation of co-residency was primarily justified on grounds of protecting the women's colleges. It was believed that, should the men's colleges open their doors to women, they would probably 'cream off' the most able candidates. Co-residency was, from the start, seen by both advocates and opponents to pose a threat to the future of the women's colleges. St Hugh's Principal, Kathleen Kenyon, voiced such fears in her speech to Congregation in 1972. Like the other female Principals, she did not oppose the admission of women into men's colleges, yet she expressed grave concerns about the detrimental effects this process might have on her own institution. '[T]here is a real risk,' she warned in 1972, 'that we shall drop back into being second class citizens.' For 'at the undergraduate level girls may, on grounds of both social mix and the attraction of ancient and famous college names, put mixed colleges first, and we shall lose the best applicants'.[41] As Carol Dyhouse has argued, status has always been bound up with gender within educational institutions and particularly at the ancient and monastic universities of Oxford and Cambridge.[42] Whereas in 1920 the introduction of female undergraduates was believed to lower the status of Oxford University, by the 1970s the acquisition of a few especially bright girls at some of the men's colleges was seen to enhance their standing. And yet, female-dominated institutions continued to be viewed as irretrievably low-status. Kathleen Kenyon, for example, went on to argue that the women's colleges could not possibly compete with the newly mixed men's colleges by introducing co-residency themselves because

[o]nly men who failed to make the grade at a men's college
would try to creep in this way, and only a man who saw no hope
of getting a fellowship elsewhere would accept one at a college
where it would require an effusion of time of some thirty years
before petticoat government disappeared.[43]

The rest of Kenyon's presentation did not shirk from standing
up for her institution, delivering a fiery denunciation of women's
marginalisation within the University which none too subtly
pointed to the belated nature of the men's new-found enthusiasm
for gender equality. Yet Kenyon's arguments also implied that St
Hugh's only flourished because the best women students had no
choice but to apply there. What had become of the early twentieth-century pride in all-female institutions? Why was Kathleen
Kenyon not celebrating the destruction of the last bastion of male
privilege in the University? Certainly, some of her colleagues at
St Hugh's felt that their Principal's speech was overly defeatist
and gratuitously depreciative of their college.[44] But perhaps all
was not as it seemed, for the politics surrounding the introduction of co-residency were far from straightforward, and the 'real'
feminist position was hard to identify. Again the complexities of
ensuring that women were able to reach their full potential in a
male-dominated institution became apparent. While some urged
the need to do away with special treatment for women, including
their exclusion from the men's colleges, others questioned the
benefits of merely superficial forms of equality. 'Feminism' was
used both genuinely and opportunistically in the ensuing debates
and interpreted in a variety of ways: many arguments thus combined pro- and anti-woman sentiments in a confusing manner.

Gender equality had been forced into the University's consciousness by the WLM and the generally more egalitarian
atmosphere engendered by the 1962 Education Act. The 1972
co-residency debates could not avoid nodding in the direction of

the women's movement, even if all reference to 'women's liberation' was merely rhetorical. Opponents of co-residency, meanwhile, were careful to insist that they were not 'anti-feminist'.[45]
The most common argument initially made by those men's colleges who wished to admit women was that it would open up
more places for women in the University – at present they made
up only 20 per cent of Oxford undergraduates.[46] Though no
longer limited by statute, the numbers of women students were
kept down by the fact that they could only apply to five out of
more than thirty colleges, meaning that competition for places
at the women's colleges was far greater than at the men's. Yet it
was not straightforwardly altruistic or feminist motives that led
that first group of men's colleges to open their doors to women.
While many male dons were undoubtedly keen to create more
opportunities for women, they were also attracted by the prospect of improving their college's academic standing by luring the
cleverest female candidates away from the women's colleges.[47]

Oxford's undergraduate representative bodies were also in
favour of going mixed on the basis that this would increase the
overall numbers of female students. In 1971 the Student Representation Committee submitted a report to University Governing Body declaring that 'The only feasible way to increase
the proportion of women at Oxford is to admit them to the
present men's colleges.'[48] Yet such arguments did not always place
the interests of women first. Rather than couched in explicitly
feminist terms, co-education was supported by (mainly male)
student leaders on the grounds that it was the only possible progressive position. As the historian Marie Hicks has pointed out,
they tended to focus upon the social and intellectual benefits of
interaction between the sexes, and often seemed more concerned
with how this would improve the lives of men, than with fighting
for sexual equality.[49]

Women students tended to support co-residency for very
different reasons. In 1974, St Hugh's JCR passed overwhelmingly a motion to 're-affirm' their support for co-residency. The
motion stated that the current moratorium of five years, pre-
venting more men's colleges from admitting women until 1977,
should be abolished. Whereas senior members of the college had
seen this as necessary to prevent mass exodus to the men's colleges, St Hugh's junior members believed the moratorium to be
a discriminatory practice, unfairly limiting the number of places
available to women students. This was also the view of a group
called 'Women Against the Quota', who that same year picketed
Congregation and invaded the student union to press for all colleges to be opened to women.[50] St Hugh's Tutor, Theo Cooper,
who was also acting as the first female Senior Proctor at the time,
defended the quota against student protests – claiming that it was
not a restriction but a guideline based upon predictions of how
many 'good woman candidates' might apply. The five men's colleges had agreed not to give places to more than twenty women
per year in order to protect the women's colleges – a decision
premised on the assumption that there was an overall shortage of
'good women'.[51]

In light of such statements about the lack of female talent
available, it is easy to see how St Hugh's students felt betrayed
by the refusal of their tutors to give their wholehearted support
to co-residency. The belief that the numbers of clever women
were far more limited than numbers of clever male applicants
was widespread and frequently referred to by the more reaction-
ary elements of the men's colleges. Opponents of co-residency
declared that 'there is no untapped pool of feminine talent available', nor did they believe that 'there are vast untapped depos-
its of women more able than the less able men we at present
take' – suggesting that the ratio of clever women to men would

never exceed the 1:4 reflected in the University's current intake.[52] Yet members of the women's colleges, such as Kathleen Kenyon, must also have accepted that this was the case, for otherwise they would not have expressed such concern about the impact of men's colleges going mixed.

In response, some of the more intransigent male supporters of co-education accused the women's colleges of acting selfishly, preferring their own institutional success over widening women's educational opportunities. One article in the *Oxford University Gazette* referred to them as 'Uncle Toms' – women complicit in a patriarchal system who cared only for their own privileged position in their master's house.[53] While the attitudes of some members of the women's colleges did undoubtedly reveal the difficulties of trying to act at once in the interests of their own institutions and for women in general (a fairly demanding task in any situation), more robust feminist arguments were also in evidence. Many members of St Hugh's SCR, for example, supported increasing the number of places for women at Oxford. In 1964, when the prospect of admitting women to one of the men's colleges was first raised, Theo Cooper, Betty Kemp, Mary Warnock and Susan Wood were among the sixteen female Oxford dons who signed a letter to the *Observer* registering their support for New College's proposal to introduce 'joint education'.[54] It was not that the women's colleges had any uncertainty about the issue in principle – of course they were in favour of improving the position of women in Oxford and increasing numbers. Their issue was with the manner in which this principle was to be implemented. At this stage, many supported what looked to be the most viable approach of a small number of men's colleges admitting women, thus giving applicants of either sex a choice of mixed- or single-sex without having too great an impact on the women's colleges. Susan Wood recalls that for many, it was the 'Gadarene swine-like rush' of the rest of the men's colleges to snap up the women after the moratorium had been lifted that angered many in the women's colleges.[55]

Although initially supportive of the moves to co-residency, Mary Warnock had changed her position by 1972, arguing that the present scheme would not achieve its stated goal of improving educational opportunities for women. For, to admit women 'as a minority group into what will continue to be a men's college is precisely not to be given equality of status'. Mary Warnock was not hopeful about how the process of co-residency would play out in a University where men always seemed to be at an advantage. Admitting a handful of women into a few of the men's colleges was not going to address the reasons that fewer women than men applied to Oxford in the first place, and why even fewer went on to become academics. Without confronting systemic inequalities, co-education would not work in women's interests. Moreover, if women were accepted into men's colleges it would not be long before women's colleges would have to start accepting men. This, warned Warnock, could have an even more disastrous effect upon women's position in the University. For by reforming out of existence the one place where they could be sure of avoiding discrimination in favour of male candidates, full integration at the Fellowship level could lead to a situation where even the old women's colleges employed only a single 'token' female Fellow.[56]

St Hugh's goes mixed, 1977–87

Warnock was, of course, correct in thinking that the admission of women into men's colleges would soon lead to discussions about the need for the women's colleges to become co-educational. This question dominated at St Hugh's throughout the 1980s, during which arguments about the inadequacy of a gender-blind approach to managing women's position in the University, and the need instead to address their distinctive needs as women, became ever more prevalent. In 1977, at the end of the five-year moratorium, the committee appointed to review the trial period of co-residency presented its report. It recommended that there ought to be no more restrictions and any college wishing to go mixed should be free to do so. Co-residency had increased the proportion of female students from 20 to 23 per cent, while the standard of entry (based upon their A-Level results) had only fallen slightly – bringing them into line with the male candidates who had always on average been of a slightly inferior calibre. Moreover, the Sex Discrimination Act of 1975 now made it illegal to impose a quota upon the number of women students a mixed college was permitted to admit. In response to this report, many of the same arguments and concerns about the impact of co-residency upon the women's colleges were repeated, though by now the transition to co-education appeared inevitable.[57]

In 1979 St Anne's and LMH went fully mixed and St Hugh's began to admit male Fellows. Given the grave warnings of Mary Warnock, only seven years before, about the effects that such a move would have upon women academics, it seems slightly strange that this decision should have been remembered as a relatively uncontroversial one.[58] Possibly the idea of men and women working together within the University had become so common by this point, particularly since St Hugh's was already employing men as short-term lecturers, that it did not feel as though it represented a big shift in the organisation of the college.[59] Some members, however, did recognise that the admission of men at a senior level made the acceptance of male undergraduates at some point inevitable, for no other college occupied the same anomalous halfway house.[60] In 1980 the maths tutor Mary Lunn took a motion to Governing Body calling for St Hugh's to admit male undergraduates. Her main reasons for supporting such a move were academic – St Hugh's had achieved poor results in examinations for the last two years, while the number of first-choice applicants at admissions was 'dangerously low'. She felt that there were clever boys being rejected because there were not enough places for them (an interesting reversal of the arguments made about a lack of places for women students in the early 1970s – even by 1988 men still constituted more than 60 per cent of undergraduates), and the situation was particularly acute in the sciences. Mary Lunn finished with 'a plea for all tutors of subjects like my own, who are tired of teaching an excessive number of the feebler undergraduates and who see a clear remedy'.[61] Already in 1980 the majority of Governing Body was in favour of going mixed, but with twelve votes in favour and nine against they had not secured the two-thirds majority they needed.

Rachel Trickett, who had by now succeeded Kathleen Kenyon as Principal, was strongly opposed to going mixed. Whereas the advocates of admitting men tended to focus on the supposedly 'gender-neutral' issue of the academic benefits it would bring, those who wanted St Hugh's to remain as it was tried to frame the debate around the question of whether women did better in mixed- or single-sex institutions. Trickett argued that female students in all-women colleges had more time to concentrate on their work and, free from the pressures of having to compete with men, were better able to build up their confidence and develop their talents.[62] She felt strongly enough on this question to make her case to the national press while the debate in her own college raged on. In 1981 she told the *Observer* of how she had recently dined in a newly mixed men's college. When she asked her undergraduate host why there were only four women students in Hall that night, he had replied: 'Oh … they don't dine much, you know, they're generally making supper for their boyfriends.'[63] By the 1980s Trickett's sentiments were supported by the majority of the JCR and the Middle Common Room (MCR) of graduate students. Shortly before Governing Body first debated the question in 1980, the JCR had its own discussion – when only four members voted to admit men against sixty-one who wished to retain the status quo. The results of this vote were conveyed to Governing Body and from then on St Hugh's undergraduates sought to influence the decision of the college authorities as much as possible.[64] The MCR also lobbied the Governing Body, pointing out that the support provided by an all-female community at undergraduate and graduate level was crucial, especially to those who wished to pursue an academic career.[65]

Many by this time were arguing that the end of single-sex colleges would lead to a reduction in the numbers of women Fellows. While the former men's colleges were extremely slow in appointing women to their Fellowships, men very quickly began to take up the places previously reserved for women at St Anne's, Lady Margaret Hall and St Hugh's. Only one year after they had admitted male Fellows LMH had seventeen men, St Anne's had sixteen, St Hugh's had eleven men on their academic staff of about forty-one. By contrast, Brasenose still had no women at a senior level six years after going mixed, while Jesus – the best of the men's colleges in this respect – had five women in a staff of close to 80.[66] Rachel Trickett stated that she would not be in favour of opening up all-women institutions to men until it was possible to have a Mistress of Balliol as well as a male Principal of Lady Margaret Hall.[67] It was also feared that going mixed would reduce the number of places open to women at the undergraduate level too. The old men's colleges continued to admit only very small numbers of female applicants each year, and even with three remaining women's colleges, female undergraduates were in the minority overall. If places at St Hugh's were given over to men, this number would decrease even further.[68]

Support for St Hugh's to remain single-sex was by now often regarded in the press and in the University itself as the 'feminist' position.[69] Certainly the JCR's opposition was part of a general feminist culture among students at the time.[70] Their defence of their all-women community also reflected wider shifts within the British women's movement which, by the 1980s, placed increasing emphasis on the need for women to create their own spaces separate from those of men. Whereas in the mid-1970s the more politicised and progressive elements of the JCR were strongly in favour of admitting men, by the early 1980s the 'radical' position had switched to advocating that St Hugh's remain single-sex.[71] In many ways, the alliance that emerged between the Principal and her left-leaning undergraduates was an odd one. As one journalist commented, 'a few of her students no doubt think Miss Trickett is so far to the right, so much of the Establishment, as to be unsightable', for Trickett was indeed a self-identified 'conservative ... [and] paid up member of the Church of England'.[72] Some have suggested that, despite their feminist rhetoric, SCR opponents of going mixed did not give sufficient thought to how an all-female institution could continue to thrive in an otherwise co-educational University.[73] Yet although much opposition to co-residency may well have been motivated by loyalty to the status quo, this was wholly in keeping with a pre-existing tradition of conservative feminism at St Hugh's, allowing for a wholly sincere appeal to the college's founding values.

Rachel Trickett, for example, reminded Governing Body that 'we were founded to foster and encourage the education of women', and suggested that, instead of admitting men to raise academic standards, the college might more actively recruit 'highly intelligent perhaps feminist girls who really want to be at a women's college'.[74] She certainly appears to have courted this element in the JCR, giving a talk in 1982 on 'Women in Education' which included a detailed history of the college as well as pessimistic predictions about the difficulties women academics would face should the remaining women's colleges go mixed.[75] The JCR responded enthusiastically to this invocation of St Hugh's founding values, and they too subsequently argued that turning St Hugh's into a 'male dominated academic institution' would be 'contrary to the original endowment of the college'.[76] Such a break with the past also had important financial implications. For, as both Trickett and the JCR pointed out, the large fund-raising drive for the college centenary aimed to generate pride in St Hugh's hundred-year-long record of women's education, and was primarily targeted at Old Members, many of whom opposed the admission of men.[77]

In spite of the varied arguments put forward in favour of staying single-sex, St Hugh's Governing Body did finally vote in 1985–6 to admit men: the first male candidates were interviewed in December 1986 and matriculated in October 1987.[78] Those in favour of co-residency had always affirmed their commitment to a form of gender-neutral equality, which they offered as a counter to the more separatist feminist arguments put forward by the advocates of single-sex education. Mary Lunn, for example, had maintained that the college needed to teach women students how to mix with men at an earlier stage, rather than wait until they found themselves struggling in the workplace, ill-equipped to negotiate the inequalities of the real world.[79] By 1986, many Fellows felt exhausted by the last seven years of uncertainty, and were keen to move on from what one don remembered as the 'poisonous' atmosphere the disagreement had at times produced. Susan Wood decided to change her position and vote in favour of co-residency simply because she felt that this was the only way to settle the issue.[80] Marilyn Butler, a strong supporter of single-sex colleges, decided, when taking up a post at Cambridge, not to choose one of the remaining women's colleges because she could not bear the thought of having to go through it all over again.[81] Perhaps such fatigue explained why, in the newly mixed college, those who had argued so strongly against the pitfalls of co-education did not put an equal-opportunities policy in place, nor any other measures to ensure that women were not dominated by the male intake. Instead, the main aim of the Steering Committee for the Admission of Men concentrated on ensuring that gender 'ghettos' were not created when allocating rooms in college and that men and women students mixed as much as possible.[82]

During the first year of the new admissions, tutors were left to admit students on the basis of academic merit and to put aside questions of gender balance. Such a policy, however, soon created problems when, during the second year of interviewing male applicants alongside women, places were offered to seventy-nine men and only forty women. Some subjects, such as Law, did not accept any female candidates at all. The Principal was dismayed by the results: 'I assure you that we did not plan to admit twice as many men as women. It just came out that way,' she told the press; 'I am very concerned.' Yet Trickett believed that this gender imbalance was due to the fact that when tutors 'tried to get the best people they can', they inevitably ended up with more men than women because 'too many of the best women are applying to the former men's colleges'.[83] The JCR tried to offer constructive advice. It did not advocate positive discrimination but it did call on the SCR to more actively pursue female candidates who had put down St Hugh's as their second or third choice and to strengthen links with secondary schools to attract larger numbers of female students in the first place.[84] Yet the Fellowship continued to feel powerless to affect the situation. The Governing

Body's report on admissions acknowledged the problem of large numbers of men being accepted, but concluded that: 'There seems no easy counter to this, except by an increase in the number of good female applicants.'[85] The possibility that the interview process itself might inherently discriminate against women who, it had been frequently pointed out during the debates over going mixed, were often less outspoken and less confident than men, was not given official consideration.

The JCR remained strongly opposed to admitting men even after the Governing Body had made its final decision.[86] It went on strike during the 1986 Open Day, refusing to offer any help or endorsement of this important event.[87] Undergraduates also voted to keep the position of JCR President women-only and prohibit male students from standing for the position. This amendment remained in place for over a year despite threats by the college authorities that such a move was illegal and would lead to the confiscation of JCR funds.[88] To mark the arrival of the first male students, St Hugh's Women's Group organised a protest street party in St Margaret's Road.[89] Charlotte Hume, an undergraduate at the time, remembered how '[t]he first mixed year was a real test of patience for everyone and there were numerous rustications. There seemed to be extremes in behaviour. Blue-stocking women appeared more uptight and some men took behaving badly to an art-form.' One of the first male students, Jason Hollands, for example, passed a motion at his first-ever JCR meeting to stop students referring to the common room as the 'Winnie Mandela Room' (as a former generation of female students had proudly titled it) and return to the more traditional 'Junior Common Room'. Perhaps Hollands felt it necessary to assert himself in the face of 'jokes from members of other colleges about being at a girls' college' – something which was also associated during these years with not being clever enough to get into a 'proper' college.[90] Even by the 1980s, female-dominated institutions were still low-status, while the entry of men was often implicitly assumed to bring increased prestige – something that some of the first male students were well aware of. 'I decided early on that I wasn't going to spend three of the best years of my life apologising for my sex,' declared Simon Dickson. 'St Hugh's needed men to raise its profile across the University as a whole … As things stood in 1987, the College was – in University-wide terms – a backwater.'[91]

St Hugh's did ultimately adjust to becoming a mixed college. The JCR President wrote a diplomatic report for the *Chronicle* at the end of the academic year of 1987/8, recording that 'on reflection the first year of men at St Hugh's reveals a smooth and successful transition'.[92] By 1989, the JCR had agreed to remove the amendment restricting the post of JCR President to women only, and put in place a joint post to be filled by one man and one woman. This only lasted for two terms however, and was removed partly in the belief that the college was now ready to practise gender equality without having it forced upon them (there was not another female JCR President until 1994, and there have only been two more since then). When this author applied to St Hugh's as an undergraduate in 2000, I was only vaguely aware that it had once, in the distant past, been a women's college and I was certainly ignorant of the significance of this to past generations of students. St Hugh's as a mixed college had acquired a new identity, not unrelated to its former life as an all-women institution. It promoted itself in its prospectus as 'unstuffy', 'friendly' and open to students from 'non-traditional' backgrounds. Its wider reputation confirmed this – St Hugh's was, like the other former women's colleges, considered to be more progressive and less tradition-bound than the older former men's colleges, and attracted many students precisely for these reasons. The low prestige of St

Hugh's as a women's college had been translated into a more positive outlook that valued the ways in which it stood out from the more traditional Oxbridge model. For this, perhaps, we should be grateful to that committed element of the JCR who fought for St Hugh's to 'stop apologising for being a women's college'. For although they lost the fight against going mixed, they succeeded in developing a sense of pride in, what was now a voluntary, exclusion from the establishment.

4

WHO CLEANS A ROOM OF ONE'S OWN?

Scouts, students and domestic labour, 1886–2011

'We took each other for granted. They did their job, we did ours.'
St Hugh's undergraduate, matric. 1950

'I don't really remember them much. Which is worrying.'
St Hugh's undergraduate, matric. 1965

'They didn't know anything!'
'Hadn't a clue!'
Retired scouts recalling St Hugh's undergraduates, 2009

D OMESTIC STAFF have a shadowy presence in the history of St Hugh's. They are not mentioned in the official accounts left for us by former Principals and undergraduates; and they are encountered only occasionally, and then fleetingly, in the college archives. Yet chance references remind us that domestic staff were, from the very beginning, a constant presence at St Hugh's. Indeed its first residents were Mrs Ward, the housekeeper, and Annie Beck, the house and parlour maid, who arrived early in 1886 to prepare for the first four students.[1] We also encounter servants at the centre of some of the most significant events in the history of the college. In 1924, for example, when Principal Jourdain dropped dead from a heart attack after receiving a rebuke from the Chancellor of the University, it was Mabel, the parlourmaid, who discovered her body.[2] In fact, the very fabric of St Hugh's grew up around the assumed presence and labour of domestic staff: Main Building and the Mary Gray Allen wing were built with specially designed servants' quarters, while any plans to expand the college had to consider the accommodation of domestic workers well into the twentieth century.

Domestic staff or 'college servants', as they were known until very recently, are essential to the smooth running and therefore ultimate success of the college. For students to study and for tutors to teach it is necessary also that rooms are tidied, food is served, and bathrooms are scrubbed clean. 'Scouts' (the Oxford term for cleaners and dining-room staff), along with kitchen staff, form a key part of St Hugh's and need to be included in its history. Exploring this 'other' side of college life not only tells a part of the story that has previously been forgotten or ignored, but also suggests new ways of looking at those aspects of St Hugh's that *have* formed an integral part of its historical narrative. For, as this chapter will reveal, the life of the mind at St Hugh's has been intimately bound up with the details of domesticity; while the roles and aspirations of undergraduates were forged in relation to those women who cooked and cleaned for them. St Hugh's evolving institutional identity, its expansion and professionalisation, is especially clearly viewed in terms of the transformation of the role of the 'college servant', especially in the last few decades.

The figure of the female servant was important to broader discussions of what it meant to be both 'feminine' and 'feminist', and the history of domestic service is inseparable from a history of the 'new' middle-class professional woman created at St Hugh's. Looking at them together disrupts one of the most important paradigms for understanding the history of women's education, namely Virginia Woolf's 'room of one's own'. A very different narrative of the changing role of twentieth-century women emerges once we ask who it was that cleaned this room. What was the 'reality' behind the popular perception of the female servant, what kinds of women worked at St Hugh's and what motivated and compelled them to take on domestic work? Domestic staff were in the ambiguous position of being both members of and workers for the college. Many scouts formed positive and close relationships with students, yet the idea that they are 'part of the family' has always sat uncomfortably along-side the potential for exploitation within the workplace. From the First World War onwards, both scouts and students began to question what seemed to be outdated hierarchical relationships enshrined within the Oxford colleges, resulting in moments of dramatic conflict as well as more sustained attempts to organ-ise the domestic workforce. Recently, the more traditional and informal aspects of the domestic side of St Hugh's have given way to a managerial and businesslike approach. What does this tell us about the changing nature of the Oxford college and higher education more generally, and what does it mean for the lives of those whose work remains so crucial to the whole of the Uni-versity community?

The other women: servants, 'ladies' and feminists

It is in the domestic sphere that gender identities and class divi-sions between women are most clearly revealed. And in the late nineteenth and early twentieth century, the figure of the female servant was central to the identity of the kinds of middle-class women – both feminine and feminist – that graduated from St Hugh's. The Victorian servant served as a counterpoint to representations of her mistress as 'the angel in the house'. The hard manual labour performed by domestic servants both literally and metaphorically protected their female employer from contamination by the 'dirty' world of work, bolstering the idealised vision of middle-class femininity as physically delicate and morally superior.[3] This strange paradox of what constituted true 'womanhood' was clearly evident during the early days of the Oxbridge women's colleges. Then, the concern over whether women students were physically strong enough to cope with rigorous study did not extend to those other female residents of the colleges who rose at 6 every morning to lug buckets of coal up the stairs.

Even by the mid-twentieth century servants were perceived by many as irrevocably and unfathomably *different* from the women who employed them. In 1940, soon after graduating from Somerville College, Celia Fremlin went to work as a char in order to explore the mysterious world of the 'domestic'. Fremlin's stated aim was to remedy a situation in which 'the trouble is that the two of you speak different languages; you think different thoughts, you live in different worlds. In a word, you belong to different classes of British society.'[4] In light of such attitudes it becomes easier to understand how servants could have remained absent from the official records of St Hugh's, despite having lived alongside students and tutors. Yet perhaps this insistence upon the cultural gulf between servants and ladies was a reaction to the fact that, in everyday life, the relationship between middle-class women and their servants was defined less by distance or difference, than by intimate physical proximity.

In many ways, the Victorian servant was required to offer her own body as a replacement for that of her mistress; cooking and cleaning for her but also dressing her, fetching small items, and adjusting the physical environment for her comfort. This created a relationship that was not only deferential but also stifling and infantilising.[5] Even by the 1920s and 30s, middle-class women remained vastly dependent upon their servants. Alison Light, in her work on Virginia Woolf, reveals the extent to which a woman otherwise so proud of her independence was left 'pathetically stranded' without her cook and maid – 'unable to invite [her] friends to dinner or even answer the front door'.[6] While most homes now employed far fewer servants, houses were also smaller, forcing mistress and maid to live together in an even more confined space.[7] The lack of physical distance, combined with the erosion of social hierarchies in the world at large, also made it more difficult to maintain distinctions of status and authority. By the interwar period the 'servant question' had become particularly explosive terrain for the kinds of women graduating from the Oxbridge women's colleges.

For many educated women, servants continued as the 'other', representing the inverse of the modern, emancipated female. In 1935, the Somervillian novelist Dorothy L. Sayers published *Gaudy Night*, in which the central character Harriet Vane (like Sayers, a successful writer of crime fiction) struggles with the question of what it means to be a truly independent woman. The novel is set in a fictional Oxford women's college, and throughout the book the college scouts are depicted as ridiculous and grotesque figures – the mirror image of the community of female scholars they live alongside. During a thunderstorm, which members of the Senior Common Room find thoroughly enjoyable, the servants succumb instead to superstition and lack of self-control, with 'Carrie in hysterics, and Cook thinking her last hour had come, and Annie shrieking to heaven that her darling children would be terrified ... and one of the kitchen maids having an outbreak of religious blues.'[8] The scouts represent just those unattractive 'female' qualities – ignorance, irrationality, and emotional incontinence – from which modern independent women such as Harriet Vane (and Dorothy L. Sayers) most wished to distance themselves.

Worst of all, the female servants reject the values, achievements and intellectual freedom that are the result of fifty years of struggle by the pioneering community of college women. Annie the scout tells Harriet that:

> it seems to me a dreadful thing to see all these unmarried ladies living together. It isn't natural, is it? It seems a great shame to keep up this big place just for women to study books in. I can't see what girls want with books. Books won't teach them to be good wives.

Yet Sayers's venomous depiction of working-class women also reveals her own unease with the feminist rejection of domesticity and the choices it has led her heroine to make. On the one hand, ridiculing servants provides a reassuring way for Sayers to distance herself from a life of domestic drudgery which her university education and modern views have enabled her to escape. On the other, the female servant becomes a threatening figure – the focal point for Sayers's ambivalence over whether feminism also compels a renunciation of femininity.[9] Harriet Vane's dilemma throughout the novel is whether she, in rejecting conventional marriage and family life, is also denying her true womanly nature. Could it be that the uneducated college servants were in fact more feminine than some of the strange hybrid creatures that held college Fellowships?[10]

Gaudy Night is reflective of a wider discomfort within twentieth-century feminism with the question of domesticity and domestic labour. For so many middle-class feminists over the course of the century, domesticity represented their confinement in the home while freedom was equated with fulfilment outside it. Yet the view that, as Alison Light puts it, 'the domestic is something one rises above in order to get on with the real business of life' does not solve the problem of how the work gets done.[11] By the interwar period, a significant minority of middle-class women were now able to acquire a university education and pursue a professional career. Yet the women's movement, and the social changes that enabled such a development, left unchallenged power relations within the family and the gendered division of labour.[12] Women were still responsible for the work of keeping house and raising children, and if they wished to work outside the home it was necessary to employ servants to do the work within it. Their position was made more difficult after the First World War when new employment opportunities in factories and shops began to attract young working-class women away from domestic service, creating a 'shortage' of servants.[13] The feminist response was to call for improvements in the conditions of domestic service, for mistresses to treat their maids more kindly, but they did not critique the fundamental inequality of such a relationship.[14] While feminists of the period frequently discussed how to combine their careers with raising a family, they rarely suggested that the answer was to restructure the division of labour within the home, compelling their husbands to take on a greater share of the domestic work.[15] Instead, working-class women were required to carry the burden of professional women's new-found freedom.[16]

The class conflict inherent in this version of emancipation also lay at the heart of the famous feminist motif of 'a room of one's own', a concept that has become central to historical narratives of the women's colleges. The first women's colleges are often seen as the embodiment of Virginia Woolf's vision of intellectual and spiritual freedom, whereby women would have space and

A room of one's own at St Hugh's, c. 1928. (St Hugh's College Archive)

time free from domestic duties to develop their creative powers. Woolf's essay 'A Room of One's Own' was first delivered as a lecture in 1928 at Newnham and Girton colleges in Cambridge. There Woolf reiterated the complaints of the first generations of women students, who found university a welcome relief from the constant round of social calls and family duties that prevented them from pursuing their studies at home. Woolf surely did not need, therefore, to remind her audience that 'women never have half an hour … that they can call their own'.[17] The founders of the first women's colleges had insisted that girls should be permitted to study away from home in a residential community of like-minded scholars, and in providing their students with their own study-bedrooms, they asserted women's right to a room of their own long before Woolf's famous essay.[18]

Well into the twentieth century, students at St Hugh's frequently cited having their own room, providing full control over how and when to study, as the most important factor in their intellectual development.[19] A room of one's own often came to symbolise the wider psychological independence of college life for, as Virginia Woolf was well aware, 'intellectual freedom depends upon material things'.[20] St Hugh's students were also clear that one of the primary benefits of college was that it freed one from domestic chores. One Old Student, at St Hugh's in the 1970s, recalls with wonder this 'pampered' lifestyle: 'In fact, now I think of having my room done; meals bought, prepared and washed up; buildings maintained and insured; *everything* taken care of so that I could learn interesting things and stretch my mind – well, when can I come back?' The luxury of not having to perform any domestic labour was perhaps most apparent to students from less well-off backgrounds. One account of St Hugh's in the 1930s, by the daughter of an impoverished schoolteacher, conveys the enchantment of a room of one's own while also reminding us what, or rather who, made such a thing possible:

> For the first time in my life I had a 'room of my own', having always had to share with my sister at home. It was a delight to arrange it to my taste, putting up the curtains and disguising the bed in the day time with a matching cover, filling the shelves with my own books and brightening a corner with a vase of flowers. I was greatly surprised on the second morning when a little maid came in while I was still abed to clean the grate, lay a fire and fill a coal scuttle. Never having been waited on before, I felt vaguely guilty.[21]

Domestic life at St Hugh's, then, offers a microcosm of one of the key contradictions of twentieth-century feminism. The college gave one group of women an immensely important, if ultimately limited, kind of freedom, which was entirely reliant upon the labour of another group of women. We know a great deal about the women who enjoyed a room of one's own; we will now explore the lives of those who cleaned it.

St Hugh's domestic staff, 1886 to the present day

Domestic workers have always constituted a significant proportion of college members. By 1915, when St Hugh's had grown too large for the houses in Norham Gardens and plans were being made for the new buildings, the Council predicted that accommodation would need to be provided for sixty-three students and seven servants.[22] By the 1920s just over thirty domestic staff were employed.[23] Their numbers continued to rise, over the course of the century, and today the college employs seventy-five domestic staff to cater for 655 students, eighteen administrators and sixty-two Tutors and Fellows.[24] Yet the St Hugh's archives, which hold a rich collection of official papers, committee minutes, college publications, newsletters, diaries, personal correspondence and memoirs, have frustratingly little to tell us about domestic workers. The college wage books are one of the few surviving records concerned with the scouts, and yet even here (up until the 1950s) they are referred to by their first names only. And so we are left wondering what kinds of women Dorothy, Winifred, Eva, Hilda, Ivy and Kathleen might have been.[25]

St Hugh's is not exceptional in this sense. Only one historical work has ever been published about Oxford college servants, while histories of women's education have never before looked at domestic workers.[26] Some of the most fruitful insights into the lives of servants at St Hugh's come from trying to interpret these absences. The silence of the archives reflects contemporary expectations of a 'green-baize-door society'[27] which believed that servants should remain invisible while also always being on hand. It acts as a reminder of how social hierarchies were established and maintained through the segregation of space and material culture.[28] This was certainly a concern for those planning St Hugh's first purpose-built site. A letter was sent, for example, by a

St Hugh's college servants, c. 1928. (St Hugh's College Archive)

Council member specifying that 'servants' rooms be together and not scattered among students', and the architects were also asked to provide servants with their own separate passageway by which to reach the front door.[29] Although the role of college 'servant' has undergone fundamental changes since the early years of St Hugh's, scouts today still describe how 'we try to be as invisible as possible'. Maintaining a separation between the domestic and academic work at St Hugh's, they claim, makes it 'more comfortable for everybody'.[30]

The role of Oxford 'college servant' is as ancient as the University itself and brings with it almost as many traditions. By the mid-nineteenth century the college scout had entered into the mythology of the Oxbridge undergraduate – part of his world of hard drinking, high living and practical jokes.[31] The scout began to acquire a recognisable set of cultural characteristics – known primarily (and in no particular order) for his loyalty, his comic nature and his drunkenness. Female servants, like the women's colleges themselves, entered this tradition-laden world relatively late in the day. Women domestics were rarely able to share in the dubious prestige accorded to 'the most obliging man in Europe', and in the early days St Hugh's servants were organised more along the lines of a modest North Oxford family home.[32] Only a housekeeper and parlourmaid are mentioned in early accounts of the college, though it is probable that a 'daily' or 'char' woman would also have come in on a regular but part-time basis. Vera Brittain suggested that the tiny budgets of the early women's colleges compelled them to economise on servants and perform more of the domestic labour themselves. Yet accounts from St Hugh's suggest that it was the maids who shouldered most of the financial hardship: 'Finances were meagre ... Except for making beds and doing the cooking they [the two resident maids] did everything, grates, lamps [gas was still used because Wordsworth couldn't afford to install electricity], cleaning. They must have served St Hugh's for about 15 hours a day ...'[33]

The domestic side of St Hugh's, however, quickly expanded and began to be more closely modelled on that of the men's colleges. By 1914 a bursar had been employed to oversee domestic and administrative work and more formal hierarchies were introduced into the now much larger body of staff.[34] By the mid-Twenties the female staff wore uniforms, and in 1930 the college was budgeting to employ thirty-six maids plus an unspecified number of 'daily women' to cater for a projected figure of 155 students and eight tutors.[35] As the century progressed, different departments emerged, dividing those who answered to the cook from those who worked for the SCR, who in turn often saw themselves as superior to the JCR scouts.[36]

When the college first opened, the women who came to work as maids would have been far more representative of the 'average' woman than those who came as students. For at the end of the nineteenth century over a third of all women in waged work were employed in domestic service and in 1881 a third of *all* women aged from fifteen to twenty were classified as such.[37] Service was by far the largest area of women's employment in Oxford at the turn of the century, accounting for almost half of the city's female wage earners. The social investigator Violet Butler believed that it attracted 'quiet' and 'steady-going' young women, while their 'livelier' sisters were more likely to be employed in shop work, the dress industry or as unskilled bookbinders and printmakers at the University Press. Butler also reckoned that Oxford's live-in servants tended to come either from very poor families unable to keep them, or from the better class of artisan, those who occupied the red-brick cottages of Jericho and St Clements with their 'fair gardens' and starched muslin curtains.[38]

Domestic work was also an obvious choice for those migrating from the impoverished rural communities surrounding Oxford which were hit particularly badly by the agricultural recession in the last quarter of the nineteenth century.[39] Servants tended to be very young (42 per cent were under the age of twenty in 1880), and almost invariably unmarried.[40] In 1898 St Hugh's employed two maids, Kate Thomas (who had come to the college in 1888) and Ellen; a cook, Mrs Davies; and a 'char', Mrs Beauchamp.[41] Kate and Ellen were probably younger single women, who would typically have entered service at the age of fourteen and then worked for about ten to fifteen years before marrying.[42] It was rare for married women to be employed as live-in servants unless their husbands were groundsmen or caretakers, but daily 'charring' was often taken on by the wives of seasonal labourers or men either too ill or unwilling to support their families.[43]

The First World War brought about dramatic changes to patterns of female employment and domestic service, and between 1914 and 1918 almost 400,000 servants left domestic work for the armed forces, war production or munitions factories. Having experienced higher wages and greater freedom, many declined to return to service once the war had ended.[44] The expanding areas of light manufacturing and retail work now held more appeal, so that by the 1920s the number of female servants accounted for only 25 per cent of those in paid employment.[45] In the 1930s, however, high unemployment coupled with a coercive unemployment benefits system forced many back into service.[46] It was not until after the Second World War, therefore, that domestic service stopped being one of the main employment options for young working-class women. By the 1950s domestic labour in the home was increasingly the preserve of the unwaged housewife and in 1951 only one in ten women were employed as cleaners.[47]

This national picture, however, was subject to significant regional variations. Servants at St Hugh's in the early twentieth century also chafed against long hours and strict rules. One maid, for example, asked to be allowed to stop work at 10 p.m. and for permission to speak to her brother when she met him in the street – requests which Principal Jourdain dismissed as ridiculous.[48] Yet it was not always easy to find alternative work, even after the First World War, in a town where the University remained one of the most important employers. In fact, the numbers of women working as college servants probably rose during this period as male scouts were attracted away from the colleges by the much higher wages of the Morris Motor Factory in Cowley and women stepped into their vacated positions.[49] In the late 1920s and 30s, therefore, St Hugh's continued to employ many fourteen- and fifteen-year-old girls straight from school (we see them in the front row of the servants' 1928 portrait). Following the Second World War, as domestic service became something that women could move more easily in and out of at different stages in their lives, scouting at St Hugh's was increasingly taken on as a part-time job fitted in around women's family commitments.[50] Pat Spring started working for this reason in the late 1970s:

> I was a single Mum and had a young daughter. I came up and I got the job ... Then in [19]84 my daughter was getting to be a teenager – and I used to come back in the evenings as well.

Scouting appealed to working mothers especially because they finished work before the end of the school day, and also because, until recently, they were able to bring their children into college during the holidays.[51]

No statistics are available for the ethnicity of St Hugh's domestic staff, but anecdotally it appears that in the last decade a greater number of recent migrants have been employed. Historically, jobs in Oxford colleges were most commonly advertised by word of mouth – creating close-knit communities of friends, acquaintances and often family members working in the same place.[52] This practice has continued among migrant communities, so that St Hugh's has, through local networks, attracted many Polish workers – in contrast to a nearby college which has become a popular place of employment for Chinese migrants.[53] Some of these domestic workers were highly skilled professionals in their countries of origin, such as one who was a speech therapist in Poland before coming to the UK to work first in McDonald's and then at St Hugh's.[54]

Domestic staff at St Hugh's and the other women's colleges have, in the main, been female – the exception to the rest of the university where traditionally scouts were exclusively male. For many centuries, the monastic exclusion of women from the University extended even to female servants. Medieval statutes banned them entirely, specifying that even the 'latrix', working at her linen outside the college, had to be of 'such age and condition that no sinister suspicion can, or ought to follow her'.[55] By the nineteenth century, however, though the male colleges still opposed admitting women as members of their university, they managed to tolerate the presence of the female sex making their beds, cleaning their rooms, and washing up their plates. Nevertheless, some regard for gender distinctions remained, for it was ensured that women never assumed the more prestigious position of college scout, but took on the subservient role of 'bedmaker' – carrying out the mundane tasks while the scout tended to the undergraduates' personal needs.[56] Women did not begin to take on scouting roles in the men's colleges until the twentieth century, and then only slowly and sporadically. In some places this was seen as indicative of a more general decline in standards, and it is clear that women were employed because the colleges could pay them lower wages.[57]

By contrast, the women's colleges employed almost entirely female staff. Ina Brooksbank reported in 1917 that the only male in college was the 'bicycle boy', although before the Great War had bled Oxford of its men, Miss Jourdain had planned to employ two 'man-servants' on the new site.[58] By 1920 five men were employed by the college, and although their numbers continued to rise over the course of the century, they remained a minority among the scouts.[59] Today there are two male scouts and thirty female. In the past, women had taken on some of the more prestigious roles normally reserved for men, such as Head Porter, and although in 2010 the Lodge is entirely male, female porters have remained a feature of St Hugh's throughout its history.[60]

Working lives

The college servants' working day began at 7 a.m. when they entered undergraduates' bedrooms to lay the fire and wake them in time for chapel. This practice continued into the 1950s, and even during the Second World War when St Hugh's was relocated to Holywell Manor, 'uniformed maids' knocked on each door every morning to call 'Seven o'clock Miss'. 'Rituals from the pre-war past lingered on,' recalled one student who came up just after the war. 'We never had to lift a finger for ourselves …'[61] The scout also delivered buckets of coal directly to students' rooms, a job that required considerable strength given that each bucket weighed around 18–20lb.[62] Before the Second World War this was a daily task, though at the height of rationing in the early 1950s students began to be limited to two buckets per week.[63] Scouts would then be responsible for keeping going about ten fires apiece while students were at breakfast, ensuring that rooms were warm enough to study in for the rest of the morning. Undergraduates' rooms were dusted and swept every day until the 1980s, and although strictly speaking students were required to make their own beds, some scouts remember continuing to incorporate this into their daily routine.[64] Until the war scouts also washed up any dirty crockery left over from tea and cocoa parties.[65]

The structure of the working day followed a similar pattern across the colleges. Until the 1950s it would begin very early in the morning and finish usually just after lunch, which scouts were often responsible for clearing away and washing up. College servants then had the afternoon off, enough time for them to have a quick nap before returning to work at about 5 p.m. to serve at tea and dinner.[66] In the postwar period at St Hugh's, however, it became more common for different sets of staff to work these jobs – either as morning scouts, working from about 8 a.m. until 1 or 2 p.m., or as servery or dining-room staff working from 5 to 9 p.m. Some, however, continued to work double shifts when they needed extra money, and today many of those who work the five-hour morning shift have to take another job elsewhere.[67]

Serving in Hall was highly skilled and elaborate work. Until the 1980s, High Table was laid with silver cutlery, every piece 'counted up' and 'counted down' to ensure that nothing had gone missing. The work took on a ritualistic element: 'I … can still do it in my mind …', recalled Eileen Lydon, who began working at St Hugh's in 1972. 'I can still tell you how many cruets, how many spoons … There were eight salt cellars and eight tiny little spoons, and there were five peppers, and they used to have to be put in different parts of the High Table … they all had their certain kinds of napkins – cloth napkins … everybody had their own.' These tiny details were in fact important indicators of status and college rank. Table napkins, for example, 'had to be placed by seniority. You had the Principal's first, then the Vice-Principal, and it went all the way down … I mean it used to take ages.'[68]

In many ways, domestic staff acted as the tutors' personal servants. The old system of bells which allowed employers to call for service from any room at a moment's notice was replaced in the new St Hugh's buildings with internal telephone lines between the pantry and the Principal's rooms, the Vice-Principal's rooms, the tutors' common room, the nurses' bedroom, the Lodge, and the servants' hall.[69] Perhaps because of the practice of tutors 'living-in', this culture of personal service continued late into the twentieth century. The SCR retained a considerable degree of control over those staff specifically assigned to them. 'They were very demanding,' recalls one retired scout. On formal nights staff were not permitted to go home until all the guests had left and tutors gone to bed. Drinking in the SCR in front of the open fire might go on until late in the evening, after which SCR scouts had to tidy the common room and clear out the grate.[70] Domestic staff also tended to the needs of Fellows and Tutors after they had retired to their rooms.[71] One source of particular resentment was the bell, built into the floor by High Table, which Fellows could step on during meals to gain the attention of staff. This bell remained in use until the arrival of Principal Andrew Dilnot.[72]

In the days of chaperone rules the scouts were expected to take on a formal disciplinary role. Servants had to report to the college authorities if a student was late in returning at night or seen with a man in her room after hours. Annie Lydbury and Elsie Maddock, resident maids at St Hugh's throughout the 1920s and 30s, were still remembered sixty years later by one Old Student for the vigilance with which 'they kept a strict eye on our ... behaviour and punctuality'.[73] Maids were often placed on night duty, charged with waiting up for those students with late leave and checking that they returned at the appointed hour.[74] This was a tedious task, and sometimes Gertrude Thorneycroft, the Bursar in the 1930s with strongly left-wing sympathies, would waive late rules in order to 'save the maids'.[75] Yet this disciplinary role also gave the servants a considerable amount of power, which in turn could provide a source of financial reward. In the early 1950s, the Porter was allowed to keep the half-crown fines charged to students if they returned after 11.15 p.m. This of course encouraged a particularly scrupulous attitude on his part: as one student recalls, 'He was not above haggling over half a minute or even a few seconds past the proscribed time.'[76] In the 1970s scouts were still expected to report breach of the male visitors rule, though by this time they preferred to turn a blind eye rather than exercise their disciplinary authority.[77]

The scout's job also entailed a considerable amount of emotional labour. Remembered by one student as 'the real guardians of the college', scouts took responsibility for comforting homesick freshers, waking undergraduates after all-night essay crises, calming them down before exams, showing them how to cook, and providing 'motherly' or 'common-sense' advice.[78] Sometimes, servants were also the purveyors of rather more tangible sources of comfort, such as the 'cheap American cigarettes harvested from American servicemen' which were sold on to students in the early 1950s.[79]

Such 'perquisites' were important, since traditionally colleges had paid very low wages on the assumption that a significant portion of one's income would be made up by tips from under-graduates.[80] St Hugh's students were still tipping scouts, at a rate which the JCR was free to decide upon and raise when they felt necessary, until 1970.[81] It has been calculated that the average wage of a senior scout in the men's colleges in the 1920s was £104 per annum. At St Hugh's in 1926 a full-time resident scout earned about £90 once the value of her board, determined by the college to be worth about half her pay, had been factored in. In cash terms she would have walked away with about £45.[82] Wages at St Hugh's appear to have been about average for domestic service at the time, which often paid less than other working-class jobs.[83]

They were also, of course, far lower than the incomes of St Hugh's professional employees. The Bursar, by this period, was earning at least £300 per annum, the Principal £600, and the tutors a base rate of about £300. Over the course of the century, the 'real value' of domestic staff wages appears to have been rela-tively stable – perhaps somewhere around what has now become the official minimum wage.[84] This meant that incomes often fell short of a *living* wage. In 1971, for example, it was reported that most domestic staff in the University did not even earn equiva-lent to social security payments.[85] Scouts today are paid £6.72 an hour (16 per cent above the national minimum wage of £5.80) and St Hugh's has a policy to pay at the median average of other Oxford colleges.[86]

Before the Second World War jobs in the women's col-leges were more secure than in the men's, where scouts were expected to find alternative work during the vacation periods.

By contrast St Hugh's employed its domestic staff for the whole of the year because they were needed to cater for the meetings and conferences hosted outside term.[87] The newer buildings of the women's colleges also provided mod cons such as electricity, hot water and indoor bathrooms much earlier than at the men's, greatly reducing the amount of heavy labour that domestic staff were expected to perform.[88] On the other hand, the reduced incomes of the women's colleges could make for poorer working conditions. Certainly, scouts at St Hugh's did not have to serve their undergraduates lavish meals in their rooms, clear up after drunken parties, or spend all night queuing for theatre tickets for their spoilt young wards.[89] Yet this also meant that they missed out on the often considerable perquisites that such personal services could entail. Moreover, women's colleges did not feel themselves financially equipped to provide domestic staff with adequate pensions. In *Gaudy Night* we hear of how the college has managed to 'squeeze out a tiny pension' for Agnes, the retired Head Scout, supplemented by 'a little scheme by which she takes in odd jobs of mending and so on for the students and attends to the College linen'.[90] In 1928 St Hugh's did establish a pension scheme for servants over the age of sixty-five who had worked there for more than fifteen years, which paid 1 per cent of their final income plus an amount calculated according to housing and fuel costs (£50 per annum for female former residential staff).[91]

Domestic staff at St Hugh's, unlike those at the men's colleges, were also offered room and board, and before the Second World War a fairly large proportion of domestic staff lived in. When the college was still occupying houses in Park Town, two resident maids had to sleep in the kitchen throughout the winter of 1892–3 because the renovations to the college houses had not been completed.[92] In the new buildings, however, rooms were set aside for this purpose on the first floor of Main Building, the East

Wing of MGA, and each of the Woodstock Road houses had its own resident maid or maids.[93] A handful of staff were still resident in Main Building in the 1970s, while the Woodstock Road houses became home to housekeepers, including Mrs Windscheffel, a German–Romanian refugee and widow who lived at number 78 in the 1980s and 1990s, until her death.[94] The specially designed servants' rooms were slightly smaller than those of the students and some of them had bars on the windows.[95] Their original furnishings, many of which were hand-picked by Miss Jourdain, consisted of one 'stained chest of 5 drawers', a 'Black Framed Mirror', a 'stained washstand', 'Toilet Ware', a 'Bentwood Chair', a 'Cork Carpet as Fitted', and an 'Axminster rug'. Each room housed two or three maids who shared the one bed with its 'woollen mattress' and 'iron bedstead'.[96]

The appeal of residence was that it was cheaper than living-out, although St Hugh's, ever mindful of every penny of its inadequate income, carefully calculated the value of living-in, and deducted it from wages accordingly – something it did not do for professional members of staff whose income was paid on top of their residences. Servants were also charged a laundry fee, ten shillings per month in the 1920s, reduced to eight shillings by the mid-30s, presumably for washing and starching their uniforms. Normally, one of the benefits of working in larger establishments rather than private houses was that servants got to eat well. Yet, given the complaints of the undergraduates about the mushroom 'tails' and 'bone soup' that were regularly served up, it seems unlikely that mealtimes would have been seen as much of a perk.[97] Accommodation at St Hugh's before the Second World War was probably better than what most servants were used to at home, and working conditions in general were no worse than in other colleges or domestic service posts.[98] Yet this did not prevent some of them from fighting to improve their situation.

Part of the family?

Are domestic staff college members, or just employees? Are they workers, or part of the family? Servants have often been viewed by historians as separated off from the rest of the working class; isolated in the home of their employer and less likely to develop class solidarity or consciousness of themselves as workers.[99] Brian Harrison, a leading historian of the University of Oxford, suggested that college servants' proximity to the rich and powerful inspired not hostility, but admiration and emulation. Furthermore, the divisions (and rivalries) *between* colleges, and the separation of departments *within* them, made it difficult to unite domestic staff across the University as workers with common cause.[100] Scouts have often been characterised as conservatives; hostile to trade unions and siding with the world of Oxbridge privilege against their own class.[101] The situation was, in fact, far more complex than this, and recently historians have begun to strongly criticise an approach which interprets domestic service in the black and white terms of either 'deference' or 'defiance'.[102]

Today, St Hugh's longest-serving scouts certainly consider themselves part of the college and are proud to have known some of its most famous students. Lydon and Spring, for example, still remembered in detail the time that the fourteen-year-old maths prodigy Ruth Lawrence spent at St Hugh's between 1983 and 1985.[103] Even those scouts who are not local to Oxford and do not plan to settle permanently at St Hugh's identify in different ways with the University's ancient traditions.[104] It is perfectly possible, however, for expressions of positive affinity with the college to coexist with a rigorous critique of managerial practices and working conditions.

The position and identity of domestic staff in the women's colleges was further complicated by the claim that these institutions were modelled not on a workplace, but on a family home. Within this, domestic staff were often positioned as maternal figures, and students especially have described their scouts in these terms. An Old Student arriving at St Hugh's in the 1940s described being 'cosseted like a newborn kitten' by the college maids,[105] while one of the first male students at St Hugh's in the 1980s went so far as to describe his scout Rose as 'my second mother'.[106] The familial terms in which Old Students so commonly described their relations with domestic staff should not always be taken at face value, and might equally be seen as a convenient way of masking the inequalities of such a relationship.[107] Nevertheless, some scouts also reported feeling motherly towards their undergraduates, and protective of those who had not yet acquired life skills as basic as knowing how to do their laundry or fry an egg. They often went beyond their brief, helping with extra domestic chores or taking time to listen to students' problems.[108] Affectionate relationships did sometimes emerge, and it was not uncommon to exchange Christmas presents and stay in touch long after graduation.[109]

St Hugh's could also act as an extension of the scouts' own family home, for along with bringing their children to college in the vacations, they often worked with other members of their family. One scout today has worked at St Hugh's with both her mother and her daughter; Janet and Gale Burke (two sisters) cleaned Main Building together for many years; and it has been common practice for the children of domestic staff to work at St Hugh's part-time or in the school holidays. The reminiscences of Eileen Lydon, for example, interweave an 'official' account of St Hugh's history – Principals, tutors, famous names – with more intimate family stories involving her daughter, who worked alongside her in the Senior Common Room.[110]

While domestic staff do, at times, see themselves as part of a bigger college family, the blurring of boundaries between the home and the workplace has not prevented various moves to organise themselves as workers. In 1919, as part of a broader surge of working-class militancy following the First World War, efforts were made to form 'A Trade Union of College Servants'. Some of the servants' complaints were, they felt, the result of the war and the 'consequent high price of living', though others focused on longstanding problems such as 'being dependent more or less on tips or gratuities which often failed to materialise'.[111] It does not appear that this union was ever formed, but the poor conditions endured by domestic servants more generally were certainly a popular subject for debate throughout the interwar period.[112] The 'rights of domestic servants' were even discussed at St Hugh's when, in 1930, it hosted the conference of the National Council of Girls' Clubs. Miss E. Godfrey of Shoreditch condemned the long hours that young servant girls were forced to work and the difficulty of training for an alternative occupation, though it is not recorded whether her speech concerned itself with the conditions of St Hugh's scouts.[113]

The possibility of organising a scouts' union continued to be occasionally discussed after the Second World War,[114] but did not achieve much success until the early 1970s. Again, renewed energy to organise reflected the growing strength of workers' and social movements in wider society, but at Oxford it was the women's colleges who seem to have provided much of the early impetus. In 1971 St Hilda's JCR started an inquiry into the conditions of its domestic staff, to coincide with a meeting called by the Oxford Women's Action Group to discuss the formation of a Women Scouts' Union.[115] Although this meeting was not a success (only one scout turned up), it did mark the beginning of a series of efforts over the next two years, during which a number of scouts began to speak openly about low pay and long hours, and to join the National Union of Public Employees (NUPE). Scouts and trade unionists accused college authorities of trying to deter their employees from joining a union and threatening those attempting to organise their fellow workers.[116] The situation came to a head at another of the women's colleges, St Anne's, in the autumn of 1972 when Frank Keen was fired – allegedly for his union activities. The planned one-day protest strike ended up lasting twenty-one days, during which about a third of the domestic workforce besieged the college and prevented delivery of crucial supplies, causing the central heating to be turned off because of a shortage of oil. To the surprise of many, the strike was a success: the college agreed to arbitration and Frank Keen was reinstated. NUPE described it as a 'landmark', the first-ever instance of industrial action by domestic workers in eight hundred years of the University history.[117] If only for a few weeks the whole of Oxford was forced to acknowledge what a crucial role domestic workers played, and how much power they had over the colleges should they choose to use it.

The St Anne's strike was officially supported by its own and numerous other JCRs, including St Hugh's, as well as by student bodies such as the Student Representation Committee (the forerunner to the Student Union) and the Oxford Women's Action Group.[118] It occurred just at a moment in which relations between domestic staff and students were undergoing an important shift. In the early twentieth century, while servants were sometimes referred to affectionately in student publications, the hierarchical relationships which structured life at St Hugh's were seen as quite normal.[119] Rather than question the divisions that existed between them and these 'other women', students were more likely to see their difference as comical or distasteful. In 1921, the student literary magazine The Imp published a 'humorous' piece about one of the St Hugh's scouts. 'Mrs Brown's Soliloquy' poked fun at her way of speaking and tendency to interrupt students from their studies with her chatter:

> 'There, my dear, I've spread yer a nice tray for tea, with some nice butter an' a nice disherjam, and four nice cups for yer visiters, all as nice as I kin mike it.' 'Well now, I'll jest do yer room up a bit, shall I Miss? ... Miss X., now, she's a tidy little thing, too. I'm very fond of 'er ... I 'opes as 'ow she'll marry some nice man if she do marry – one with a bit of money like.' (Exit, panting, leaving me to recover).

As with Dorothy L. Sayers's portrayal of her college scouts, here it is Mrs Brown's concern for domestic details (she insists on removing invisible cobwebs from the ceiling before the student invites her guests in) and her concern for silly matters such as marriage that highlight her difference from the undergraduate author.[120] Other reminiscences of student life at St Hugh's between the wars also comment upon the *difference* of the servants. Annie Lydbury and Elsie Maddock are described as 'raw-boned black-and-white garbed attendants', while another remembers the strange and unpleasant cooking smells that emanated from the servants' quarters.[121]

It is possible that some of the barriers between students and scouts were broken down by the Second World War, during which many middle-class women performed manual labour for the first time in their lives. The war work of one St Hugh's undergraduate, for example, consisted of 'chambermaiding' the doctors' quarters at the Radcliffe Infirmary, after which she would at the very least have acquired some sense of what it was like having to clear up after others.[122] Nevertheless, many reminiscences of St Hugh's in the postwar period suggest that students continued to take for granted the work of the domestic staff, to the extent that they have no memory of them at all. Many alumni simply replied to the section on relations with domestic staff in the anniversary questionnaire with answers such as 'I hardly saw any of them', 'I don't remember anything unusual', 'Didn't impinge on us'. By the late 1960s and early 1970s, however, with student radicalism at its peak and less well-off students benefiting from free university education, some undergraduates began to view the college's domestic arrangements in a new light. In 1968, the JCR voted to open its facilities to the scouts, and in 1970 it agreed that the JCR committee should meet with scouts and maintenance men on a monthly basis to discuss issues of common interest.[123] In 1972, one student was shocked to learn from her scout that the 'unbearable drudge' of working at St Hugh's had apparently caused at least two of the resident staff to experience mental health problems. This prompted her to suggest that the JCR 'make some protest about the exploitation of resident staff', which led to a heated debate in which other students began to notice – as if for the first time – the indignity of having to put hot water bottles in tutors' beds and serve tea trussed up in 'black dresses and pinnies'. They even began to question the necessity of employing servants at all – couldn't students clean their own rooms?[124]

Yet in spite of the democratic impulses of this generation of students, traditional hierarchies and class barriers proved exceptionally difficult to overcome. In 1971, Isabel Morgan, an undergraduate, and her scout Trish[125] found this out the hard way. Trish and Isabel were about the same age (Trish was slightly younger than the students she looked after), and, on discovering a shared interest in reading and a shared history of being labelled 'troublemakers' (Isabel by her form mistress, Trish, rather more seriously, by the police), they became friends. They spent a lot of time chatting in Isabel's room, when Trish was probably supposed to be working, and one evening they sat together on the lawn outside Main Building and shared a bottle of wine. The following day,

Trish was fired for 'fraternisation'. The college authorities never clearly stated whether this was because of her friendship with Isabel, though when Morgan visited the Bursar to protest, she was told: 'There are two classes in Britain; why do you choose to make your friends amongst the lower classes?'[126] Isabel was also bitterly disappointed by the response of her fellow students, for, while some were upset by what had happened, many regarded a 'no scout–student fraternisation' rule as perfectly reasonable.[127]

While such an episode is an extreme and possibly exceptional case in the history of the college, it nevertheless clearly illustrates the limitations of the comforting notion that domestic staff were simply part of the family. Other scouts who worked at St Hugh's in the 1970s remember far less violent, though no less entrenched, class divisions. Principal Trickett, politely described by one as a 'really strait-laced type of person', would not reply when scouts informed her that it was time for dinner, giving instead only the slightest of nods. 'Very, very, very few of them acknowledged you in the corridor [when] you walked past them', recalls another scout. 'Now they say, how are your children – everybody chats to you.' While the longer-standing scouts feel that relations between domestic staff and the rest of St Hugh's have become far more friendly and informal in recent decades, others still experience a lack of respect. Those who have migrated from elsewhere especially felt themselves to be the victims of stereotypes. People often assume they are stupid 'because we don't speak perfect English', while the repetitive nature of their work – the knowledge that 'the next day there will be mess again' – means that it is undervalued. These scouts did not blame the students or tutors for thinking this way; instead they accepted that 'that's the way it is'. As one pointed out, 'Everywhere you go in the world it's the same. People who are cleaners, they are always … just the cleaners.'[128]

From home to workplace: continuity and change since 1970

The role of domestic staff at St Hugh's has been transformed over the last forty years through the 'modernisation' of the college. Perhaps the most significant shift in the working life of the scout was caused, indirectly, by the student agitation of the late 1960s and early 70s. Oxford undergraduates began to demand a bigger say in how their university was run – and control over the domestic side of college life formed an important part of this. Protests against high college fees frequently entailed a condemnation of outdated practices such as the obligatory number of formal dinners, where one was waited on 'by an army of maids in uniform'.[129]

Such critiques placed domestic staff in a strange position, for while students ostensibly rejected the servitude upon which so much past privilege had been founded they were also potentially putting scouts out of a job. At St Anne's, for example, much of the pressure on the college to economise – which had caused many scouts to fear for their jobs in the period leading up to the strike – was the result of student demands for the college to do everything it could to reduce costs.[130] At St Hugh's, the JCR President wrote to the Principal in 1971, protesting against the rise in maintenance charges. Not only were the new rates higher than those at other colleges, '[m]any of the "extra" services we get we do not want – like daily scouts, formal meals (instead of self-service) ...'[131] Yet the effect of doing away with extraneous services such as teas served in Hall, which were ended in 1968, was that staff numbers were cut accordingly.[132]

Throughout the 1970s the college authorities struggled to find ways to economise on the domestic side of college life. A 'Report on Domestic Cleaning Arrangements' in 1980 recommended that the opportunity presented by the retirement of a number of old staff that summer be used to 'rationalise' domestic work by requiring the new staff to work harder and take a shorter coffee break in return for a 'small adjustment in the hourly rate'.[133] St Hugh's, like other colleges, was beginning to be managed as a business rather than a somewhat haphazard family home. But this process came about only very slowly, for not only the domestic staff, but also many Tutors and Fellows were attached to the old ways of doing things. The cost of living of resident domestic staff had always been closely scrutinised by the college, and this simply continued. Resident staff in 1978 were reminded at an annual wage review of the 'estimated value of the accommodation, lighting and heating with which they were provided free of charge'.[134] The women's colleges' senior common rooms had never enjoyed the lavish lifestyle of the men's colleges, although after the Second World War they did acquire many of the traditional Oxbridge perks such as a wine cellar. Yet, from the point of view of the scouts, the SCR budget in the 1970s was very generous when it came to dining – 'They had port coming out of their ears,' remembers one.[135] By the end of the 1980s, however, as Rachel Trickett's Principalship drew to a close, it was becoming clear that this liberal approach to SCR expenditure was far from economically viable.

Belts began to be tightened when Derek Wood became Principal in 1991, but by the time Andrew Dilnot took over, the college was running at a loss. So Dilnot began an even more thorough reorganisation which aimed to reduce wastage and improve facilities. Mary Kerr, who became Bursar in 2004 (combining the role of Estates and Domestic Bursar), took this forward, seeing it as her task to 'professionalise' the domestic side of college. Kerr's appointment was, in itself, something of a novel departure for St Hugh's, for she was employed because of her experience in the business world (banking and then consultancy) and in managing large operations. She was shocked, on arrival, to discover what she saw as the extremely amateurish manner in which the domestic side of college had until then been run. Very few staff even had contracts, there were large discrepancies between wages and holiday allowances, and very little transparency. Kerr set about introducing a 'performance management system' which aimed to make clearer to employees what was expected of them and also what they could expect from the college. Wages were improved and disciplinary procedures tightened up, so that now, for example, when staff take time off for sickness they know they will have to face a 'back-to-work' interview on their return. Kerr believes that the difficult financial position in which the college found itself at the beginning of the twenty-first century actually provided the opportunity to modernise an outdated system. This put St Hugh's ahead of many of the richer colleges, which preferred to stick to the older way of managing domestic staff, an attitude summed up by Mary Kerr as 'We pay them less, for a lower performance, and they are part of the community.'

St Hugh's is clearly no longer run along the lines of a family home, and much of its income is generated by its conference business, for which it has to ensure very high standards of accommodation and service. This fundamental shift in the college's identity has not come about without some dissent. Kerr recalls that some of the Fellows objected to the new ways of managing domestic staff:

> Because academics don't relate to that. They are not managed
> in that way themselves, so, you know, in this very kind of liberal
> community that we live in I had quite a bit of resistance in the
> beginning from certain Fellows who said 'oh well, that's not fair'
> ...[136]

Some of the scouts also resent the loss of flexibility in their jobs while other members of the college continue to enjoy the liberal atmosphere more traditionally associated with places of learning. Only scouts and kitchen staff are asked to clock in and out at the end of each day, something that is not required of administrative staff and academics. This was singled out for criticism by one domestic worker, who commented: '[I]t is said that everyone is treated the same. I am afraid that is not so.'[137]

Has the increased professionalisation of St Hugh's also meant that domestic staff no longer identify as part of the community? Scouts are still permitted to share college facilities, such as the library and the gym, and two years ago they began to be assigned 'Bod Cards' – passports to the University's famous libraries and ancient buildings. There was a marked contrast, however, in attitudes between staff I interviewed still working today and those who had joined St Hugh's forty years ago. Pat Spring believed that the difference is that it is now possible to leave here at the end of the day and forget about your work. Even ten or twenty years ago, domestic workers were far more immersed in the life of the college and vice versa. The head chef in the 1970s, for example, used to come in every morning, seven days a week. When he left, the shock was so great that he could no longer bear to talk about St Hugh's. By contrast, some of the more recently employed scouts preferred to leave college as soon as their shift was over, for the sense of 'freedom' they obtained from leaving their workplace behind at the end of the day.[138]

It would be wrong, however, to overstate the changes that the role of scout has undergone in the last forty years. Some University historians have suggested that by the 1970s scouts had 'vanished', in that the old traditions which made their post so distinctive had been done away with.[139] Instead, it has been claimed, colleges are now run by mere 'women cleaners' and 'kitchen staff', who do not have the same degree of 'devotion' exhibited by the scouts-proper of the pre-war period.[140] Yet continuity remains as important a theme as change in the history of St Hugh's scouts. For a start, domestic staff at the women's colleges never provided their undergraduates with the same degree of personal service offered in the men's, and their rather less luxurious domestic arrangements pointed in the direction that all Oxford colleges would eventually have to follow.[141] Moreover, compared with the Redbricks and New Universities, domestic arrangements in Oxford – silver service every week at Formal Hall, accommodation cleaned on a daily basis – appear to many outsiders as relics from a Victorian past.

It is even possible to see the last decade or so as a period of return to older ideas about service and domestic labour. Since the 1990s, it has become vastly more common for women working outside the home to employ another woman as a cleaner or 'help', and in 2009 one in ten British households employed some form of domestic staff.[142] This means that students today might even be *more* likely to have experienced a non-family member picking up after them than were their counterparts thirty or forty years ago. It has also been noted that, since the introduction of ever-increasing tuition fees, undergraduates tend to have a stronger sense of the 'value' of the university experience they 'purchase' and therefore higher expectations of the standard of accommodation provision.

Far from being modern or novel practices, it is possible to view the performance management of the last few years as the re-emergence of more traditional ideas about the role of domestic staff. For example, by the interwar period the servants' traditional garb of 'cap and apron' had become an important cultural symbol of servitude.[143] Servants at St Hugh's had to carry on wearing the 'black and white pinnies' until the 1970s, much later than most, and in fact they only enjoyed a relatively brief moment of sartorial freedom before uniforms were brought back at the beginning of the twenty-first century to create a more professional appearance for conference guests.

They did their job, we did ours

This chapter has attempted to make visible an otherwise obscured aspect of the history of St Hugh's. The portrait of domestic workers provided here is necessarily patchy and anecdotal, the limited evidence-base precluding a more generalised sociological survey. Yet I have also aimed to make sense of the invisibility, to see it as reflective of a division of labour whereby, in the words of one Old Student, 'they did their job, we did ours'. The separation of domestic work from academic work served a crucial ideological function in the emergence of the women's colleges. It signalled the right of young women to focus their energies on a sphere of labour previously reserved for men – intellectual, creative, productive rather than reproductive and, crucially, not necessarily directed towards the needs of others. At a time when there was a great deal of anxiety over whether middle-class women could or should work outside the home, it proved useful and reassuring to emphasise the difference between the 'professional' work for which St Hugh's trained its students and the kind of work performed by working-class women. Feminists in the first half of the century replicated this paradigm when they equated emancipation with a rejection of domestic labour or invested the figure of the domestic servant with an outdated and regressive form of womanhood.

At the same time, the separation of domestic from academic work at St Hugh's was only ever at a superficial level and in fact the two were continuously interconnected. Successful academic production was dependent upon the labour of domestic staff who kept scholars warm, well fed, and sometimes even emotionally looked after. More than this, however, the college structure combines the domestic and the intellectual in a highly distinctive manner, in that Oxford is one of the few universities to bring together research, teaching and living under one roof. If one was to attempt to measure the economic productivity of St Hugh's, therefore, it would be impossible to separate out which work and whose work contributed to the final result of an internationally renowned educational institution. This situation also means that the jobs of Oxford academics entailed an interest in and contribution to seemingly trivial domestic matters. The St Hugh's Fellow Margaret Jacobs, for example, sat on a committee in the 1970s which spent not insignificant amounts of time discussing agenda items such as 'The Cheese Alternative' and debating whether this dessert option ought to be offered every day or only at weekends.

Feminist scholars, not to mention women themselves in their capacities as mothers, wives, partners and family members, have long pointed out how difficult it is to get people to recognise that work performed within the home is in fact *real* work. This extends into waged labour too, whereby work traditionally associated with women and the domestic sphere tends to be low-paid and undervalued. The history of domestic service at St Hugh's is no exception, and while traditional forms of workplace organising failed in the past to unite domestic workers and win gains across the University, this has not been because staff have remained unaware or uncritical of their conditions. Today some scouts and students, inspired by worker–student alliances successful on a number of US campuses, continue to campaign for a living wage in the Oxford colleges. Some of the most recent work on the history of domestic service has argued that it is patronising to view it solely in terms of exploitation and oppression. Historians have stressed that, for many, going into service was a rational economic choice; that their work was often recalled in a positive light; and that some developed intimate relationships with their employers. The story of domestic staff at St Hugh's encompasses a range of experiences, which varied over time. Exploitation, however, is not just about whether people are nice or nasty. It is inherent to a division of labour in which one group directly benefits from the low-paid work of others. The history of scouts at St Hugh's provides a glimpse of how such exploitation not only structures working life but also fundamentally determines human relationships, shaping the identities and interactions between different groups of college women.

5

WHOSE EDUCATION IS IT ANYWAY?

Class, funding and protest, 1886–2011

Anyone who has ever been a member of the University of Oxford will know that, in this supposed bastion of privilege, class politics remain alive and well. The subject of class – be this in relation to students' social backgrounds or Oxford's prestigious position vis-à-vis the civic universities – is at once discomfiting and compelling, and neither the University's critics nor its supporters have ever been able to avoid it for long. Elitism and exclusivity remain central to Oxford's identity. While many members worry that this creates a distorted picture which might repel potential applicants, others see it as a major selling point. Myths of privilege and exclusion are frequently invoked when considering the more concrete issue of Oxford's finances – both in terms of the government's willingness to fund an institution whose 'accessibility' is questioned, and in relation to the changing funding sources available to individual students. These issues were as important 125 years ago as they are today, though they were conceived of and responded to very differently. St Hugh's was born out of a desire to provide higher education to women from poor families. Though the college's policy of charging lower fees had quickly to be abandoned as financially unviable, St Hugh's retained a reputation for being 'not so snotty' as the other women's colleges and continued to attract a significant minority of students from less wealthy backgrounds. The social or class background of Oxford undergraduates (including those at St Hugh's) has interested historians for some time, but their findings need to be considered in the context of a broader analysis of the economics of education. The changing identity of St Hugh's student body will thus be considered not only in terms of demographics, but also in relation to how students perceived the meaning and purpose of their education.

The relative poverty of the women's colleges in their early years places them outside the dominant narrative of pre-Second World War Oxford as a place of luxury and privilege. Unlike their male counterparts, they rarely attracted students from the upper echelons of society and instead filled many of their places with women who pursued a university education out of economic necessity. Even before the introduction of substantive state funding post-1945, St Hugh's was home to small numbers of working-class students who managed to survive through a combination of scholarships, loans, charitable funds and frugal living. The distinctive social and economic positioning of St Hugh's during this period generated a complex set of attitudes towards education, combining liberal and utilitarian thinking in a manner that was often contradictory and sometimes frustrating. Higher education was fundamentally transformed between 1945 and 1979 when universities were expanded and made free to all. By the 1960s 'students' were beginning to be viewed as a distinct social grouping, often associated with a set of counter-cultures and/or radical politics. The Oxford colleges, especially St Hugh's, are usually seen as marginal to the 'student power' movements of the late 1960s and early 1970s. Though there were frequent clashes with University authorities, they were not comparable to the upheavals at the Sorbonne, Berkeley, or the London School of Economics. If we take a micro view of these processes of social change, however, it is apparent that their impact was felt at St Hugh's in muted but nevertheless transformative ways. The JCR's protests over inadequate domestic arrangements, for example, point to the emergence of new ideas about the educational community, whereby students began to demand the right to have a say in how their institution was governed.

From the late 1970s onwards, state funding for universities was gradually cut back and a market-driven view of education gained ground. The impact of these national debates was experienced at St Hugh's in terms of rising college prices and diminishing student grants. Throughout the 1980s and 1990s students organised to resist such policies, yet the self-interested nature of their actions did not preclude wider discussions about the implications of student poverty for the accessibility and democratisation of an Oxford education. When tuition fees were reintroduced in 1998, St Hugh's was one of the centres of the campaign for non-payment. This was accompanied by an intensification of the debate on class and access, during which Oxford came under the scrutiny of the national press. St Hugh's undergraduates of the early twenty-first century were far more embattled and caught up in day-to-day economic pressures than their 1970s predecessors, with less time to devote to discussing alternative visions of education. For many, the rising cost of university and the need to find employment after graduation has seen the consumer model of higher education win out. Nevertheless, struggles around the introduction of tuition fees, top-up fees, and funding cuts continue to throw up questions of who and what education is for.

Struggling to survive in a place of privilege, 1886–1945

'I thought it might be well to start a hall of a rather less expensive character than Lady Margaret,' wrote Elizabeth Wordsworth, recalling how St Hugh's came to be founded, '[e]xperience has shown that it was in the long run an impracticable idea.'[1] Wordsworth's awareness of the need for a more affordable women's college reflected the concern of many university reformers in the late nineteenth and early twentieth century, who argued that the high cost of studying at Oxford excluded many who were both deserving and in need of higher education. The lavish lifestyle of Oxbridge students and high college living standards were pointed to as a particularly prohibitive expense.[2] Keble College had been founded in 1870 to cater for less wealthy male students by practising 'economy and simplicity of living', and Wordsworth looked to it as her model for St Hugh's.[3] The 'poor' students Wordsworth hoped to attract were certainly not working-class in the sense of coming from labouring families, but rather the 'shabby-genteel' daughters of impoverished sections of the professional classes. For such women, with fathers unable to support them, a university education was promoted as the best way of securing against downward mobility.[4] Orphans were another group for whom a middle-class upbringing meant little if their fathers had failed to provide for them after death, and such unfortunate young women appear frequently in the college registers of the 1880s and 1890s.[5]

St Hugh's was successful in appealing to those who could not have afforded to study elsewhere, initially charging a minimum of £45 a year for food and lodging, as compared with Somerville, which charged £60, and Lady Margaret Hall, which asked for £75.[6] It continued to offer some smaller rooms at a cheaper rate into the early decades of the twentieth century and, until the move to permanent buildings, students could volunteer to share rooms for half the usual rate.[7] It was thus possible for Ethel Wallace to come to St Hugh's in 1908, having previously believed that expense made Oxford an 'unobtainable dream'. With only her mother and a bursary from the Clergy Orphan Fund to support her, Wallace managed to eke her way through the three years by choosing the cheapest of colleges and sharing her bedroom with another student.[8]

Yet St Hugh's soon had to start charging the same fees as the other women's colleges, for it became clear that the financial demands of running such an institution made it impossible to subsidise even the poorest of students.[9] Until 1923 women's colleges received no state funding, and were forced to compete in a 'free market' against subsidised co-educational colleges, and against any number of other worthy causes for wealthy benefactors.[10] The Anglican colleges were even worse off than Girton, Newnham and Somerville, possibly because clerical ambivalence towards women's education deterred potential benefactors from donating large sums of money.[11] The Oxford and Cambridge Act (1923) provided funding for the University for the first time, some of which filtered down to women tutors, but the colleges themselves have always been ineligible for state support.[12] St Hugh's could only offer modest scholarships, of lower value than those at the other women's colleges, which did not even cover the lowest rate of room and board.[13] The most generous was the Clara Mordan Scholarship, bestowed in 1897 at £40 a year, followed by an exhibition of £35 and a closed scholarship (for students from the Alice Ottley School) also for £40.[14] In 1916 the Old Students raised enough money to establish a scholarship of £30, and in 1921 they added an exhibition of £20. Because female students were excluded from applying to University-wide scholarships competition for support from the women's colleges was intense, and in 1918 157 candidates competed for a total of nineteen open scholarships and exhibitions.[15]

St Hugh's was keenly aware of the financial hardship faced by some of its students. Along with the other women's colleges, St Hugh's organised the Bertha Johnson Loan Fund (est. 1895) and the Poor Students' Fund which lent sums of between £5 and £10 to students 'who, intending to earn their own living, need help to enable them to continue their education'. The qualifying criteria, however, were strict and somewhat humiliating, and students had to provide references proving both their poverty and their good character. A report on the recipient's academic progress was made to the Loan Committee every term, and if she was found to be slacking or struggling with her work payments might be suspended.[16]

Though staff at St Hugh's were concerned by the plight of their poorer members, they were far from being advocates of the right to education regardless of ability to pay. Though obtaining a scholarship was almost the only route by which a student without private means could attend St Hugh's, the college awarded them not to the neediest but to the most talented. In 1922, Somerville College resolved 'that while the status and title of scholar be awarded purely on grounds of merit, the emoluments of a scholar be only granted to those in need of assistance'. Somerville suggested to St Hugh's that they might also pursue such a policy, but although some on the Council were in favour, St Hugh's ultimately opposed 'associating the name of scholar with financial need [rather] than with intellectual ability'. Instead, St Hugh's Council suggested asking the parents of scholars who came from wealthy families to donate their emoluments to a fund for 'poor and deserving students'.[17] The principle of reserving some free places for any girl capable of meeting the same academic standard as that of her wealthier peers was, however, firmly rejected.[18]

The first State Scholarships for attending university were introduced in 1920. Prior to this, as many educational reformers pointed out, girls were particularly disadvantaged in the scramble for what little charitable funding existed. The Board of Education's Consultative Committee, considering the situation in 1916, concluded that it was unseemly for girls to compete for the same entrance scholarships as boys. As a result, the Oxford women's colleges lobbied the Board of Education, demanding in 1918 that a certain proportion of the proposed scholarships be reserved for women. They argued that under the present system talent was being wasted: 'We have reason to believe that there are girls who would benefit by a University education who for the lack of a sufficient number of scholarships are debarred from coming to Oxford.'[19] At first the government responded positively to their request and allocated scholarships equally between boys and girls. But in 1930 boys were allocated 188 scholarships and girls only 112. Local Authority Grants also became available in the interwar period, though the amounts varied drastically according to the area, and during the Depression some only offered loans. Students might also receive a scholarship from their secondary school, though, again, girls tended to lose out because their institutions were less well endowed than the older boys' public schools. A number of students at St Hugh's also held Board of Education Scholarships, which indentured them to teach on leaving university, sometimes for as long as ten years.[20]

Oxford was still significantly more expensive than the civic universities: in 1933 it was estimated that it cost £130 per annum to go to a provincial university but between £160 and £240 for a woman to study at Oxford (the men's colleges were even more costly).[21] Few scholarships were adequate to cover costs, and they were often measured on the assumption that parents would be able to at least partially contribute. Nevertheless, a handful of students from impoverished families (a few even from traditionally 'working-class' backgrounds) made it to St Hugh's during this period, cobbling together a number of funding sources in order to survive. M. King, at Oxford in the 1930s, remembered how

> I could go to College only if I found financial help, so that an Exhibition at St Hugh's opened the door for me – I already had to refuse a place at Somerville because there were no emoluments, but I did manage to win a County Scholarship of £30 a year, and a Leaving Exhibition from school of £45 a year. My Exhibition was also £45 and I was given a 'Training Grant' for teaching ... College fees were £50 a term and this I could manage as long as my parents kept me during the vacations.[22]

King emphasised that she 'was by no means the only student in this position', a view that is borne out by the reminiscences sent in by alumni from this period.[23] One undergraduate studying in the 1920s, for example, was forced to mount up a considerable debt to the Bertha Johnson Loan fund, which, combined with the loans she received from the Local Education Committee (grants were suspended during this period), became a real burden after graduation when she was struggling to survive on her meagre teacher's salary.[24] Many who studied at St Hugh's between the wars affirm that the college's reputation as a cut-price institution lasted much longer than its policy of low fees, making it the college of choice for those who could only just afford to come to Oxford. Nevertheless, such young women remained a minority in a predominantly middle-class institution.

Before the Second World War, the women's colleges, unlike the men's, were not places where the wealthiest of society wished to send their daughters. As one historian put it: women's education 'worked very hard to become respectable, but smart it never was'.[25] In the period before the First World War, 3 per cent of students at the women's colleges were the daughters of men in what we might consider to be 'working-class' jobs (tradesmen and clerks) compared with 5 per cent in the men's colleges. At St Hugh's, this figure (for 1886–1920) was slightly higher – standing at 4.7 per cent, though 3.85 per cent of these were daughters of clerks rather than manual labourers.[26] Such examples crop up occasionally in the College Register (in the 1880s St Hugh's accepted a butcher's daughter and in the 1890s one father is listed as 'bank clerk') but they remain the exception. Daughters of professional men formed the largest group, counting for 38 per cent of women at Oxford before the First World War.[27] At St Hugh's, 23 per cent of students up until 1920 came from professional families, a figure which rises to 46 per cent if Church of England clergy are included in this category. In general, students were less likely than their male counterparts to come from the upper and lower extremes of the social spectrum and were instead more 'solidly' middle-class.

The numbers of St Hugh's undergraduates from working-class occupational backgrounds increased slightly after the First World War: 8.8 per cent in the 1920s and 1930s and rising to 16.6 per cent in the 1940s. However, Sarah Curtis's survey of 1,092 students at St Hugh's between 1917 and 1979 found that until the 1940s, four out of ten fathers were themselves university graduates – a considerable proportion given that even by the late 1920s and early 30s only 6 per cent of those who had attended secondary school went on to university.[28] Girls' secondary education is a slippery indicator of social status, since fee-paying institutions cannot be neatly categorised into 'public' and 'private' in the manner of boys' schools.[29] St Hugh's did attract some girls from the most prestigious (and expensive) schools such as Roedean, Wycombe Abbey and Cheltenham Ladies', which modelled themselves on leading boys' public schools such as Eton, Winchester and Harrow. Thirty-eight per cent of those in Curtis's study who studied at St Hugh's in the 1930s specified that they had attended such institutions.[30] Prior to 1945 there was no state sector within secondary education – instead the government funded small numbers of free places in local authority and endowed grammar schools. From 1907 onwards these schools were offered a higher rate of grant on condition that they made at least a quarter of places available to scholars from the state-funded elementary schools.[31] St Hugh's accepted a significant proportion of students from these 'direct grant' schools, which provided the main, though extremely narrow, route by which girls from working-class families made it to Oxford.[32]

Different people often mean very different things when they refer to themselves or fellow students as 'working-' or 'middle-class'. Class as a historical category can never be reduced simply to family income or social background. At the start of the twentieth century, for example, a clergyman's daughter, however poor, was still considered a lady, whereas a tradesman's daughter, even if she came from considerable wealth, might be seen as lowering the tone of the more prestigious women's colleges.[33] In order to understand how class 'worked' at St Hugh's we need to look not just at who was able to attend but also how they experienced the college once they arrived. A number of students recall St Hugh's as an unusually accepting place, especially compared with the other women's colleges where some comment on being made to feel 'socially not quite up to it' during the joint interviews.[34] Conspicuous spending habits were not, on the whole, fashionable at St Hugh's and this had something of a levelling effect, allowing for a greater degree of social interaction between students from different backgrounds.[35] Such recollections, however, must be interpreted with care, for it tended to be those from more comfortably-off families who spoke most enthusiastically about the lack of 'social snobbery' at St Hugh's.[36] How 'not having much money' was defined was also extremely subjective and accounts of the interwar period reveal large discrepancies in income. Ida Moberly (m. 1920), for example, cheerfully described herself as 'always bankrupt', though her godmother gave her £10 each term for 'incidental expenses' such as theatre tickets, occasional clothing items and cigarettes. By contrast, one student in the late 1920s had only £1 per term spending money.[37]

Many grammar school girls recall feeling like outsiders at St Hugh's. They lacked the manners, connections and sense of entitlement exhibited by a small but influential group of students from the top public schools. Young women with friends, brothers and cousins at other colleges had a considerable advantage over those who had no family history of studying at Oxford. Naomi Papworth, a young Jewish woman who came to St Hugh's on a scholarship, found her more established peers deeply intimidating:

> They knew the ropes and seemed very self-assured. I was very conscious of making mistakes which caused their eyebrows to rise. I said 'Broad Street' instead of 'the Broad', and didn't know about 'the House' and 'the Bod' and 'the Radder'.[38]

Barbara Castle, the future Cabinet Minister already active in the Labour Party when she arrived at St Hugh's in 1929, found these privileged young women 'amicable enough but they came from an alien world. My passion for politics was a joke to them and they enjoyed mimicking my northern accent.'[39] Ina Brooksbank also found her northern background a social impediment, remembering how 'We were regarded almost with surprise because we spoke English ... [and] had decent table manners.'[40] For one 'presumably very clever student from the East End' the challenge of adapting to such a different environment proved impossible to bear. Having had to endure the humiliating experience of being taught how to use a bath by her fellow students, it is hardly surprising that she chose not to remain at St Hugh's.[41]

Despite the good intentions of many individuals and a genuine desire to open the door to those 'less fortunate than ourselves' the middle-class legacy of the early movement for women's education weighed heavily upon the college. St Hugh's founders, like the rest of 'that phalanx of formidable women staring down from the walls of the University women's club', had been unquestioningly concerned with the needs of middle-class women. 'They were pioneers alright,' noted St Hugh's graduate Valerie Pitt, 'but they were … highly privileged pioneers and they were all, damn them, *ladies*.' The upper-middle-class Anglican values that dominated St Hugh's in its early years were felt by some to have generated a culture of 'amazing insularity' – one that prevailed up until the Second World War. Even as late as the 1940s, Pitt felt that students were seldom required to question their own ethos or the assumptions they brought with them from home.[42] Such attitudes could exclude not only along class lines but also those of race and religion. When Nancy Salinger came for an interview at St Hugh's in 1929, neither Miss Seaton nor Miss Gwyer 'seemed very interested in me or my English work. Miss Gwyer's main concern was whether I would require Kosher food.' Ten years later an 'intolerant' bursar dismissed all religious dietary requirements as 'fads and fancies', and in general the need for 'special', in other words *different*, treatment was looked down upon by the college authorities.[43] 'Inward looking and unambitious', was Nancy Salinger's verdict – a college crippled by 'polite conformity' and 'oh so complacent middle-class values …' Yet for Salinger, as well as for Naomi Papworth, studying at St Hugh's allowed them to encounter different kinds of religions and cultures, an experience which they both subsequently described as emancipatory. Such cultural dissonance could be both exclusionary and liberating, and was only possible because of the presence of small numbers of students from 'non-traditional' backgrounds:

middle-class insularity may have dominated, but it was no longer hegemonic.[44]

St Hugh's distinctive cultural and socio-economic make-up created a somewhat peculiar mixture of educational values. Visions of women's education, especially, were marked by a longstanding tension between liberal and utilitarian approaches.[45] In their different ways, both Elizabeth Wordsworth and Emily Davies argued for women's right to the former – an education directed not towards a particular profession but *knowledge* in a more general sense. Annie Moberly inherited the difficult task of reconciling Wordsworth's lofty visions with the need of many of her students for a qualification that would enable them to find professional employment as teachers.[46] Teaching remained one of the most popular careers for St Hugh's graduates into the 1970s. Of all who replied to Curtis's survey, 38 per cent had become school-teachers, though its popularity showed a marked decline from the 1950s onwards (when 43 per cent went on to teach) to the 1970s (when only 19 per cent of respondents had gone on to acquire a teaching qualification).[47] Despite this overriding vocational path, the tradition of liberal education, of commitment to learning for its own sake, remained strong at the Oxford women's colleges. In a Gaudy speech in 1955, Mary Proudfoot (née MacDonald) spoke half-jokingly, yet affectionately, of her time at St Hugh's in the early 1930s when, 'not obliged by hard circumstance to regard learning as a means to some other end', she and her friends had been able to nurture a 'passionate interest in the location of West Saxon saucer brooches, in Homeric archaeology, in Anglo-Saxon philology and so on'.[48]

Such an approach clearly had its benefits – whether or not a woman intended to become a schoolteacher she was expected to develop a broad interest in her subject rather than pursue a more narrow vocational form of training. Yet some students saw their tutors' commitment to pure scholarship as a sign of disengagement from the real world. 'Scholarship and education were, to these women, a high calling, a mission in remote lands,' recalled Nancy Salinger, who felt 'alienated' by their refusal to take on the challenges of the modern world.[49] There were, however, exceptions – Agnes Headlam Morley came to St Hugh's as tutor in Politics, Philosophy and Economics in 1930, boasting considerable 'worldly connections' in diplomacy and international relations.[50] She transformed Salinger's attitude to learning, inspiring her to 'work and read voraciously and to pursue my work doggedly through the libraries ... I would go after dinner to read her my essay and stay till 10.30 p.m. arguing about politics and economics.'[51]

Salinger was encouraged by her PPE tutor to pursue postgraduate research, but not all students were fortunate enough to find such a source of inspiration. Some felt that the tutors assumed 'that we had come to Oxford because of our love of learning and not in order to qualify for earning a living'. Others, conversely, believed that 'the women dons saw Oxford as a teachers' training college ...' Both attitudes resulted in an almost total absence of advice about future careers and a strong aversion to personal ambition – a relic, perhaps, of Elizabeth Wordsworth's distaste for women pursing education for personal gain.[52] Naomi Papworth's 'tentative suggestion' that she would like to pursue postgraduate research into the history of working-class political organisations was quickly dismissed by Miss Gwyer. Instead she was directed towards the University Women's Appointments Bureau, which 'gave a choice of teaching, social work or a secretarial course'.[53]

Few students felt able to challenge such attitudes, and even those who campaigned for social change in the outside world never thought of applying their radical politics to their own education. 'We were very docile as far as the syllabus was concerned,' recalled Naomi Papworth, who at the same time was an active socialist in the University Labour Club.[54] For those students from less well-off backgrounds, rebellious behaviour or assertions of independence would have seemed ungrateful to parents who had made considerable sacrifices to send them to college. Such young women felt obliged to work very hard, too anxious about how they would earn a living in the future to participate in many of the other activities the University had to offer.[55] One student felt that an otherwise positive experience of St Hugh's had been limited by a timid and 'uncritical' attitude resulting from her working-class origins: 'If my background had been professional or academic,' she wrote, 'no doubt things would have been different.'[56] Undergraduates from wealthier backgrounds, however, were also answerable to their families, precisely because they were dependent upon them for financial support. One woman, who had come to St Hugh's in 1919, responded tersely to a question in the centenary questionnaire asking why *she* had chosen to go into higher education. Students were not financially independent in those days, she reminded the historian, and 'consequently it was *father's* decision'.[57]

Education for all? 1945–79

The postwar era brought with it a radical transformation in education funding. The Education Act of 1944 provided free secondary education to all children and established grammar schools based upon intellectual merit rather than ability to pay. Although class inequality continued to operate in less obvious ways (only 10 per cent of working-class children passed the 11-Plus in the early 1950s), grammar schools became a well-established route by which the less wealthy were for the first time able to enter Oxford in significant numbers.[58] State scholarships also increased, so that by the 1950s it was no longer only very poor students who received state assistance: in 1956–7, for example, 74 per cent of Oxbridge undergraduates were recipients of some form of financial support.[59] The number of state scholars at St Hugh's increased accordingly, reflecting what had effectively become a system of partial state subsidy.[60] Yet Oxbridge continued to be more expensive than the civic universities, and the cost of living in college often exceeded the government's maintenance allowance, which was set according to national figures.[61]

The most important change came with the 1962 Education Act, which abolished tuition fees and introduced a minimum maintenance grant to all students (both of which were now to be paid by Local Education Authorities). Students with parents on lower incomes were given a more generous grant, intended to cover all living costs. One of the arguments put forward for the abolition of means-tested tuition fees was that at present some parents were refusing to pay their assessed contribution. The views of the universities were solicited on this question by the Anderson Committee, whose 1960 report paved the way for the 1962 Act. They received a mixed response but found that many universities *were* concerned that means testing jeopardised the educational prospects of students who, for whatever reason, did not have a good relationship with their families. At Oxford, there were one or two undergraduates in each college per year, 'quite a numbering total', whose parents failed to make their contributions.[62] St Hugh's Sylvia Jones, for example, had won a means-tested County Major Scholarship in 1952, but her father refused to contribute because he was against her going to university. 'I therefore found it very difficult to afford to buy many textbooks,' she remembered, 'whereas a lot of my friends did a lot better with their county scholarship grants.'[63]

Means testing was also felt to deter working-class pupils

from applying to university in the first place; either because they assumed that their parents would not be able to afford the contribution or because they wished to avoid becoming a financial burden on their families. Girls were believed to be particularly badly affected, encouraged from an early age to consider alternative careers that offered remunerative training. A draft response by the Anderson Committee suggested that means testing 'strengthens family loyalty, and in doing so strengthens the student's own sense of responsibility'. Oxford, however, professed itself in strong opposition to such a view and, along with many other universities, requested an end to such fees.[64] St Hugh's Governing Body argued for some time over its formal reply to this question, though in the end it voted by a small majority to support the abolition of parental contributions.[65] Some at St Hugh's had long been concerned that means testing damaged women's chances of a university education. In her 1953 Gaudy speech, Principal Proctor told her audience that although most of the barriers that had previously prevented the poor child from attending university had by now been removed, she nevertheless suspected that parents whose incomes were not much above the upper income limit, and who had sons at public schools and universities, might well decide that they could not afford a university education for their daughters.[66]

Following the postwar changes, St Hugh's student body began gradually to diversify, with the college proving itself open to an increasing number of applicants from grammar schools. In 1975 51 matriculating undergraduates came from state schools (36 of them grammar schools) and only 47 from Independent schools. St Hugh's retained its reputation for being less 'snotty' than the other women's colleges, and a number of state-school students recall being encouraged by their teachers to apply to the college on this basis.[67] Angela French came on a State Scholarship in

1958 and felt 'proud that St Hugh's had been founded for the less well-off'. Others continued to feel a tiny 'working-class/ grammar school' minority 'amongst the upper-middle classes and privately educated'.[68] Yet even those who complained about such an imbalance felt that 'St Hugh's seemed less class ridden than most men's colleges'.[69] St Hugh's students were also now less isolated from the 'working world' than in previous generations. Formerly, vacation work had been strongly disapproved of by the college, making life very difficult for those who needed an extra source of income. Yet from the mid-Sixties onwards it became much more common for students to undertake paid work in the holidays, often for the extra cash it provided but also because of a growing notion that it was useful to broaden one's 'experience' beyond the sheltered life of St Hugh's.[70]

As Britain's student population grew in size and social diversity, university campuses across the country became increasingly politicised spaces – and St Hugh's was no exception.[71] Conflict between Oxford students and University authorities in the late 1960s and early 1970s remained relatively small-scale compared with those in the rest of Europe and the USA.[72] The women's colleges, especially, were looked upon as a gentle backwater during the rising tide of student unrest. When the Dean of St Hugh's wrote to the Heads of colleges in 1968 to inform them of a slight extension to men's visiting hours, the Sub-Rector of Exeter College commented wryly: 'it all seems very mild in comparison with what is happening elsewhere.'[73] It was certainly true that St Hugh's JCR was primarily concerned with domestic matters, and this has often been taken to indicate a lack of interest in wider politics.[74] Yet to assume that 'politics' can only exist on a meta-level ignores the way that ideologies and desires are enacted in the everyday. The numerous petitions, direct actions and even rent strikes that took place at St Hugh's in the late

1960s and early 1970s, to protest against the low standards and high cost of living, clearly demonstrate that the domestic sphere *can* be 'political'. Such activity signalled not only an increasingly intransigent student body, but also their wish for a more participatory form of education.

Food was a particularly hot political issue – not surprising, given that complaints about its dire quality had been voiced by generations of students. In fact, even the more respectful and obedient undergraduates of the 1920s had considered organising 'food strikes' to draw attention to the disgusting nature of their nightly fare.[75] In 1948, when such radical forms of protest were unheard of among the student populace, plans were made by strike organisers to form a roadblock on the Banbury Road with placards advertising their mistreatment to passers-by.[76] Students adopted contemporary political jargon to describe their domestic organising. In the early 1960s the term 'eat-in' had been coined to refer to a form of counter-boycott whereby students would descend en masse upon the dining hall to expose the college's failure to provide enough food despite refusing to allow undergraduates to opt out of the meals charge.[77] It was not until the start of the 1970s, however, that the JCR began to adopt forms of protest that forced the college authorities to take their demands seriously. At Oxford, 1968 had marked a turning point in relations between the University and its undergraduates, when a radical subsection of students began to engage in a series of large-scale and antagonistic protests and occupations.[78] The minutes of JCR meetings from this period attest that the effects of these wider upheavals in the University were beginning to be felt at St Hugh's. Minutes of meetings from the 1960s record growing JCR frustration with their tutors' interference in non-academic aspects of student life. Yet they also show that many undergraduates felt powerless to change the situation.[79] By the early 1970s, however, a much more confrontational culture had emerged. A prospective JCR President, for example, appealed to her voters with the promise to organise 'firm direct action' to force the college authorities to do their bidding.[80]

In Michaelmas 1971, St Hugh's undergraduates went on strike against the increased maintenance charge, which exceeded that recommended by the government's Department for Education and Science. JCR President Catherine Dooley accused the SCR of a callous disregard for the undergraduates' wellbeing, informing Kathleen Kenyon that '[t]he JCR does not trust the college to keep down its costs', and believes that it is run 'by people unqualified to maintain an establishment of this size and complexity'.[81] The Governing Body was 'astonished at the offensive tone of the letter', yet it was not the students who found themselves answerable to their superiors, but the Principal who had to agree to interrogation by the JCR. The college Treasurer also had to provide written justification of her decision to raise rents, which included a detailed account of the college's financial difficulties. An early draft of this document even pleaded with students on the basis that St Hugh's Fellows had to put up with considerably lower salaries than tutors at other colleges, and although this was subsequently deleted, it suggests that the SCR must have felt themselves to be in an extremely vulnerable position to even consider disclosing this fact. By the end of October, eighty-eight students were still refusing to pay the full amount, though they were offering cheques for what they considered to be a fair price. Although the Governing Body did not back down on the rent increase, they did agree that they were not in a position to discipline the non-payers, or even force them to pay the shortfall until the following term.[82]

This rent strike became the model for similar actions over the course of the decade, which occurred almost every time the college

CHERWELL

Friday
15th
October

Vol 141
No. 2
3p

ST HUGH'S BATTELS ROW

New Health Appointment

INCREASED BATTELS CHARGES HAVE CAUSED A FURIOUS REACTION AMONGST ST. Hugh's undergraduates. The college raised them to £11.50 per week. £93 per term, without significant consultation with the JCR. This makes them £12 p.a. more than the LEA's allow for in maintenance grants.

A JCR meeting at the end of last term overwhelmingly deplored the increase and the way they were introduced, wished to have a breakdown of college finances made public, and sought representation on the Finance Committee. It pledged it's support for any of its members who might be victimised for following its instruction not to pay more than the LEA's allowance.

This term the tension has increased. The Principal met interested members of the JCR on Sunday and seemed staggered at the poverty of some of them. Moral Tutors have been talking to their students. There was a meeting of Governing Body on Monday night and the JCR meets tonight; the Vice-President Elect of the NUS will speak. Eighty undergraduates have signed a petition pledging not to pay their college bills until satisfactory action is taken, but paying of bills has in any case been suspended. As in other colleges recently the whole question of JCR-SCR relations has been raised by this issue, and is perhaps of more profound importance.

PETE ADAMS

MORE NEWS ON PAGE 2

ST. HUGH'S LATEST

At an emergency meeting of the JCR on Tuesday John Randolph, an NUS official spoke, giving some very useful background information. In the NUS-DES negotiations on grants, it is apparent that the differential for Oxford and Cambridge could be ended as part of the final agreement.

Although this is the only recent issue on which the JCR has expressed itself forcibly in word and deed it is unclear whether at next Monday's fully constitutional meeting the JCR will decide to continue refusing to pay the £4 per term until definite concessions are received or make the best of the muddle and keep the peace.

ACTION COMMITTEE: left to right; top row, Nicky Bagley, Liz Bond, Katy Church; bottom row, Sarah North, Catherine Doolay.

The University is to appoint a suitably qualified full-time health counsellor early in 1972.

This follows the Brock Committee report on student health which recommended that a University medical counselling service should be set up on lines similar to that already successfully established at Cambridge. The main purpose of the service would be to help students suffering under psychological stress and would also assist in the diagnosis of mental illness. The estimated cost of the unit would be about £5000 per annum.

The general effect of the decisions taken by Council and the Conference of Colleges will be a reliance on an extended and improved college doctor system, supplemented by the University medical counselling service under its own committee of management.

POOL PLAN

The plans for a university swimming pool are progressing fast. The pool will be built in Iffley Road and will cost £150,000. The colleges and other sources have raised half the sum and the Rhodes Trustees have contributed the rest. The plan envisages a 25 metre pool with six lanes and possibly a learners' pool.

APPLICATIONS DOWN

The number of applications from school leavers to enter the University fell last year by 151. Of the 3,851 who applied 1,872 were admitted and of these 646 were given awards.

St Hugh's students fight it out in 'Battels Row', 1972. (Bodleian Libraries N.G.A. Oxon.b.181; front page) tried to increase the maintenance charge.[83] Although non-payers were usually in a minority, and the SCR seldom backed down once a price had been set, Governing Body increasingly found itself having to consult and negotiate with the JCR; as a result of which rents rose less quickly than they might have done.[84]

The background to this upsurge in domestic militancy was partly economic. By the 1970s, governments were already beginning to retreat from the generous funding policies of the 1960s,[85] and in 1971 grants ceased to rise in line with the cost of living – creating an ever-increasing deficit between what colleges felt it necessary to charge and what students felt able to pay.[86] But there was also an important ideological context to the JCR's activities. The JCR President may have reassured alumni that the events of 1968 had failed to have much impact at St Hugh's, but this momentous moment in the history of the student movement did not pass the college by entirely. 1968 was also the year in which St Hugh's students were first granted formal representation in college government, when the Joint Committee, consisting of both Fellows and Junior Members, was created.[87] The SCR probably hoped that this would amount to nothing more than a bureaucratic reshuffle, but JCR members were soon using their position on Joint Committee to demand greater decision-making powers in the college as a whole. In 1970 they began to request representation on Governing Body, eventually forcing the SCR to give observer rights to two undergraduate members. The following month, the JCR published confidential Joint Committee minutes to expose the SCR's failure to consult students over proposed rent increases.[88] In the face of further rent rises in 1971 JCR members began to demand the right to attend Finance Committee, in order to scrutinise the SCR's claims that the college had no choice but to increase maintenance to cover costs.[89] Governing Body argued fiercely over this, but eventually, under pressure from Kathleen Kenyon, they agreed to allow the JCR President and Treasurer to attend Finance Committee meetings at which non-confidential matters were discussed.[90]

JCR sources from this period reveal a surprisingly clear set of ideas behind the push for greater participation in college affairs. There was a powerful sense that students had the right to govern their own educational communities and decide for themselves what best suited their educational needs. In May 1971, for example, the JCR followed standard form by thanking the SCR for extending visiting hours, but added that it rejected 'entirely the SCR's assumption that it has the right to impose such restrictions'.[91] St Hugh's students also actively supported the national campaign against Minister for Education Margaret Thatcher's proposals to place student unions under the financial aegis of their colleges. The JCR made their position clear in the *St Hugh's Chronicle*, stating firmly that: 'As students we feel we are best able to decide how our money should be spent.'[92] These undergraduates strongly resisted accusations that their desire for greater autonomy implied indifference to the wellbeing of St Hugh's. To the contrary, insisted JCR President Catherine Dooley, 'The JCR cares about the college, but not in the way that some SCR members appear to expect, i.e. "St Hugh's, right or wrong."'[93] In arguing for representation on the Governing Body, students put forward an alternative understanding of their relationship to the college:

> The case for student representation rests on the essential principle that every individual has the right and the duty to contribute to the governing of an institution of which she is a full member ... Students should be active participants, not passive consumers in the educative process.[94]

Caught in the crossfire, 1979–2011

St Hugh's students did not give up their desire to transform their educational environment, but the carefree optimism of the 'student power' generation became far harder to retain in the face of the severe cuts to higher education carried out by the 1979 Conservative government.[95] First to go were subsidised places for overseas students,[96] and in 1981 the Expenditure White Paper forecast a reduction in university funding of between 11 and 15 per cent.[97] At St Hugh's a decrease of undergraduate numbers was imposed and college fees raised in 1982.[98] Student grants, meanwhile, continued to fall in real terms, creating the new (or rather returning to the old) phenomenon of student debt.[99] In 1990 all maintenance grants were frozen at their existing levels, from then onwards to be topped up by loans. Students' right to housing benefit and social security during the vacations was also withdrawn. At St Hugh's, students' complaints about financial hardship began to be taken seriously by the administration, despite the fact that continued undergraduate resistance to rising college prices caused the college much inconvenience.[100]

A turning point was reached in 1998, when the newly elected Labour Government introduced tuition fees – requiring all students to pay an upfront fee of £1,000, subject to means testing. The St Hugh's Principal, Derek Wood, was extremely concerned about the impact this would have on both hardship and access. He publicly condemned the government's actions on a number of occasions: in speeches to the Association of Senior Members; at the lunch organised for parents of first-year undergraduates; and in two annual reports to the *St Hugh's Chronicle*.[101] Wood described himself as a 'creature of the 1944 Education Act' – a grammar school boy who was able to attend University College Oxford and go on to become a QC, thanks to the postwar government's commitment to free education. His own background, recalled here in an interview, was an important factor in his decision to speak out against tuition fees:

> No higher education anywhere in the family. Big families. Both sides – none of them went to grammar school or anything like that… Grants all the way through. Full grant at Oxford. Full maintenance grant. All my fees paid … I had to do a bit of work to earn money in the summer vacation but otherwise I could ostensibly go up to the Institute of Classical Studies in Gordon Square and read Livy in the Christmas and Easter vacations.

Wood's father had been a tailor and his mother a shopworker, and without a generous system of higher education funding in place he would not have been able to go to university. Although in 1998 tuition fees were initially relatively low, Wood believed that future generations of students from less wealthy backgrounds would be denied the opportunities that had been so crucial to his own success, feeling 'very strongly – emotionally – that this was a retrograde step'.[102]

Wood recalled that his opposition to tuition fees was supported by many other St Hugh's Fellows; especially the influential economics don Theo Cooper. Feelings also ran very high amongst the undergraduate body, many of whom denounced the idea of students becoming consumers in a free market of higher education. Campaigners for free education argued that not all students sought a degree to increase their earning power, and those who wished to pursue more 'socially responsible' careers such as teaching or working in the voluntary sector might now be deterred by a burden of debt which encouraged them instead to go after the largest salaries. The value of higher education, it was argued, could not be measured simply in terms of the individual economic benefits of possessing a degree.[103] Some students continued to defend a more expansive vision of education, insisting that University ought to be open to everyone who wished simply to develop their creativity or better equip themselves to fight social injustice.[104]

Oxford became one of the centres of national student opposition to tuition fees, producing a spate of protests which included handing over fake £1,000 notes to the University administration; rowers in torpids sporting black armbands to signify the 'death' of free education; large demonstrations on the streets of Oxford; and a one-day national student 'strike'.[105] The campaign's main focus, however, was on the tactic of non-payment, whereby students aimed to make the system of tuition fees unworkable through collective refusal to hand over their fees.[106] When the first generation of 'student-consumers' arrived in Oxford in October 1998, St Hugh's proudly boasted the largest contingent of non-payers throughout the University. Student activists already studying at St Hugh's worked hard to catch Freshers when they arrived and convince them not to pay their fees until they had attended the JCR meeting and heard the arguments against doing so. In a referendum in which only first years were able to vote, forty out of ninety-one undergraduates chose to refuse payment, in defiance of threats by the Bursar that this made them ineligible to receive their loan cheques.[107] On the whole, however, St Hugh's Governing Body did not actively seek to discipline non-payers.[108] Instead, it was up to the University authorities to threaten expulsion, so that at the end of Michaelmas term the forty protesters donned black armbands and at last handed over their cheques.[109]

The fight against fees did not force the government to change its policies. Non-payment campaigns continued at St Hugh's for another two years, though by 2000 only one student took a stand.[110] Such action did, however, succeed in highlighting the need to improve access to Oxford University in general. Throughout the non-payment campaigns, the *Oxford Student* newspaper (funded by the Oxford University Student Union, or OUSU) published numerous articles condemning Oxford's bias towards undergraduates from wealthy backgrounds. In 1998, only 7 per cent of pupils nationwide attended fee-paying schools, yet they made up 56 per cent of Oxford's undergraduate population.[111] That same year, two Oxford dons published a report which suggested that applicants from independent schools were 30 per cent more likely to be offered a place than equally qualified state school pupils.[112] Derek Wood did not support his students' campaign of non-payment but he did share their concern that tuition fees would further deter working-class students from applying to Oxford. At St Hugh's, moves to improve access had initially been made by the undergraduates who, in 1988, visited comprehensive schools to encourage more applications 'from those who might otherwise not think of joining us here'.[113] When Wood arrived in 1991, he was keen to strengthen the college's 'outreach' programmes, organising a number of weekends for teachers from state schools with the aim of demystifying the Oxford admissions process. Most Fellows strongly supported these moves to widen access, although Wood remembers resistance from one don who insisted that the college ought to try to recruit students from 'good stable' (the well-known public schools) on the grounds that if St Hugh's agreed to take their 'less bright' pupils then they might be more willing to send their cleverer candidates next time![114]

The wider University was also beginning to take measures to improve access, and in 1997 an Admissions Working Party was formed at the behest of the student union. Its senior members, however, rejected OUSU's proposal to ask for lower grades from comprehensive school candidates. In the furore surrounding tuition fees, the national media seized upon the concerns and statistics generated by these internal discussions to turn Oxford elitism into headline news. According to one report, Oxford was even more class-ridden than Cambridge, accepting students from narrower social strata than its East Anglian rival. The *Independent* newspaper printed an exposé on the 'formalised' links discovered between Oxford colleges and top public schools.[115] In 2000, a highly qualified state school student, Laura Spence, accused Magdalen College of discrimination when they denied her a place to read Medicine. In the wake of this, media attacks on Oxford intensified to the degree that the OUSU newspaper accused journalists of jeopardising the Access Scheme by mischaracterising the University as 'full of posh kids who laugh at poor people'.[116] Oxford's admissions process came under scrutiny not only from the press, but also from teachers keen to secure their pupils places at the University. Derek Wood commented that while Magdalen had been accused of acting unfairly towards state schools, he, along with the heads of seven other colleges, had 'received an indignant letter from the headmaster of a famous independent school accusing us of bias in the other direction'. This was not the first time, he claimed, that Oxford had been 'caught in the crossfire'.[117]

Almost a decade and a half later, tuition fees do not yet appear to have had the dramatic impact upon admissions rates that many predicted.[118] At Oxford, the ratio of students from state versus independent schools (the most common, though often not very accurate, shorthand way of measuring class) has stagnated at roughly equal numbers – 'disgraceful inequalities' according to some, but without any sharp changes since 1998.[119] St Hugh's admissions have also remained relatively stable and between 2002 and 2009 the college accepted 48.5 per cent of students from state schools and 51.5 per cent from independent.[120] St Hugh's also has a hardship fund in place for students experiencing economic difficulties, which supplements the University bursaries that have been available to students from low-income families since 2006.[121] In 2004 the government transferred upfront costs to a graduate tax and brought in a small grant for students from families in the lowest income bracket. Such measures, however, were accompanied by the introduction of variable or 'top-up' fees, which effectively increased charges by allowing individual universities to set their own prices up to a 'cap' of £3,000. As this book goes to press, the Con-Dem Coalition Government has announced plans to allow universities to raise fees to a two-tier cap of either £6,000 or £9,000 per annum.[122] Derek Wood believes that in 1998 he had failed to predict the extent to which students would be willing to take on very large amounts of debt to pay for their university education – and this has been the reason why the numbers of applications show little diminution until now. Wood is less confident, however, that this willingness to 'live with debt' will continue 'following the current economic crisis and the most likely further hike in university fees'.[123]

In 1999 Barbara Castle returned to her old college where, in a speech to Fellows and Old Students, she told of how she had almost been prevented from taking up her place at St Hugh's. In 1929, Castle's success in her final school exams won her a State, a City, and a School Scholarship. Yet none of these provided any financial support because, under the means-testing system, her father's income was considered too high. Means testing had failed to allow for the fact that Castle already had two older siblings at University (one of them at St Hugh's), which already absorbed a considerable amount of the family income. Her father hopelessly concluded that Barbara would not be able to go to Oxford after all. Her mother, however, marched down to Bradford Town Hall wielding a 'meticulous' breakdown of their weekly expenditure, which managed to convince the council that they did not even have enough money left over to 'purchase a newspaper'. Barbara was eventually given a £50 grant and a loan to match, which just about covered the cost of studying, though the loan remained a 'millstone round [her] neck' for many years to come. 'That is why,' Castle declared seventy years later, 'I am so against this system of means testing.'[124] Castle was understandably worried about a return to the bad old days. The odds were heavily stacked against a lower-middle-class girl of her own generation attending University, yet her political career had spanned the gradual introduction of free education. She had watched the erosion of HE funding in the 1980s and 1990s, and now, at the end of the twentieth century, she was to witness her own party reprivatising University education.

Thinking about the economics of education is not only to ask 'who' education was for, but also how the purpose of that education was redefined and re-imagined over time. The sense of entitlement and intellectual prosperity conveyed in the writings of the student militants of the 1970s cannot be reduced to something as crude as a student grant and yet would also never have been possible without such a thing. On the 125th anniversary of the college, with universities about to face cuts on a potentially unprecedented scale, those days seem a long way off, threatening to generate nostalgia for a time of ease that never really was. Yet the legacy of free education and the student radicalism that accompanied it has not been entirely eradicated. In a small community such as St Hugh's – one which retains a strong sense of its own history – cultures of resistance are more easily passed on between generations. And former students will always be on hand, just as Barbara Castle was, to caution their successors against allowing hard-won gains to be lost without a fight.[125] Students today may be facing similar economic pressures to their 1930s counterparts, yet unlike such women they do not question their right to be at Oxford and, as students of St Hugh's, they are no longer made to feel members of a second-rate institution.

AMONGST WOMEN AND
BETWEEN MEN

25 years of co-education

S T HUGH'S BEGAN LIFE as an institution on the margins.
Part of a university which refused to acknowledge its existence, it was a college on the edge of town, and on the edge of
the male academic world. For its first few years it could not even
be certain of its independent status, with some viewing the new
Hall not as a women's society in its own right but as a 'halfway
hostel' for Lady Margaret Hall. As St Hugh's began to establish
itself as the third of the Oxford women's colleges, it remained
caught between different and sometimes opposing worlds. It was
founded in the face of considerable opposition to women's education, yet its early supporters prided themselves on their cautious
and non-confrontational approach. Elizabeth Wordsworth was
repelled by the more radical manifestations of the women's rights
movement, yet her college was to acquire financial security only
at the bequest of a militant suffragette. St Hugh's was established
on a 'definite Church basis', out of a desire to ensure that women's
education did not fall to the radicals and the secularists, and yet
it was the Anglican clergy who made up some of the college's
most powerful opponents. Generations of St Hugh's students had
also to inhabit this paradoxical world – subject to a high degree
of discipline in order that they might acquire greater freedom.
Their education equipped them to become pioneers on behalf of
their sex at the same time as teaching them to conform to Victorian standards of feminine conduct. Their sexually segregated

community taught female undergraduates to value the intellects and company of other women, while leading also to frustration with its narrow outlook and enforced intimacy.

The ability to negotiate such contradictions and to make the most of its marginal position was thus essential to St Hugh's formative identity. When, following the Second World War, the college began to move closer to the mainstream of University life, the transition proved complicated and sometimes painful. The question of how to make sense of a feminism born of necessity in an increasingly integrated society remained a pressing one well into the 1980s. Yet this was not the only way in which St Hugh's tradition of conservative feminism proved problematic – for any analysis which seeks to take seriously the gendered power dynamics of the movement for women's education must also pay attention to the hierarchies that existed within the women's colleges themselves. Looking at the relationship between different groups of women at St Hugh's, between those who taught and studied and those who performed the domestic work, provides a different perspective on the history of higher education. It reminds us not only that women were excluded from the University of Oxford on grounds of class as well as gender, but also that the construction of a new model of educated 'modern' womanhood was contingent upon a devaluing of other forms of labour performed within St Hugh's. The democratisation of higher education was not a smooth or linear process, though a fundamental transformation did take place over this period. St Hugh's benefited from publicly funded free education, and never quite forgot its founding pledge to cater to young women from less wealthy backgrounds, placing it just outside the charmed circle of Oxbridge privilege.

In 1969, however, the story of St Hugh's ceased to be one primarily about women and began to include men at the centre of its narrative. John Wilkinson (Geography) arrived at St Hugh's that year as the college's first male lecturer (he subsequently became St Hugh's first male Fellow in 1979). The start of his thirty-year career at St Hugh's was marked at High Table by Principal Kathleen Kenyon delivering the Latin Grace in the masculine, after which she announced 'that's the last time I'll be doing that'. Yet Wilkinson recalled that, overall, his reception at St Hugh's was a friendly one, more so than at St Hilda's (with whom he shared his lectureship), where the female dons were far more 'formidable'.[1] Derek Wood also remembered a warm welcome when he became the first male Principal in 1991. The college had been co-educational for almost five years by then, and although a few Old Students 'were quite distinctly angry about the appointment of a man', longstanding Fellows, such as Margaret Jacobs and Ann Smart, supported his application. Wood represented a break with the past in a number of ways, for he was the first Principal to come from a professional rather than academic background, as well as the first non-Anglican. Although, by this time, St Hugh's could hardly be described as a Church institution, Trickett nevertheless felt it necessary to enquire of Wood whether his Jewish background would prevent him from supporting the work of the college chapel. Reassured that this would not be a problem (Wood simply insisted on Old Testament passages when he was called upon to read the Lesson), Trickett was extremely helpful to Wood when the time came for him to take over the Principalship.[2]

In 1986, when St Hugh's at last decided to admit male undergraduates, Rachel Trickett declared that the college would remain committed to promoting the cause of women's education. 'I have no doubt,' she wrote in her report to the *Chronicle*, that 'we shall all of us work, as we have in the past, to maintain the standards and the aims intended by our founder and our first Council.'[3] Trickett's remarks were no doubt directed at the many Old Students who feared that the arrival of men would change the college's unique 'character' and 'cohesion'.[4] Such concern intensified when, in 1987, the intake of men vastly exceeded the number of women candidates admitted. Later that year St Hugh's undergraduates pledged 'to remain true to tradition as an educational institution which fosters women's education at the highest level', visiting thirty-five 'target' schools to encourage more female applicants.[5] Male undergraduates have, however, continued to slightly out-number women, with women making up 47 per cent of those admitted in 2010.[6] As a co-educational college, then, St Hugh's has ceased to bolster the number of women in a university where men make up over half (53.4 per cent) of undergraduates, and where male applicants have a slightly higher chance of gaining a place than female applicants.[7] Men also dominate the academic staff to a degree that would have shocked earlier generations of St Hugh's dons. Today there are only nine female Fellows com-pared with forty-eight male Fellows, with an overall percentage of female academic staff of 24 per cent compared to the national average of 40 per cent.[8] As Trickett predicted, a male Principal of St Hugh's was quick in coming, though we wait in vain for a Mistress of Balliol. The literary scholar Marilyn Butler, a Fellow at St Hugh's from 1973 to 1986, bucked the trend to become Provost of Exeter College, though she remained highly critical of the fact that by the turn of the twenty-first century, women made up only 19 per cent of Oxford academic staff. As she reminded us in 2000, 'Having SCRs that congratulate themselves for having over 20 per cent women is hardly going to tell women students that they should and can aim as high as they like.'[9]

Over the last twenty-five years, however, men have made an active and important contribution to St Hugh's, and their presence has not dampened the college's sense of pride in its feminist heri-tage. Such a tradition remains important to past students who have chosen to remain part of the college community after graduation. Since 1986, the Association of Senior Members has hosted a number of feminist 'themed' events on 'Women in Politics: The Suffragettes and Beyond' and 'The Glass Ceiling'; while formal speeches at Gaudies and college reunions have often taken St Hugh's 'trailblazing' foremothers as their subject.[10] Very soon, however, a large proportion of graduates will have only known the college as a co-educational institution, meaning that 'nostalgia for the kind of feminine solidarity most of us enjoyed as undergraduates' will no longer be enough to sustain the feminist legacy.[11] If St Hugh's is to continue to further the cause of women's education, it needs to assert this tradition as something that all its members – women and men – can lay claim to and proudly promote within the rest of the University.

The continuation of gender inequality at Oxford (not only are there fewer female undergraduates and dons, but women are also less likely to achieve a First Class degree) is not a matter of concern only for the former women's colleges, but must be addressed by the whole of the University.[12] Challenging it is not simply about increasing numerical representation, but also involves scrutinising and re-evaluating our assumptions about what constitutes a 'good' education.[13]

It is important to pay attention to areas of exclusion, not simply to find ways to integrate 'minority' groups but also to discover what is missing from the mainstream and to reshape our provision accordingly. St Hugh's College never was and never wanted to be a provider of radical educational alternatives, and it was motivated far more by a desire to be accepted into the academic establishment than by a critique of the status quo. And yet, the marginal position into which St Hugh's was forced generated a current of stubborn pride in its outsider status – a tradition that might still prove useful in reminding Oxford of the riches on offer if it would only open its doors a little wider.

SELECT BIBLIOGRAPHY

ST HUGH'S COLLEGE ARCHIVE (SHCA)

College papers

'Finance Committee Minutes' (II.6.1 [SHG/B/5/2/1], 1913–20)
'General Papers from Daily Life of College' (I.10–18, 1919–36)
'JCR Minutes and Papers' (VI.22, 1955–71)
'JCR Miscellaneous Papers' (VI.24, 1970s–90s)
'Main Building' (III.20)
'Minutes of Accommodation Committee' (II.13.1–7 [SHG/B/8/1])
'Minutes of the Bertha Johnson Loan Fund Committee' (II.12, 1895–1915)
'Minutes and Papers of Council' (II.1.1– 5 [SHG/B/2/1-], 1890–1930)
'Minutes of Governing Body' (II.1 [SHG/B/1–3], 1930–2001)
'Minutes of the Scholarship Committee' (II.4 [SHG/B/1/1], 1912–24)
'Minutes of the Steering Committee for the Admission of Men' (II.30, 1987)
'Miscellaneous Papers' (I.13)
'Miscellaneous Papers of the Dean' (VI.28–9, 1968–70s)
'Oxford Students' Debating Society: Minutes of Proceedings' (VI.18,
    1901–15)
'Papers Concerning Relations with JCR' (VI.17B)
'Papers of the Central Scholarship Committee' (VII.7–9 [SHG/C/3/5],
    1953–61)
'Papers of the Delegacy for Women Students' (VII.12 [SHG/C/2/6],
    1918–20)
'Papers on "The Row"' (I.16 [SHG/A/5])
'Photograph Album' (SHG/M/4/3, 1928)
'Principal's Copy of General Accounts' (IV.2, 1889–1922)
'Principal's Papers for Steering Committee for the Admission of Men' (II.30)
'St Hugh's College Scrapbook' (I.8)
'Undergraduate Newssheets' (VI.26, 1980s–90s)

'Weekly and Monthly Wages' (IV.38–58)

College publications

Clapinson, Mary (ed.), *St Hugh's College in the Twentieth Century: A Record of the Colloquium held at the College on 18th September 1999*

Papers on the history of the College

'Centenary Questionnaire: Papers of Sarah Curtis' (X.19, 1984)
'Papers compiled by Laura Schwartz' (uncatalogued, 2008–2010 [includes personal correspondence, transcripts of interviews])
'Replies to Questionnaire for Domestic and Maintenance Staff' (uncatalogued, 2009)
'Replies to Senior Student Questionnaire' (uncatalogued, 2009)
'Reminiscences of St Hugh's' (X.8–9, 1984)

Personal papers, writings and correspondence

Ady, Cecilia, 'Papers' (VIII.7–12, *c.*1900–1957)
Brooksbank, Ina, 'Correspondence' (X36, 1917–20)
Deneke, Helena, 'Memoir' (I.16, 1967)
McNeill, Molly, 'Correspondence' (X.35, 1916–17)
Proctor, Evelyn, 'History of St Hugh's' (VIII.16)
Rogers, Annie H., 'The Position of Women at Oxford and Cambridge' (I.8, 1896)
Wordsworth, Elizabeth, 'Sermon Manuscripts' (XIII.3, 1900–1910)

PUBLISHED WORKS

'An Appeal against Female Suffrage', *The Nineteenth Century*, 25/CXLVII (1889), pp. 781–8
Adams, Pauline, *Somerville for Women: An Oxford College 1879–1993* (Oxford: Oxford University Press, 1996)
Anderson, R. D., *Universities and Elites in Britain since 1800* (Basingstoke: Macmillan, 1992)
—, *British Universities Past and Present* (London: Hambledon Continuum, 2006)
Batson, Judy G., *Her Oxford* (Nashville: Vanderbilt University Press, 2008)
Battiscombe, Georgina, *Charlotte Mary Yonge: The Story of an Uneventful Life* (London: Constable, 1943)

—, *Reluctant Pioneer: A Life of Elizabeth Wordsworth* (London: Constable, 1978)

Bickerton, Fred, *Fred of Oxford: Being the Memoirs of Fred Bickerton, until Recently Head Porter of University College, Oxford* (London: Evans Brothers Limited, 1952)

Binfield, Clive, *Belmont's Portias: Victorian Nonconformists and Middle-Class Education for Girls* (Leicester: Friends of Dr. William's Library [Leicester Printers Ltd], 1981)

Birch, Dinah, *Our Victorian Education* (Oxford: Blackwell Publishing, 2008)

Bodichon, Barbara Leigh Smith, *Women and Work* (London: Bosworth & Harrison, 1857)

Brittain, Vera, *The Women at Oxford: A Fragment of History* (London: George G. Harrap, 1960)

—, *Testament of Youth: An Autobiographical Study of the Years 1900–1925* (Glasgow: Fontana Paperbacks, 1979)

Brown, Nigel, *Variable Tuition Frees in England: Assessing Their Impact on Students and Higher Education Institutions: A Third Report* (Universities UK, 2010)

Bryant, Margaret, *The Unexpected Revolution: A Study in the History of the Education of Women and Girls in the Nineteenth Century* (London: University of London Institute of Education, 1979)

Burgon, John William, *To Educate Young Women Like Young Men, and with Young Men, – A thing Inexpedient and Immodest: A Sermon Preached Before the University of Oxford in the Chapel of New College on Trinity Sunday (June 8th, 1884)* (Oxford & London: Parker & Co., 1884)

Burstyn, Joan, *Victorian Education and the Ideal of Womanhood* (London: Croom Helm, 1980)

Bush, Julia, *Women against the Vote: Female Anti-Suffragism in Britain* (Oxford: Oxford University Press, 2007)

—, '"Special Strengths for Their Own Special Duties": Women, Higher Education and Gender Conservatism in Late Victorian Britain', *History of Education,* 34/4 (July 2005), pp. 387–405

—, 'The National Union of Women Workers and Women's Suffrage', in Myriam Boussahba-Bravard (ed.), *Suffrage Outside Suffragism: Women's Vote in Britain, 1880–1914* (Basingstoke: Palgrave Macmillan, 2007), pp. 105–31

Caine, Barbara, *English Feminism, 1780–1980* (Oxford: Oxford University Press, 1997)

Castle, Barbara, *Fighting All the Way* (London: Macmillan, 1993)

Cobbe, Frances Power, *Female Education, and How It Would Be Affected by University Examinations: A Paper Read at the Social Science Congress, London, 1862* (3rd edn; London: Emily Faithfull, 1862)

Curthoys, M. C., and Howarth, Janet, 'Origins and Destinations: The Social Mobility of Oxford Men and Women', in M.C. Curthoys and M.G. Brock (eds), *The History of the University of Oxford* (VII; Oxford: Oxford University Press, 2001), pp. 571–95

Curtis, Sarah, 'Origins and Outcomes', in Penny Griffin (ed.), *St Hugh's: One Hundred Years of Women's Education in Oxford* (Basingstoke: Macmillan Press, 1986), pp. 244–83

Davidoff, Leonore, '"Mastered for Life": Servant and Wife in Victorian and Edwardian England', *Journal of Social History*, 7/4 (1974), pp. 406–28

Davidoff, Leonore, and Hawthorn, Ruth, *A Day in the Life of a Victorian Domestic Servant* (London: George Allen, 1976)

Davies, Emily, *The Higher Education of Women* (London: The Hambledon Press, 1988 [first published 1866])

de Bellaigue, Christina, *Educating Women: Schooling and Identity in England and France, 1800–1867* (Oxford: Oxford University Press, 2007)

Delamont, Sara, *Knowledgeable Women: Structuralism and the Reproduction of Elites* (London: Routledge, 1989)

Delap, Lucy, 'Feminist and Anti-Feminist Encounters in Edwardian Britain', *Historical Research*, 78/201 (August 2005), pp. 377–99

—, 'Bedmakers of St Catherine's', *St Catherine's College Magazine* (2008)

—, *Knowing Their Place: Domestic Service in Twentieth Century Britain* (Oxford: Oxford University Press, forthcoming 2011)

Deslandes, Paul R., *Oxbridge Men: British Masculinity and the Undergraduate Experience, 1850–1920* (Bloomington & Indianapolis: Indiana University Press, 2005)

Dunbabin, J. P. D., 'Finance Since 1914', in Brian Harrison (ed.), *The History of the University of Oxford* (VIII; Oxford: Oxford University Press, 1994), pp. 639–82

Dyhouse, Carol, *Girls Growing Up in Late Victorian and Edwardian England* (London: Routledge & Kegan Paul, 1981)

—, *Feminism and the Family 1880–1939* (Oxford: Basil Blackwell, 1989)

—, *No Distinction of Sex? Women in British Universities, 1870–1939* (London: UCL Press, 1995)

—, 'Troubled Identities: Gender and Status in the History of the Mixed College in English Universities Since 1945', *Women's History Review*, 12/2 (2003), pp. 169–93

—, *Students: A Gendered History* (Abingdon: Routledge, 2006)

—, 'History and Policy Papers: Going to University: Funding, Costs, Benefits', *History and Policy* (2007); http://www.historyandpolicy.org/papers/policy-paper-61.html

Edwards, Elizabeth, 'Homoerotic Friendship and College Principals, 1880–1960', *Women's History Review*, 4/2 (1995), pp. 149–63

—, *Women in Teacher Training Colleges: A Culture of Femininity* (London & New York: Routledge, 2001)

Evans, Joan, 'Editor's Preface', *An Adventure* (5th edn; London: Faber & Faber, 1955)

—, *Prelude and Fugue: An Autobiography* (London: Museum Press, 1964)

Fletcher, Sheila, *Feminists and Bureaucrats: A Study in the Development of Girls' Education in the Nineteenth Century* (Cambridge: Cambridge University Press, 1980)

Glenday, N., and Price, M., *Reluctant Revolutionaries: A Century of Headmistresses 1874–1974* (London: Pitman Publishing, 1974)

Gore, Charles, 'The Religious Aspect of the Women's Movement', *The Religious Aspect of the Women's Movement: Being a Series of Addresses delivered at Meeting Held at the Queen's Hall, London, on June 19, 1912* (2nd edn; London: The Collegium, 1912), pp. 30–8

Griffin, Penny, 'Preface', in Penny Griffin (ed.), *St Hugh's: One Hundred Years of Women's Education in Oxford* (Basingstoke: Macmillan, 1986), pp. xi–xii

Harrison, Brian, 'Tape Recorders and the Teaching of History', *Oral History*, 1/2 (1972), pp. 3–10

—, 'College Servants in Corpus Forty Years Ago' (forthcoming, 2011)

Haynes, Renée, *Neapolitan Ice* (London: Chatto & Windus, 1928)

Heeney, Brian, *The Women's Movement in the Church of England 1850–1930* (Oxford: Clarendon, 1988)

Hicks, Marie, 'Integrating Women at Harvard and Oxford, 1964–77', in Laurel Thatcher Ulrich (ed.), *Yards and Gates: Gender in Harvard and Radcliffe History* (Basingstoke: Palgrave Macmillan, 2004), pp. 245–70

Horn, Pamela, *The Rise and Fall of the Victorian Servant* (Dublin: Gill & Macmillan, 1975)

—, *Life below Stairs in the Twentieth Century* (Stroud: Sutton Publishing, 2001)

Howarth, Janet, 'Public Schools, Safety Nets and Educational Ladders: The Classification of Girls' Secondary Schools, 1880–1914', *Oxford Review of Education*, 11/1 (1985), pp. 59–71

—, 'Review: Anglican Perspectives on Gender: Some Reflections on the Centenary of St Hugh's College, Oxford', *Oxford Review of Education*, 12/3 (1986), pp. 299–304

— and Curthoys, Mark, 'The Political Economy of Women's Higher Education in Late Nineteenth and Early Twentieth Century Britain', *Historical Research*, 60/142 (1987), pp. 208–31

—, 'Introduction', *The Higher Education of Women by Emily Davies* (London & Ronceverte: The Hambledon Press, 1988)

—, 'Women', in Brian Harrison (ed.), *The History of the University of Oxford* (VIII; Oxford: Clarendon Press, 1994), pp. 345–75

—, 'Introduction: Writing University History', *Oxford Review of Education*, 23/2 (1997), pp. 147–50

—, 'The Edwardian Reform Movement', in M.G. Brock and M.C. Curthoys (eds), *The History of the University of Oxford* (VII; Oxford: Oxford University Press, 2001)

—, '"In Oxford but … not of Oxford": The Women's Colleges', in M.G. Brock and M.C. Curthoys (eds), *The History of the University of Oxford* (VII.2; Oxford: Oxford University Press, 2001), pp. 237–307

—, 'Johnson [née Todd], Bertha Jane (1846–1927), Promoter of Women's Higher Education', *Oxford Dictionary of National Biography* (online edn; Oxford: Oxford University Press, 2004)

—, 'Jourdain, Eleanor Frances (1863–1924)', *Oxford Dictionary of National Biography* (online edn; Oxford: Oxford University Press, 2004)

—, 'Moberly, Charlotte Anne Elizabeth [Annie] (1846–1937)', *Oxford Dictionary of National Biography* (online edn; Oxford: Oxford University Press, 2004)

—, 'Rogers, Annie Mary Anne Henley (1856–1937)', *Oxford Dictionary of National Biography* (Oxford: Oxford University Press, 2004)

—, 'The Church of England and Women's Higher Education', in Peter Ghosh and Lawrence Goldman (eds), *Politics and Culture in Victorian Britain* (Oxford: Oxford University Press, 2006), pp. 153–70

Iremonger, Lucille, *The Ghosts of Versailles. Miss Moberly and Miss Jourdain and Their Adventure: A Critical Study* (London: Faber & Faber, 1956)

Jeffreys, Sheila, 'Does It Matter If They Did It?', in Lesbian History Group (ed.), *Not a Passing Phase: Reclaiming Lesbians in History, 1840–1985* (1989), pp. 19–28

Kemp, Betty, 'The Early History of St Hugh's', in Penny Griffin (ed.), *St Hugh's: One Hundred Years of Women's Education in Oxford* (Basingstoke: Macmillan Press, 1986), pp. 15–47

Kohl, Benjamin G., 'Ady, Cecilia Mary (1881–1958)', *Oxford Dictionary of National Biography* (online edn; Oxford: Oxford University Press, 2004)

Levine, Philippa, *Victorian Feminism, 1850–1900* (London: Hutchinson, 1987)

—, *Feminist Lives in Victorian England: Private Roles and Public Commitment* (Oxford: Basil Blackwell, 1990)

Light, Alison, *Forever England: Femininity, Literature and Conservatism Between the Wars* (London: Routledge, 1991)

—, *Mrs Woolf and the Servants* (London: Penguin Books, 2008)

Marcus, Sharon, *Between Women: Friendship, Desire and Marriage in Victorian England* (Princeton & Oxford: Princeton University Press, 2007)

Martineau, Lisa, *Politics and Power: Barbara Castle* (London: André Deutsch, 2000)

Meade, Mrs L. T., *The Chesterton Girl Graduates: A Story for Girls* (London: W. & R. Chambers Limited, 1913)

Moberly, Charlotte Anne Elizabeth, *Dulce Domum: George Moberly, His Family and Friends* (London: John Murray, 1911)

—, *The Faith of the Prophets* (London: John Murray, 1916)

—, *Five Visions of the Revelation* (2nd edn; London & Oxford: A.R. Mowbray, 1939)

Olivier, Edith, 'Preface', *Five Visions of the Revelation* (2nd edn; London & Oxford: A. R. Mowbray, 1939), pp. 1–3

—, *Four Victorian Ladies of Wiltshire* (London: Faber & Faber, 1945)

Pederson, Joyce Senders, *The Reform of Girls' Secondary and Higher Education in Victorian England: A Study of Elites and Educational Change* (New York & London: Garland Publishing, 1987)

Platt, Christopher, *The Most Obliging Man in Europe: Life and Times of the Oxford Scout* (London: George Allen & Unwin, 1986)

Pugh, Patricia M., 'Perham, Margery Freda (1895–1982) Writer on African Affairs and University Teacher', *Oxford Dictionary of National Biography* (online edn; Oxford: Oxford University Press, 2004)

Roberts, Adam, 'Morley, Agnes Headlam (1902–86), Historian', *Oxford Dictionary of National Biography* (online edn; Oxford: Oxford University Press, 2004)

Rogers, Annie H., *Degrees by Degrees: The Story of the Admission of Oxford Women Students to Membership of the University* (Oxford: Oxford University Press, 1938)

Sayers, Dorothy, *Gaudy Night* (London: New English Library, 1996 [first published 1935])

Soutter, Ann (ed.), *St Hugh's Register, 1886–1959* (forthcoming 2011)

Spender, Dale (ed.), *Time and Tide Wait for No Man* (London: Pandora Press, 1984)

Stedman Jones, Gareth, 'The Meaning of the Student Revolt', in Alexander Cockburn and Robin Blackburn (eds), *Student Power/ Problems, Diagnosis, Action* (Harmondsworth: Penguin, 1969), pp. 25–56

Strachey, Ray, *The Cause: A Short History of the Women's Movement in Great Britain* (London: Virago, 1978)

Sutherland, Gillian, 'The Movement for the Higher Education of Women: Its Social and Intellectual Context in England, c.1840–80', in P. J. Waller (ed.), *Politics and Social Change in Modern Britain: Essays Presented to A. F. Thompson* (Sussex: Harvester Press, 1987), pp. 91–117.

—, 'Review Essay: The House That Jill Built', *Oxford Review of Education*, 23/2 (June 1997), pp. 245–50

—, 'Anne Jemima Clough and Blanche Athena Clough: Creating Educational Institutions for Women', in Pam Hirsch and Mary Hilton (eds), *Practical Visionaries: Women, Education and Social Progress 1790–1930* (London: Pearson Education, 2000), pp. 101–14

—, *Faith, Duty and the Power of the Mind: The Cloughs and Their Circle 1820–1960* (Cambridge: Cambridge University Press, 2006)

Tamboukou, Maria, *Women, Education and the Self: A Foucauldian Perspective* (Basingstoke: Palgrave Macmillan, 2003)

Thane, Pat, 'Review Article: Scholars or Amazons?', *Oxford Review of Education*, 23/2 (June 1997), pp. 253–8

—, 'Girton Graduates: Earning and Learning, 1920s–1980s', *Women's History Review*, 13/3 (2004), pp. 347–61

Thomas, Keith, 'College Life, 1945–70', in Brian Harrison (ed.), *The History of the University of Oxford: The Twentieth Century* (VIII; Oxford: Oxford University Press, 1994), pp. 189–215

Todd, Selina, 'Domestic Service and Class Relations in Britain 1900–1950', *Past and Present*, 203 (2009), pp. 181–204

Trickett, Rachel, 'The Row', in Penny Griffin (ed.), *St Hugh's: One Hundred Years of Women's Education in Oxford* (Basingstoke: Macmillan, 1986), pp. 48–61

—, 'Women's Education', in Penny Griffin (ed.), *St Hugh's: One Hundred Years of Women's Education in Oxford* (Basingstoke: Macmillan, 1986), pp. 5–14

Vicinus, Martha, *Independent Women: Work and Community for Single Women, 1850–1920* (London: Virago Press, 1985)

—, 'Distance and Desire: English Boarding School Friendships, 1870–1920', in Martin Bauml Duberman, Martha Vicinus, and George Chauncey Jr. (eds), *Hidden from History: Reclaiming the Gay and Lesbian Past* (New York: New American Library Books, 1989), pp. 212–29

—, *Intimate Friends: Women Who Loved Women, 1778–1928* (Chicago & London: University of Chicago Press, 2004)

Vickery, Margaret Birney, *Buildings for Bluestockings: The Architecture and Social History of Women's Colleges in Victorian England* (Newark & London: University of Delaware Press, 1999)

Warnock, Mary, 'Women's Education and Its Future', in Penny Griffin (ed.), *St Hugh's: One Hundred Years of Women's Education* (Basingstoke: Macmillan, 1986), pp. 284–98

—, *A Memoir: People and Places* (London: Gerald Duckworth, 2000)

Watson, Judith, and Church, Andrew, 'Funding the Future: The Attitudes of Year 10 Pupils in England and Wales to Higher Education' (National Union of Students, 2008)

West, Priscilla, 'Reminiscences of Seven Decades', in Penny Griffin (ed.), *St Hugh's: One Hundred Years of Women's Education* (Basingstoke: Macmillan, 1986), pp. 62–243

Whiteley, L. D., *The Poor Student and the University: A Report on the Scholarship System* (London: George Allen & Unwin, 1933)

Wiggins, Sarah, 'Gendered Spaces and Political Identity: Debating Societies in English Women's Colleges, 1890–1914', *Women's History Review*, 18/5 (2009), pp. 737–52

Wolstenholme, Elizabeth, 'The Education of Girls: Its Present and Its Future', in Josephine Butler (ed.), *Woman's Work and Woman's Culture* (London: Macmillan & Co., 1869), pp. 290–330

Woolf, Virginia, *A Room of One's Own* (Harmondsworth: Penguin Books, 1975 [first published 1928])

Wordsworth, Christopher, *Christian Womanhood and Christian Sovereignty: A Sermon* (London: Rivingtons, 1884)

Wordsworth, Elizabeth, *First Principles in Women's Education* (Oxford: James Parker & Co., 1894)

—, *Glimpses of the Past* (London & Oxford: A. R. Mowbray, 1912)

MAGAZINES AND NEWSPAPERS

The Cherwell
The Fritillary

The Imp
Oxford Journal Illustrated
Oxford Magazine
Oxford Student
Oxford Times
Oxford University Gazette
St Hugh's Chronicle
St Hugh's Club Paper

OTHER ARCHIVES

Bodleian Library, Oxford
Oxford University Archive, Oxford
Wiltshire & Swindon History Centre, Chippenham
Women's Library, London

UNPUBLISHED WORKS

Eccles, Kathryn, 'Women Students at the University of Oxford, 1914–39: Image, Identity and Experience' (University of Oxford, unpublished doctoral thesis, 2007)

Wiggins, Sarah, 'Politics and Political Culture in English Women's Colleges, 1890–1914' (London: Royal Holloway, University of London, unpublished doctoral thesis, 2003)

NOTES

INTRODUCTION

1. Elizabeth Wolstenholme, 'The Education of Girls: Its Present and Its Future', in Josephine Butler (ed.), *Woman's Work and Woman's Culture* (London: Macmillan & Co., 1869), pp. 290–330 (p. 328).

2. Josephine Butler, *The Education and Employment of Women* (Liverpool: T. Brakell, 1868), p. 7. For examples of this theme within feminist writings earlier in the century, see Mary Wollstonecraft, 'A Vindication of the Rights of Women', in Janet Todd (ed.), *Mary Wollstonecraft: Political Writings* (London: William Pickering, 1993), pp. 67–296; Eliza Sharples, 'The Third Discourse of the Lady of the Rotunda', *Isis* (1832); Frances Wright, 'Lecture 1. On the Nature of Knowledge', in Frances Wright (ed.), *Course of Popular Lectures as Delivered by Frances Wright, in New York, Philadelphia, Baltimore, Boston, Cincinnati, St Louis, Louisville, and other Cities, Towns and Districts of the United States. With Three Addresses on Various Public Occasions and a Reply to the Charges Against the French Reformers of 1789* (4th edn; New York: Office of the Free Enquirer, Hall of Science, 1831).

3. Barbara Leigh Smith Bodichon, *Women and Work* (London: Bosworth & Harrison, 1857).

4. Ibid., p. 11; Frances Power Cobbe, *Female Education, and How It Would Be Affected by University Examinations: A Paper Read at the Social Science Congress, London, 1862* (3rd edn; London: Emily Faithfull, 1862), pp. 4–5; Emily Davies, *The Higher Education of Women* (London: The Hambledon Press, 1988 [first published 1866]), pp. 38, 44.

5. Wolstenholme, 'Education of Girls', p. 318.

6. Butler, *Education and Employment of Women*, p. 4.

7. Bodichon, *Women and Work*, p. 18; Elizabeth Sewell, *Principles of Education Drawn from Nature and Revelation and Applied to Female*

Education in the Upper Classes, 2 vols (I; London: Longman, Green, Longman, Roberts, & Green, 1865), pp. 260–2.

8. Davies, *Higher Education of Women*, pp. 71, 76–8.

9. N. Glenday and M. Price, *Reluctant Revolutionaries: A Century of Headmistresses 1874–1974* (London: Pitman Publishing, 1974); Philippa Levine, *Feminist Lives in Victorian England: Private Roles and Public Commitment* (Oxford: Basil Blackwell, 1990), pp. 128, 36–7.

10. The domestic model remained, however, an important influence into the 1860s, complicating schoolmistresses' relationship with their professional role and the 'public values' they passed on to their students: Christina De Bellaigue, *Educating Women: Schooling and Identity in England and France, 1800–1867* (Oxford: Oxford University Press, 2007).

11. Sheila Fletcher, *Feminists and Bureaucrats: A Study in the Development of Girls' Education in the Nineteenth Century* (Cambridge: Cambridge University Press, 1980). See also Joyce Senders Pederson, *The Reform of Girls' Secondary and Higher Education in Victorian England: A Study of Elites and Educational Change* (New York & London: Garland Publishing, 1987).

12. Gillian Sutherland, 'The Movement for the Higher Education of Women: Its Social and Intellectual Context in England, *c.* 1840–80', in J. Waller (ed.), *Politics and Social Change in Modern Britain: Essays Presented to A. F. Thompson* (Sussex: Harvester Press, 1987), pp. 91–116.

13. Janet Howarth, 'The Church of England and Women's Higher Education', in Peter Ghosh and Lawrence Goldman (eds), *Politics and Culture in Victorian Britain* (Oxford: Oxford University Press, 2006), pp. 153–70. For the non-conformist contribution to women's education, see Clive Binfield, *Belmont's Portias: Victorian Nonconformists and Middle-Class Education for Girls* (Leicester: Friends of Dr William's Library [Leicester Printers Ltd], 1981).

14. Margaret J. Tuke, *A History of Bedford College for Women, 1849–1937* (London: Oxford University Press, 1939); Gillian Sutherland, 'The Plainest Principles of Justice: The University of London and the Higher Education of Women', in F. M. L. Thompson (ed.), *The University of London and the World of Learning, 1836–1986* (London & Ronceverte: The Hambledon Press, 1990), pp. 35–56.

15. Carol Dyhouse, *No Distinction of Sex? Women in British Universities, 1870–1939* (London: UCL Press, 1995), p. 14.

16. Janet Howarth and Mark Curthoys, 'The Political Economy of Women's Higher Education in Late Nineteenth and Early Twentieth Century Britain', *Historical Research,* 60/142 (1987), pp. 208–31.

17. Joan Burstyn, *Victorian Education and the Ideal of Womanhood* (London: Croom Helm, 1980).

18. For women's education in Cambridge, see Alice Gardner, *A Short History of Newnham College Cambridge* (Cambridge: Bowes & Bowes, 1921); Ray Strachey, *The Cause: A Short History of the Women's Movement in Great Britain* (London: Virago, 1978); M. Bradbrook, *'That Infidel Place': A Short History of Girton College 1869–1969* (London: Chatto & Windus, 1969); Rita McWilliams-Tullberg, *Women at Cambridge: A Men's University Though of a Mixed Type* (London: Victor Gollancz, 1975); Janet Howarth, 'Introduction', *The Higher Education of Women by Emily Davies* (London & Ronceverte: The Hambledon Press, 1988); Mary Agnes Hamilton, *Newnham: An Informal Biography* (London: Faber & Faber, 1936); Ann Phillips (ed.), *A Newnham Anthology* (Cambridge: Cambridge University Press, 1979); Gillian Sutherland, 'Anne Jemima Clough and Blanche Athena Clough: Creating Educational Institutions for Women', in Pam Hirsch and Mary Hilton (eds), *Practical Visionaries: Women, Education and Social Progress 1790–1930* (London: Pearson Education, 2000), pp. 101–14.

19. Rachel Trickett, 'Women's Education', in Penny Griffin (ed.), *St Hugh's: One Hundred Years of Women's Education in Oxford* (Basingstoke: Macmillan, 1986), pp. 5–14.

20. Annie H. Rogers, *Degrees by Degrees: The Story of the Admission of Oxford Women Students to Membership of the University* (Oxford: Oxford University Press, 1938).

21. Colin Matthew, 'The Early History of St Hugh's and "The Row"', in Mary Clapinson (ed.), *St. Hugh's College in the Twentieth Century: A Record of the Colloquium Held at the College on 18th September 1999* (Oxford, 1999), pp. 15–27,(15–16). See also Rogers, *Degrees by Degrees*, p. 25.

22. Vera Brittain, *The Women at Oxford: A Fragment of History* (London: George G. Harrap, 1960), p. 49.

23. Betty Kemp, 'The Early History of St Hugh's', in Penny Griffin (ed.), *St Hugh's: One Hundred Years of Women's Education in Oxford* (Basingstoke: Macmillan Press, 1986), pp. 15–47 (18, 22).

24. 'St Hugh's College Scrapbook' (I.8; SHCA [SHCA]), p. 3.

25. Kemp, 'The Early History of St Hugh's'.

26. See, for example, Penny Griffin, 'Preface', in Penny Griffin (ed.), *St Hugh's: One Hundred Years of Women's Education in Oxford* (Basingstoke: Macmillan, 1986), pp. xi–xii.

27. Somerville admitted men in 1992, while St Hilda's, the last remaining women's college, went mixed in 2008.

28. Davies, *Higher Education of Women*.

29. 'Letters received and read at the Meeting of the North of England Council for the Higher Education of Women held at Leeds, on Wednesday, April 15th, 1868', *North of England Council for the Higher Education of Women* (Liverpool: T. Brakell, 1868); Sutherland, 'The Movement for the Higher Education of Women'.

30. Butler, *Education and Employment of Women*, pp. 17–18.

31. Sutherland, 'Creating Educational Institutions for Women'.

32. Trickett, 'Women's Education', p. 8.

33. The term 'feminism' was not used in England until the 1890s, and historians have debated its utility for describing the diverse activities of those advocating women's rights in the nineteenth century. This book, however, follows convention in referring to 'Victorian feminism' according to Levine's definition as women's recognition of their collective oppression and their positive identification with each other in the context of political struggle, Philippa Levine, *Victorian Feminism, 1850–1900* (London: Hutchinson, 1987), p. 14. For problems with the term 'feminism', see Nancy F. Cott, *The Grounding of Modern Feminism* (New Haven & London: Yale University Press, 1987); Karen Offen, 'Defining Feminism: A Comparative Historical Approach', *Signs*, 14/1 (1988), pp. 119–57; Barbara Caine, *English Feminism, 1780–1980* (Oxford: Oxford University Press, 1997); Lucy Delap, 'Feminist and Anti-Feminist Encounters in Edwardian Britain', *Historical Research*, 78/201 (August 2005), pp. 377–99.

34. For more linear and progressive narratives, see Rogers, *Degrees by Degrees*; Brittain, *Women at Oxford*. Dyhouse warned against simply dismissing the achievements of the early women educationalists, but nevertheless argued that it was wrong to be complacent about the position of women at Oxford after 1920: Carol Dyhouse, *Students: A Gendered History* (Abingdon: Routledge, 2006), pp. x–xi, 84. For continued exclusion in the interwar period, see also Kathryn Eccles, 'Women Students at the University of Oxford, 1914–39: Image, Identity and Experience' (University of Oxford, unpublished doctoral thesis, 2007).

35. Martha Vicinus, *Independent Women: Work and Community for Single Women, 1850–1920* (London: Virago Press, 1985), pp. 134–5. Some continue to argue that such an approach was necessary and beneficial: Kemp, 'The Early History of St Hugh's', p. 31; Judy G. Batson, *Her Oxford* (Nashville: Vanderbilt University Press, 2008), p. xv.
36. Sutherland, 'The Movement for the Higher Education of Women', p. 94; Levine, *Feminist Lives*, p. 127.
37. For a discussion of the potential benefits and pitfalls of 'insider' histories, see Janet Howarth, 'Introduction: Writing University History', *Oxford Review of Education*, 23/2 (1997), pp. 147–50; Gillian Sutherland, 'Review Essay: The House That Jill Built', *Oxford Review of Education*, 23/2 (June 1997), pp. 245–50; Eccles, 'Women Students', p. 13.

1   FOUNDING IMPULSES

1. Kemp, 'The Early History of St Hugh's', in Penny Griffin (ed.), *St Hugh's: One Hundred Years of Women's Education in Oxford* (Basingstoke: Macmillan Press, 1986), pp. 15–47.
2. Until recently many historians believed that Yonge was Moberly's godmother, though Mrs Keble in fact took on this role: Janet Howarth, 'Moberly, Charlotte Anne Elizabeth [Annie] (1846–1937)', *Oxford Dictionary of National Biography* (online edn; Oxford: Oxford University Press, 2004).
3. For the Oxford Movement, see Robert Dudley Middleton, *Keble, Froude and Newman: Short Essays in the Early History of the Oxford Movement* (Canterbury: Gibbs & Sons, 1933); Owen Chadwick, *The Mind of the Oxford Movement* (London: Adam & Charles Black, 1960); Brad Faught, *The Oxford Movement: A Thematic History of Tractarians and Their Times* (University Park, PA: Pennsylvania State University Press, 2003); James Pereiro, *Ethos and the Oxford Movement: At the Heart of Tractarianism* (Oxford: Oxford University Press, 2008).
4. Charlotte Anne Elizabeth Moberly, *Dulce Domum: George Moberly, His Family and Friends* (London: John Murray, 1911), pp. 7–8.
5. Ibid., pp. 153, 82–3.
6. Edith Olivier, *Four Victorian Ladies of Wiltshire* (London: Faber & Faber, 1945), pp 24–7. Elizabeth strongly identified with Ethel May, a character in Yonge's novels about a family said to be based upon the Moberlys: Georgina Battiscombe, *Reluctant Pioneer: A Life of Elizabeth*

Wordsworth (London: Constable, 1978), p. 41. Annie Moberly claimed, however, that the striking resemblance between the May family and the Moberlys was coincidental: Moberly, *Dulce Domum*, p. 210.

7.   Charlotte Anne Elizabeth Moberly, 'History of St Hugh's', *St Hugh's Club Paper,* Jan. 1899.

8.   Lucille Iremonger, *The Ghosts of Versailles. Miss Moberly and Miss Jourdain and Their Adventure: A Critical Study* (London: Faber & Faber, 1956).

9.   Moberly, *Dulce Domum*, p. 296.

10.   Georgina Battiscombe, *Reluctant Pioneer: A Life of Elizabeth Wordsworth* (London: Constable, 1978), p. 125; Helena Deneke, 'Memoir' (I.16; SHCA, 1967), pp. 22–3.

11.   Deneke, 'Memoir', pp. 21–3. See also Battiscombe, *Reluctant Pioneer*, p. 125.

12.   Battiscombe, *Reluctant Pioneer*, p. 148.

13.   Evelyn Proctor, 'History of St Hugh's' (VIII.16; SHCA), p. 3.

14.   Deneke, 'Memoir', p. 23.

15.   'St Hugh's College Scrapbook' (I.8; SHCA), p. 4.

16.   Joan Evans, *Prelude and Fugue: An Autobiography* (London: Museum Press, 1964), pp. 8–9.

17.   Moberly, *Dulce Domum*, p. 117.

18.   Edith Olivier, 'Preface', *Five Visions of the Revelation* (2nd edn; London & Oxford: A. R. Mowbray, 1939), pp. 1–3.

19.   Elizabeth Wordsworth, *First Principles in Women's Education* (Oxford: James Parker & Co., 1894), pp. 17–18; Battiscombe, *Reluctant Pioneer*, p. 68.

20.   Proctor, 'History of St Hugh's', pp. 3, 5.

21.   10 May 1910, 'Minutes and Papers of Council' (II.1.2; SHCA, 1908–11), p. 28.

22.   6 Dec. 1898, 'Minutes and Papers of Council' (II.1.1 [SHG/B/2/1]; SHCA, 1890–1908), p. 109.

23.   Charlotte Anne Elizabeth Moberly, 'History of St Hugh's Part 2', *St Hugh's Club Paper,* Jan. 1900.

24.   'St Hugh's College Scrapbook', p. 22.

25.   Charlotte Anne Elizabeth Moberly, *The Faith of the Prophets* (London: John Murray, 1916); Charlotte Anne Elizabeth Moberly, *Five Visions of the Revelation* (2nd edn; London & Oxford: A.R. Mowbray, 1939).

26.   Olivier, *Four Victorian Ladies*, pp. 39–40.

27.   Iremonger, *The Ghosts of Versailles*, p. 54.

28. Wordsworth believed the mark of true femininity was the ability to perform acts of 'self-denial': Wordsworth, *First Principles*, p. 12.

29. This point is made by Howarth, 'The Church of England and Women's Higher Education', p. 153. Margaret Bryant argued that although Evangelicalism was a driving force, the Tractarian or Oxford Movement made very little direct contribution to the improvement of women's education: Margaret Bryant, *The Unexpected Revolution: A Study in the History of the Education of Women and Girls in the Nineteenth Century* (London: University of London Institute of Education, 1979), pp. 65–70.

30. John William Burgon, *To Educate Young Women Like Young Men, and with Young Men, – A Thing Inexpedient and Immodest: A Sermon Preached before the University of Oxford in the Chapel of New College on Trinity Sunday (June 8th, 1884)* (Oxford & London: Parker & Co., 1884).

31. Brittain, *The Women at Oxford: A Fragment of History* (London: George G. Harrap, 1960), pp. 24, 37; Brian Heeney, *The Women's Movement in the Church of England 1850–1930* (Oxford: Clarendon, 1988), p. 7.

32. Burgon, *To Educate Young Women*, pp. 8–10.

33. Annie H. Rogers, *Degrees by Degrees: The Story of the Admission of Oxford Women Students to Membership of the University* (Oxford: Oxford University Press, 1938), p. 19.

34. Janet Howarth, 'Review: Anglican Perspectives on Gender: Some Reflections on the Centenary of St Hugh's College, Oxford', *Oxford Review of Education*, 12/3 (1986), pp. 299–304; Howarth, 'The Church of England and Women's Higher Education'.

35. Heeney, *The Women's Movement in the Church of England*, pp. 7–8.

36. Quoted in Julia Bush, '"Special Strengths for Their Own Special Duties", Women, Higher Education and Gender Conservatism in Late Victorian Britain', *History of Education*, 34/4 (July 2005), pp. 387–405 (400).

37. Quoted in Janet Howarth, '"In Oxford but ... not of Oxford": The Women's Colleges', in M. G. Brock and M. C. Curthoys (eds), *The History of the University of Oxford* (VII.2; Oxford: Oxford University Press, 2001), pp. 237–307 (251).

38. Christopher Wordsworth, *Christian Womanhood and Christian Sovereignty: A Sermon* (London: Rivingtons, 1884), pp. 25–6.

39. Ibid., p. 33.

40. Wordsworth, *First Principles*, pp. 5–7.

41. Elizabeth Wordsworth, 'Sermon Manuscripts' (XIII.3; SHCA, *c.*1900–1910), Isaiah I–XII (1907–8).

42. Battiscombe, *Reluctant Pioneer*, pp. 174–5.

43. Ibid., pp. 100–1.

44. Wordsworth, *First Principles*. There was a strong religious dimension to nineteenth-century debates on liberal versus utilitarian education. In contrast to Wordsworth, the leading educational reformer Clara Collet promoted a wholly pragmatic vision of higher education derived from her Dissenting inheritance, whereby men excluded from Oxbridge on religious grounds earlier in the century established their own academies with a far more 'useful' approach to knowledge: Jane Miller, 'Clara Collet's Dissenting Inheritance and the Education of Women', in Mary Hilton and Pam Hirsch (eds), *Practical Visionaries: Women, Education and Social Progress 1790–1930* (Harlow: Pearson Education, 2000), pp. 115–28.

45. Wordsworth, *First Principles*, pp. 7–8.

46. Wordsworth, 'Sermon Manuscripts', Isaiah I–XII (1907–8).

47. Annie H. Rogers, 'The Position of Women at Oxford and Cambridge' (I.8; SHCA, 1896), pp. 3–4.

48. 'Scholarship Fund', *St Hugh's Club Paper*, Aug. 1909, p. 7.

49. Evans, *Prelude and Fugue*, p. 68.

50. 'St Hugh's College', *Oxford Times*, 20 Oct. 1917, p. 42.

51. Kemp, 'The Early History of St Hugh's', p. 40; Rogers, *Degrees by Degrees*, p. 51.

52. Howarth, 'Anglican Perspectives', p. 300. Wordsworth was so unwilling to publicly advocate this position that even her biographer suspected that she opposed degrees for women: Battiscombe, *Reluctant Pioneer*, pp. 137–40.

53. Battiscombe, *Reluctant Pioneer*, pp. 137–40.

54. 15 Feb. 1893, 'Minutes and Papers of Council', p. 35.

55. 1 May 1995, ibid., pp. 51–2.

56. Rogers, *Degrees by Degrees*, pp. 58–71.

57. One dust jacket described 'the fight for women's education' as 'a training ground for the more flamboyant conflicts of the suffrage movement': McWilliams-Tullberg, *Women at Cambridge*.

58. Gillian Sutherland, 'The Movement for the Higher Education of Women: Its Social and Intellectual Context in England, *c.*1840–1880', in P. J. Waller (ed.), *Politics and Social Change in Britain: Essays Presented to A. F. Thompson* (Sussex: Harvester Press, 1987), pp. 91–116. See also

Gillian Sutherland, 'Anne Jemima Clough and Blanche Athena Clough: Creating Educational Institutions for Women', in Pam Hirsch and Mary Hilton (eds), *Practical Visionaries: Women, Education and Social Progress 1790–1930* (London: Pearson Education, 2000), pp. 101–14.

59. Carol Dyhouse, *Girls Growing Up in Late Victorian and Edwardian England* (London: Routledge & Kegan Paul, 1981), pp. 59–60.

60. Jane Rendall, '"A Moral Engine"? Feminism, Liberalism and the English Woman's Journal', in Jane Rendall (ed.), *Equal or Different: Women's Politics 1800–1914* (Oxford: Basil Blackwell, 1987), pp. 112–38.

61. Levine insisted that the commitment of prominent figures such as Emily Davies, Josephine Butler, Barbara Bodichon and Bessie Raynor Parkes to a broad vision of women's rights meant that the movement ought to be conceptualised as part of nineteenth-century feminist activity: Philippa Levine, *Feminist Lives in Victorian England: Private Roles and Public Commitment* (Oxford: Basil Blackwell, 1990), pp. 127–8, 45–6.

62. Battiscombe, *Reluctant Pioneer*, p. 11.

63. Levine, *Feminist Lives*; Sara Delamont, *Knowledgeable Women: Structuralism and the Reproduction of Elites* (London: Routledge, 1989); Howarth, 'The Women's Colleges'.

64. Bush, 'Women, Higher Education and Gender Conservatism'.

65. Ibid., pp. 393, 400; Julia Bush, *Women against the Vote: Female Anti-Suffragism in Britain* (Oxford: Oxford University Press, 2007), p. 41.

66. 'An Appeal against Female Suffrage', *The Nineteenth Century*, 25/ CXLVII (1889), pp. 781–88; Bush, *Women against the Vote*.

67. Bush, 'Women, Higher Education and Gender Conservatism', p. 405. Lucy Delap also argues against dividing responses to the Woman Question into monolithic and polarised groups of 'feminists' and 'anti-feminists', and instead maintains that such debates are better understood as part of a spectrum: Lucy Delap, 'Feminist and Anti-Feminist Encounters in Edwardian Britain', *Historical Research*, 78/201 (August 2005), pp. 377–99.

68. Marcia Alice Rice, 'Dear Old Students', *St Hugh's Club Paper*, June 1898, n.p.

69. See Heeney, *The Women's Movement in the Church of England*.

70. Wordsworth, *First Principles*, p. 3.

71. Charles Gore, 'The Religious Aspect of the Women's Movement', *The Religious Aspect of the Women's Movement: Being a Series of Addresses Delivered at Meeting Held at the Queen's Hall, London, on June 19, 1912* (2nd edn; London: The Collegium, 1912), pp. 30–38.

72. Together with Edward Talbot (Keble College), Gore co-authored a collection of essays published in 1889 entitled *Lux Mundi*. More than fifty years after the Oxford Movement began, the *Lux Mundi* authors argued once again for the need to imbue the Church with a truly Catholic spirituality.

73. Walter Lock, a contributor to *Lux Mundi*, was a member of St Hugh's Council between 1894 and 1923: *St Hugh's Chronicle*, 1933–4, no. 6, pp. 25–6.

74. Scott Holland had spent Christmas with the Moberly family in 1877: Moberly, *Dulce Domum*, p. 260; Deneke, 'Memoir', p. 15.

75. 'Third Annual Report' (The Church League for Women's Suffrage, 1912), pp. 28, 1.

76. Janet Howarth, 'Rogers, Annie Mary Anne Henley (1856–1937)', *Oxford Dictionary of National Biography* (Oxford: Oxford University Press, 2004).

77. 15 May 1915, 'Minutes and Papers of Council' (II.1.3; SHCA, 1911–16), n.p. The request was declined because St Hugh's was already booked.

78. 2 June 1911, 'Minutes and Papers of Council', p. 48; 16 May 1914, 'Minutes and Papers of Council', n.p. The Union was an umbrella organisation, beginning in the 1890s and formally launched in 1895 as a network of individuals and affiliated associations working in philanthropy, education and other forms of social service. It has been described by both historians and contemporaries as 'a predominantly conservative organisation', 'flagrantly non-political' and dominated by Anglican orthodoxy; see Julia Bush, 'The National Union of Women Workers and Women's Suffrage', in Myriam Boussahba-Bravard (ed.), *Suffrage Outside Suffragism: Women's Vote in Britain, 1880–1914* (Basingstoke: Palgrave Macmillan, 2007), pp. 105–31 (105, 112). The quote is from Beatrice Webb, who eventually resigned from the executive committee because she disliked the Anglican tone of proceedings. After 1912–13 it retained many anti-suffrage members.

79. Edith Olivier, 'Diaries' (982/32–3; Chippenham: Wiltshire & Swindon History Centre, 1894–6) (Michaelmas 1896). With great thanks to Penelope Rundle for drawing attention to this source.

80. Louisa Fentham Todd, 'Dear Old Students', *St Hugh's Club Paper*, Aug. 1907, n.p.

81. E. F. Jourdain, 'Suffrage Sunday', ibid., 1908.

82. See for example M. Libetter and Agnes Ramsey, 'Postcards to the Editor', ibid.; Mary Tudor, 'Dear Old Students', *St Hugh's Club Paper,* Aug. 1909, p. 8; Leslie I.G. Bickmore, 'Senior Students' Letter', *St Hugh's Club Paper,* Aug. 1910, pp. 22–6 (24).

83. Leslie I. G. Bickmore, 'Suggested Suffrage Society', *St Hugh's Club Paper,* Aug. 1910, pp. 20–1.

84. 10 May, 19 Nov. 1913, 'Minutes and Papers of Council'. Moberly did not shy away from mentioning Clara Mordan's membership of the WSPU in her memorial: Charlotte Anne Elizabeth Moberly, 'Letter from Miss Moberly', *St Hugh's Club Paper,* Oct. 1915, pp. 24–9.

85. Quoted in Bush, *Women against the Vote,* p. 41.

86. Davison attended St Hugh's for one term in 1895, and obtained a First in Modern Languages.

87. Ethel Vaux, 'Postcards to the Editor', *St Hugh's Club Paper,* Aug. 1908, n.p; Margery Lewis, 'Accounts of Representative War Work Undertaken by Old Students', *St Hugh's Club Paper,* Oct. 1917, pp. 23–7 (25).

88. M. J. Tew, 'Postcards to the Editor', *St Hugh's Club Paper,* Aug. 1912, p. 32.

2   'A WOMEN'S COMMUNITY'

1. Many historians have noted the familial atmosphere of the women's colleges: Carol Dyhouse, *Girls Growing Up in Late Victorian and Edwardian England* (London: Routledge & Kegan Paul, 1981), pp. 68–70; Elizabeth Edwards, *Women in Teacher Training Colleges: A Culture of Femininity* (London & New York: Routledge, 2001).

2. Martha Vicinus, *Independent Women: Work and Community for Single Women, 1850–1920* (London: Virago Press, 1985), pp. 128–9.

3. Lucille Iremonger, *The Ghosts of Versailles. Miss Moberly and Miss Jourdain and Their Adventure: A Critical Study* (London: Faber & Faber, 1956), p. 63.

4. Margaret Birney Vickery, *Buildings for Bluestockings: The Architecture and Social History of Women's Colleges in Victorian England* (Newark & London: University of Delaware Press, 1999).

5. Esther M. Power, m. 1925, 'Reminiscences of St Hugh's' (X.8–9; SHCA, 1984).

6. Edwards, *Women in Teacher Training,* p. 49.

7. Vickery, *Buildings for Bluestockings*, p. 13.
8. Iremonger, *The Ghosts of Versailles*, pp. 103–4.
9. Molly McNeill (MM) to her mother (27 Oct. 1916): Molly McNeill, 'Correspondence' (X.35; SHCA, 1916–17).
10. MM to her mother (31 May 1917), ibid.
11. MM to her mother (5 March 1916), ibid.; 'Hall Notices: St Hugh's College', *The Fritillary*, June 1914, pp. 139–40; 'Hall Notices: St Hugh's College', *The Fritillary*, Dec. 1915, pp. 52–4.
12. Carol Dyhouse, *No Distinction of Sex? Women in British Universities, 1870–1939* (London: UCL Press, 1995), p. 223; Sarah Wiggins, 'Gendered Spaces and Political Identity: Debating Societies in English Women's Colleges, 1890–1914', *Women's History Review*, 18/5 (2009), pp. 737–52.
13. 4 May 1909, 24 May 1910, 'Oxford Students' Debating Society: Minutes of Proceedings 1909–1915' (VI.18; SHCA).
14. Kathryn Eccles, 'Women Students at the University of Oxford, 1914–39: Image, Identity and Experience' (University of Oxford, unpublished doctoral thesis, 2007), p. 33. Both Haynes and Lane were editors of *The Fritillary* in 1927.
15. 'Editorial', *The Imp*, Dec. 1920, pp. 1–2.
16. 19 Nov. 1915, 'Minutes of Meetings of Principals of the Women's Colleges' (Bod. MSS. Dep.d.759–60; Oxford: Bodleian Library, 1912–33), pp. 40c–41.
17. Janet Howarth, '"In Oxford but … not of Oxford": The Women's Colleges', in M. G. Brock and M. C. Curthoys (eds.), *The History of the University of Oxford* (7.2; Oxford: Oxford University Press, 2001), pp. 237–307 (275).
18. Charlotte Anne Elizabeth Moberly, 'An Appreciation', *The Imp*, Summer 1924, pp. 1–3.
19. An exception was made for Home Students, presumably because for them the prohibition would be impossible to enforce.
20. 26 Jan. 1912, 7 March 1913, 23 April 1913, 'Minutes of Meetings of Principals of the Women's Colleges' (Bod. MSS. Dep.d.759–60; Oxford: Bodleian Library, 1912–33), pp. 1, 12–13, 16.
21. 7 March 1913, ibid., p. 13.
22. 'Imp-Ressions', *The Imp*, March 1920, pp. 14–16; Ina Brooksbank (IB) to her mother (11 March 1920), Ina Brooksbank, 'Correspondence' (X.36; SHCA, 1917–20).
23. 12 May 1916, 6 Nov. 1920, 'Minutes of Meetings of Principals of the Women's Colleges', pp. 43b, 119.

24. Helen Robertson [?], 'Notes as to Daily Staff Routine' (*c.*1924), 'General Papers from Daily Life of College' (I.10–18; SHCA, 1919–36).

25. 'Regulations for Lodging Houses' (*c.*1918–21), 'Papers of the Delegacy for Women Students' (VII.12 [SHG/C/2/6]; SHCA, 1918–20).

26. Vera Brittain, *Testament of Youth: An Autobiographical Study of the Years 1900–1925* (Glasgow: Fontana Paperbacks, 1979), pp. 504–5.

27. 'A Training in Method', *The Imp,* March 1925, p. 3.

28. Brittain, *Testament of Youth,* p. 177.

29. St Hugh's students dug allotments, grew vegetables in the college garden, and worked in the Army Supplies Depot at Didcot: Betty Kemp, 'The Early History of St Hugh's', in Penny Griffin (ed.), *St Hugh's: One Hundred Years of Women's Education in Oxford* (Basingstoke: Macmillan Press, 1986), pp. 15–47 (35).

30. IB to Family (26 May 1918), Brooksbank, 'Correspondence'.

31. IB to Family (23 Nov. 1919), ibid.

32. 3 May 1920, 'Minutes of Meetings of Principals of the Women's Colleges', p. 109.

33. 1 March 1919, 17 Nov. 1921, ibid., pp. 83–4, 7.

34. See, for example, Vera Brittain, *The Women at Oxford: A Fragment of History* (London: George G. Harrap, 1960), p. 159.

35. Eccles, 'Women Students', pp. 6, 26.

36. On her return to Somerville after the First World War, Brittain wrote an article for a University magazine entitled *Outlook* in which she complained that 'With the signing of the Armistice she [the 'woman student'] has passed from the all important to the negligible': Brittain, *Testament of Youth,* pp. 482–3.

37. IB to Family (2 Feb. 1919), Brooksbank, 'Correspondence'. For women's exclusion from the Bodleian Library before the First World War, see E. M. Olivier, 'Editorial', *St Hugh's Club Paper,* Jan. 1901, n.p.

38. MM to her mother (28 Jan. 1917), McNeill, 'Correspondence'.

39. IB to Family (23 Nov. 1919), Brooksbank, 'Correspondence'.

40. E.N.S., 'Book Review: Mr Haynes, "Much Ado About Women"', *The Fritillary,* Summer 1927, p. 32.

41. Maria Tamboukou, *Women, Education and the Self: A Foucauldian Perspective* (Basingstoke: Palgrave Macmillan, 2003), pp. 78–82.

42. IB to Family (27 May 1919), Brooksbank, 'Correspondence'.

43. 31 Jan., 4 March 1924, 'Minutes of Meetings of Principals of the Women's Colleges', pp. 43, 45–6.

44. Renée Haynes, 'Editorial', *The Fritillary,* Feb. 1927, pp. 1–2.

45. B.J.S., 'Excelsior!', *The Imp,* Dec. 1929, pp. 10–11. This portrait of the over-achieving left-wing student who, in between working for a First Class degree, rides motorbikes and swims before breakfast, bears a strong resemblance to the description of Barbara Castle's 'relentless drive for perfection' given by her college friend: "'There she would be," Olive said, "creaming her face and hands at night and wearing gloves, drinking fruit juice, eating rusks and reading some obscure economics handbook all at the same time'": Lisa Martineau, *Politics and Power: Barbara Castle* (London: André Deutsch, 2000), p. 17.

46. 8 Feb. 1922, 'Minutes of Meetings of Principals of the Women's Colleges', p. 11.

47. For discussion of chaperone rules, see Gillian Sutherland, 'Review Essay: The House that Jill Built', *Oxford Review of Education,* 23/2 (June 1997), pp. 245–50; Sara Delamont, *Knowledgeable Women: Structuralism and the Reproduction of Elites* (London: Routledge, 1989); Eccles, 'Women Students'.

48. Vicinus, *Independent Women*, p. 132.

49. Such a shift can be seen as having occurred with the second generation of Principals in a number of women's colleges: see Brittain, *Women at Oxford*, p. 120; Sarah Wiggins, 'Politics and Political Culture in English Women's Colleges, 1890–1914' (London: Royal Holloway, University of London, unpublished doctoral thesis, 2003), p. 68.

50. Charlotte Anne Elizabeth Moberly, 'An Appreciation', *The Imp* (Summer 1924), pp. 1–4 (p. 4).

51. 2 March 1918, 'Minutes and Papers of Council' (II.1.4; SHCA, 1917–24), p. 18.

52. Joan Evans, *Prelude and Fugue: An Autobiography* (London: Museum Press, 1964), p. 100.

53. Janet Howarth, 'Jourdain, Eleanor Frances (1863–1924)', *Oxford Dictionary of National Biography* (online edn; Oxford: Oxford University Press, 2004). At the civic universities especially, women principals were often diverted away from their scholarly work by the burden of their pastoral and administrative duties: Dyhouse, *No Distinction of Sex?*, pp. 59, 71–2. In 1923 Cecilia Ady looked into an advertised post as head of University House, the women's residence at Birmingham University. It appears that she turned the post down because there was not enough scope for her to continue her academic work: see Beatrice Orange to Cecilia Ady (21 March 1923), 'Cecilia Ady Papers' (VIII.7–12; SHCA, *c.*1900–1957).

54. 'Jourdain was a magnificent tutor, who encouraged us to think for ourselves and do original work': Mary Hopkirk, 'An Account of Certain Events at St Hugh's College, Oxford, 1923/4, Extracted from the Diary of the President of the JCR' (MS.Top.Oxon.d.934; Oxford: Bodleian Library, 1958), p. 51.

55. 19 June 1923, 'Minutes and Papers of Council', pp. 197–8.

56. When Bertha Johnson was appointed head of the Society of Home Students (later St Anne's) in 1910 she declined payment: Janet Howarth, 'Johnson [née Todd], Bertha Jane (1846–1927), Promoter of Women's Higher Education', *Oxford Dictionary of National Biography* (online edn; Oxford: Oxford University Press, 2004).

57. 2 March 1918, 'Minutes and Papers of Council', p. 21.

58. Ibid.

59. John Hale, 'Biographical Note', in E. F. Jacob (ed.), *Italian Renaissance Studies: A Tribute to the Late Cecilia M. Ady* (London: Faber & Faber, 1960), pp. 484–8; Benjamin G. Kohl, 'Ady, Cecilia Mary (1881–1958)', *Oxford Dictionary of National Biography* (online edn; Oxford: Oxford University Press, 2004).

60. Deneke, 'Memoir' (I.16; SHCA, 1967), p. 30.

61. Kemp, 'The Early History of St Hugh's', pp. 15–47.

62. Ibid., pp. 36–9.

63. Joan Evans, 'Editor's Preface', *An Adventure* (5th edn; London: Faber & Faber, 1955), p. 17.

64. See Jourdain–Ady Correspondence (1909–12), 'Ady Papers', VIII.12A.

65. Iremonger, *The Ghosts of Versailles*, p. 121.

66. See Vicinus, *Independent Women*; Elizabeth Edwards, 'Homoerotic Friendship and College Principals, 1880–1960', *Women's History Review*, 4/2 (1995), pp. 149–63; Edwards, *Women in Teacher Training*.

67. See, for example, Eleanor Jourdain (EJ) to Cecilia Ady (CA) (24 Sept. 1910), EJ to CA (Dec. 1909[?]), 'Ady Papers'.

68. EJ to CA (4 Jan. 1911), EJ to CA (12 Dec. 1912), ibid.

69. MM to her mother (15 Oct. 1916), McNeill, 'Correspondence'.

70. MM to her mother (15 Oct. 1916), ibid.

71. MM to her mother (n.d. Oct. 1916[?]), ibid.

72. See Martha Vicinus, 'Distance and Desire: English Boarding School Friendships, 1870–1920', in Martin Bauml Duberman, Martha Vicinus and George Chauncey Jr. (eds), *Hidden from History: Reclaiming the Gay and Lesbian Past* (New York: New American Library Books, 1989), pp. 212–29.

73. Mrs L. T. Meade, *The Chesterton Girl Graduates: A Story for Girls* (London: W. & R. Chambers, 1913); D.G., 'Book Review', *The Fritillary*, June 1914, p. 125.

74. Dame Mary Cartwright, 1919–23, 'Reminiscences of St Hugh's'.

75. Meade, *Chesterton Girl Graduates*, pp. 11–12.

76. Renée Haynes, *Neapolitan Ice* (London: Chatto & Windus, 1928), p. 118.

77. Lillian Faderman maintained that, until the last quarter of the nineteenth century, 'romantic friendships' were socially acceptable and did not challenge hegemonic gender-power relations. Her argument has been strongly criticised by subsequent historians who have shown that women's relations were viewed with suspicion from the late eighteenth century onwards. Vicinus has also shown that such women were aware of the eroticised nature of their love for each other, and some, though not all, would have self-consciously acted upon it: Martha Vicinus, *Intimate Friends: Women Who Loved Women, 1778–1928* (Chicago & London: University of Chicago Press, 2004).

78. Iremonger, *The Ghosts of Versailles*, pp. 86–92.

79. Edwards, 'Homoerotic Friendship', p. 151.

80. For discussion of debates on whether 'lesbians' need to be defined by genital contact, see Sheila Jeffreys, 'Does It Matter If They Did It?' in Lesbian History Group (ed.), *Not a Passing Phase: Reclaiming Lesbians in History, 1840–1985* (1989), pp. 19–28. Sharon Marcus has criticised the 'ridiculous debate' over whether women in the past did or didn't have sex – she is instead concerned with how female marriages and female friendship (lesbian or otherwise) operated in Victorian society, arguing that they provided a crucial support to heterosexual marriage, rather than representing a threat to it: Sharon Marcus, *Between Women: Friendship, Desire and Marriage in Victorian England* (Princeton & Oxford: Princeton University Press, 2007).

81. Vicinus, *Independent Women*, pp. 158, 61.

82. Chapter 2, 'Provincial Young-Ladyhood', Brittain, *Testament of Youth*.

83. MM to her mother (27 Oct. 1916), McNeill, 'Correspondence'.

84. MM to her mother (n.d. 1917[?]), ibid.

85. Rachel Trickett recalled that it was never publicly mentioned when she first became a tutor in 1954, while Colin Matthew claimed that even in 1980 it was a touchy subject in the SCR. In 1975, anxious letters were exchanged between Evelyn Procter and Rachel Trickett regarding the interest of an American postgraduate student in the career of Cecilia Ady and the possibility that she might publish

something that would 'embarrass' the college. Rachel Trickett, 'The
Row', in Penny Griffin (ed.), *St Hugh's: One Hundred Years of Women's
Education in Oxford* (Basingstoke: Macmillan, 1986), pp. 48–61;
Matthew, 'The Early History of St Hugh's and "The Row"'; Robert
Bellow to Evelyn Procter (22 Jan. 1975), Bellow to Procter (27 July
1975), Rachel Trickett to Procter (13 Feb. 1975), 'Papers on The Row'
(I.16 [SHG/A/5]; SHCA).

86. Trickett, 'The Row'.
87. Matthew, 'The Early History of St Hugh's and "The Row"', p. 17.
88. EJ to CA (Aug. 1911), 'Ady Papers'.
89. EJ to CA (Good Friday 1911[?]), ibid.
90. IB to Family (18 Jan. 1920), Brooksbank, 'Correspondence'.
91. EJ to CA (n.d. Dec. 1914[?]), 'Ady Papers'.
92. Eleanor Jourdain, 'Statement by the Principal' (1924), 'Miscellaneous
    Papers' (I.13; SHCA).
93. Hopkirk, 'An Account', pp. 40–1.
94. Eileen Stopford, 'The Row' (I.16; SHCA), pp. 21–2.
95. A. J. Jenkinson to CA (10 Dec. 1923), 'Ady Papers'. Jenkinson referred
    to the strike action as 'the decisive factor in any action that may be
    taken by the Members of College or by the Parents and Guardians of
    the students'.
96. A. J. Jenkinson to CA (26 Nov. 1923), ibid.
97. C. M. Coate to CA (28 Nov. 1923), ibid.
98. See Hale, 'Biographical Note', p. 486.
99. Hopkirk, 'An Account'.
100. Cicely McCall to Rachel Trickett (5 June 1984), 'Papers on The Row'.
    Mary Cartwright also remembers another fellow student being sent
    down for simply being found by the Proctors standing alone in the
    middle of St Giles one evening: Mary Cartwright, 'Some Remarks
    on "The Row"' (I.16; SHCA, n.d.). For concerns about Jourdain's
    over-zealous implementation of disciplinary codes, see 10 June 1922,
    'Minutes and Papers of Council', p. 170.
101. See 'Principal's Statement' (19 Nov. 1923), 'Statement by Joan Evans'
    (10 Nov. 1923), 'Papers on The Row'.
102. Hopkirk, 'An Account', p. 15.
103. Marjorie Reeves, 'Recollections and Impressions', in Mary Clapinson
    (ed.), *St Hugh's College in the Twentieth Century: A Record of the
    Colloquium Held at the College on 18th September 1999* (Oxford, 1999), pp.
    29–32 (31).

104. Grace Jaffe [née Spurway] to CA (n.d. 1924[?]), 'Ady Papers'.
105. Alicia Percival to Rachel Trickett (5 June 1984), 'Papers on The Row'.
106. Phyllis Touch (née Wallbank), m. 1931, 'Reminiscences of St Hugh's'.
107. Priscilla West, 'Reminiscences of Seven Decades', in Penny Griffin (ed.), *St Hugh's: One Hundred Years of Women's Education* (Basingstoke: Macmillan, 1986), pp. 62–243 (117).
108. Dorothea Blott (née Bleasley), m. 1934, 'Reminiscences of St Hugh's'.
109. Anon. 8, m. 1936, ibid.; West, 'Reminiscences', pp. 114, 21–4.
110. Recalled of a fellow student by D.N. Lennie (née Thomas), m. 1936, 'Reminiscences of St Hugh's'.
111. 'Oxford Magazine' (Nov. 1936), quoted in West, 'Reminiscences', p. 116.

3 DIFFERENT OR EQUAL?

1. 'Replies to Senior Student Questionnaire' (SHCA, 2009).
2. Priscilla West, 'Reminiscences of Seven Decades', in Penny Griffin (ed.), *St Hugh's: One Hundred Years of Women's Education* (Basingstoke: Macmillan, 1986), pp. 62–243 (127, 31–2).
3. Rachel Trickett, 'Women's Education' in Penny Griffin (ed.), *St Hugh's: One Hundred Years of Women's Education in Oxford* (Basingstoke: Macmillan, 1986), pp. 5–14 (10).
4. By 1950 women students only amounted to just over one sixth of the total undergraduate body: Vera Brittain, *The Women at Oxford: A Fragment of History* (London: George G. Harrap, 1960), pp. 205, 36. See also Pauline Adams, *Somerville for Women: An Oxford College 1879–1993* (Oxford: Oxford University Press, 1996), pp. 163–4.
5. Headlam Morley was the first woman to be elected to a full professorship. Ida Mann remained Reader in Ophthalmology until 1947, during which time she held only the *title* of professor: see 'University of Oxford: Women at Oxford', http://www.ox.ac.uk/about_the_university/introducing_oxford/women_at_Oxford/index.html, accessed 25 June 2010.
6. Janet Howarth, 'Women', in Brian Harrison (ed.), *The History of the University of Oxford* (VIII; Oxford: Clarendon Press, 1994), pp. 345–75 (353–4).
7. When women were forced to compete directly with men for academic posts, universities almost invariably employed the latter. As a result, the

numbers of female academics across Britain stagnated at around 13–14 per cent between the 1930s and the 1970s: Dyhouse, *No Distinction of Sex? Women in British Universities, 1870–1939* (London: UCL Press, 1995), p. 138. See also Margherita Rendel, 'How Many Women Academics 1912–1976?', in R. Deem (ed.), *Schooling for Women's Work* (London: Routledge & Kegan Paul, 1980), pp. 142–61.

8.   Howarth, 'Women', p. 354.

9.   Brittain maintained that Oxbridge women were paid even less than their counterparts at the civic universities: Brittain, *Women at Oxford*, p. 230; 'College Expenditure on Residential Accommodation on Undergraduates' (early draft), 11 Oct. 1971, 'Minutes of Governing Body' (II.1 [SHG/B/3/1/23]; SHCA, 1970–73); Rachel Trickett, 'Memorial Address for Ida Busbridge', *St Hugh's Chronicle,* no. 63 (1988–9), pp. 29–32.

10.   Mary Warnock, *A Memoir: People and Places* (London: Gerald Duckworth, 2000), p. 18.

11.   She remembers that there was one married woman among the Fellows but that her husband was either dead or divorced: ibid., p. 112.

12.   Fernanda Perrone found that 79–85 per cent of women academics between 1884 and 1904 remained unmarried throughout their lives, although by 1924 this figure stood at 67 per cent: Dyhouse, *No Distinction of Sex?*, p. 161. Royal Holloway operated a marriage ban until 1939: see Elizabeth Kirk, 'Women Academics at Royal Holloway and Bedford Colleges, 1939–69', *Historical Research,* 76/191 (2003), pp. 128–50 (140–1). The first married Fellow at an Oxford women's college was Isobel Munro of Somerville, appointed in 1933 when she was still engaged, though she was widowed very soon after marrying: Adams, *Somerville for Women*, p. 187.

13.   Miss Spearing, for example, announced her resignation from Council 'on account of getting married': 7 May 1921, 'Minutes and Papers of Council'.

14.   Marian Basco, m. 1952, 'Reminiscences of St Hugh's'.

15.   Warnock, *A Memoir*, p. 17.

16.   Laura Schwartz, 'Interview with Former St Hugh's History Fellow and Tutor Susan Wood' (SHCA, 2009).

17.   Susan Wood, 'The Senior Common Room in the 1950s', 'Reminiscences of St Hugh's' (X.8–9; SHCA, 1984).

18.   Warnock, *A Memoir*, p. 112.

19. Elizabeth Kirk refers to this as the 'monastic ideal' and shows that it prevailed also in London women's colleges in the postwar era: Kirk, 'Women Academics', p. 140.

20. Warnock, *A Memoir*, pp. 112–13; Susan Wood, 'The Senior Common Room in the 1950s', 'Reminiscences of St Hugh's'.

21. Wood, ibid.

22. Warnock, *A Memoir*, p. 114.

23. Schwartz, 'Interview with Susan Wood'.

24. Mary Warnock, 'Women's Education and Its Future', in Penny Griffin (ed.), *St Hugh's: One Hundred Years of Women's Education* (Basingstoke: Macmillan, 1986), pp. 284–98 (289).

25. Nor was there an interest in female role models. As an undergraduate Warnock was taken under the wing of Elizabeth Anscombe, a leading philosopher and mother of four. Yet Warnock found this encounter with one of the first married women academics deeply disturbing. 'I dreaded my visits,' she later recalled, 'not only because of the exposure of my philosophical inadequacies but because of the intense smelliness of the ambience…there were toys scattered on the floor and sometimes even dirty nappies in the room. On one occasion I had a baby thrust into my arms when I arrived.' Warnock, *A Memoir*, p. 62.

26. Ibid., pp. 20–1.

27. Trickett, 'Women's Education', pp. 9–10.

28. Schwartz, 'Interview with Susan Wood'.

29. Carol Dyhouse also found in women's accounts of the civic universities in the interwar period an insistence that they had not faced any discrimination: Dyhouse, *No Distinction of Sex?*, p. 153. See also Pat Thane, 'Review Article: Scholars or Amazons?', *Oxford Review of Education*, 23/2 (June 1997), pp. 253–8.

30. 'Centenary Questionnaire: Papers of Sarah Curtis' (X.19; SHCA, 1984), #58.3.

31. Schwartz, 'Interview with Susan Wood'.

32. Dyhouse, *No Distinction of Sex?*, pp. 168–9.

33. Warnock, *A Memoir*, pp. 78–86. Warnock's friend is identified in this memoir.

34. Warnock, 'Women's Education'.

35. Schwartz, 'Interview with Susan Wood'.

36. 'St Hugh's College JCR Survey' (Oct. 1968), 'Miscellaneous Papers of the Dean' (VI.28–9; SHCA, 1968–70s); JCR Suggestion Book, 'JCR Minutes and Papers' (VI.23; SHCA, 1971–80).

37. 7 March 1973, 8 Nov. 1979, 'JCR Minutes and Papers'.

38. For example, as late as 1979 (twelve years after abortion was legalised in England) there were a number of students in St Hugh's JCR who were against the termination of pregnancies under any circumstances, 8 Nov. 1979, ibid.

39. West, 'Reminiscences', pp. 181–3.

40. 'Hebdomadal Council 24 April', *Oxford University Gazette,* 27 April 1972, p. 760; 'Co-Residence: Verbatim Report of Debate in Congregation, 30 May 1972', *Oxford University Gazette,* 7 June 1972, pp. 1053–66. Very little has been written about the introduction of co-residency at Oxbridge. For the most comprehensive accounts so far, see Carol Dyhouse, 'Troubled Identities: Gender and Status in the History of the Mixed College in English Universities Since 1945', *Women's History Review,* 12/2 (2003), pp. 169–93; Carol Dyhouse, *Students: A Gendered History* (Abingdon: Routledge, 2006); Marie Hicks, 'Integrating Women at Harvard and Oxford, 1964–77', in Laurel Thatcher Ulrich (ed.), *Yards and Gates: Gender in Harvard and Radcliffe History* (Basingstoke: Palgrave Macmillan, 2004), pp. 245–70.

41. 'Co-Residence 1972', p. 1058.

42. Dyhouse, 'Troubled Identities'; Dyhouse, *Students: A Gendered History*.

43. 'Co-Residence 1972', p. 1059. There were a few exceptions; Mrs M. E. Paul of LMH opposed any restrictions on colleges going mixed, arguing that there were enough 'good women' to fill all the places and also that the example of the London colleges showed that women's colleges could expect to attract men of high academic calibre: 'Co-Residence 1972', pp. 1063–4.

44. This was recalled by Susan Wood, 5 July 2010.

45. 'Co-Residence 1972', p. 1055.

46. This was significantly lower than the national average of female students at 36 per cent: 'Report of the Committee to Review Co-Residence', *Oxford University Gazette,* 3 Feb. 1977, pp. 461–6.

47. As Dyhouse has pointed out, the first person to propose going mixed was the Librarian of New College – a notorious conservative: Dyhouse, *Students: A Gendered History*, pp. 164–5.

48. 'Extract from Student Representation Committee to University Governing Body' (11–12 May 1971), 'Admission of Women to Men's Colleges' (UR6/w/12, file 1; Oxford: Oxford University Archive, 1971).

49. Hicks, 'Integrating Women', p. 261.

50. Senior Proctor to St Hugh's Dean (19 Nov. 1974), 'Miscellaneous Papers of the Dean'.

51. Senior Proctor to OUSU President (25 Nov. 1974), ibid.

52. Mr J. R. Lucas (Merton), 'Co-Residence: Verbatim Report of Debate in Congregation, 8 March 1977', *Oxford University Gazette*, 16 March 1977, pp. 589–94 (591); Mr R. F. S. Hamer (Christ Church), 'Co-Residence 1972', p. 1054.

53. Dyhouse, *Students: A Gendered History*, pp. 64–5. See also Dr J. M. Robertson (Merton), who asked 'on what grounds does the Council identify the cause of the women's colleges with the cause of women's education?': 'Co-Residence 1972', p. 1061.

54. The letter was published in the *Observer*, 12 July 1964, reported in Press Cutting: *Oxford Mail*, 13 July 1964, 'Admission of Women to Men's Colleges' (UR6/w/12, file 1; Oxford: Oxford University Archive).

55. Schwartz, 'Interview with Susan Wood'.

56. Mary Warnock, 'Co-Residence at Oxford?', *Oxford Magazine* (1972), pp. 5–6.

57. 'Report of the Committee to Review Co-Residence'.

58. Schwartz, 'Interview with Susan Wood'.

59. These short-term lecturers were not members of Governing Body and therefore had no say in how the College should be run.

60. Schwartz, 'Interview with Susan Wood'.

61. 13 Feb. 1980, 'Minutes of Governing Body' (II.1.29; SHCA, 1979–80), p. 134.

62. 'Notes for Speech on Principal's Writing Paper' (n.d.), 'Miscellaneous Papers of the Dean'.

63. Press Cutting: *The Observer* (27 Sept. 1981), ibid. See also Press Cutting: Stephen Glover, 'A Question of Balance: A Principal of St Hugh's Explains' (no. info), 'Principal's Papers for Steering Committee for the Admission of Men' (II.30; SHCA).

64. 3 Feb. 1980, 'JCR Minutes and Papers'.

65. Marion Hetherington (MCR President) to Rachel Trickett (n.d.), 'Principal's Papers for Steering Committee for the Admission of Men'.

66. Hicks, 'Integrating Women', p. 268. Hicks calculates twelve men at St Hugh's out of a total staff (Fellows and Lecturers) of forty, but the *Chronicle* for that year records five male Fellows and six male Lecturers: *St Hugh's Chronicle*, /52 (1979–80), pp. 3–5.

67. Hicks, 'Integrating Women', p. 268; Press Cutting: Stephen Glover, 'A Question of Balance', 'Principal's Papers for Steering Committee for the Admission of Men'.

68. This argument was made by Rachel Trickett as well as members of St Hugh's JCR: see 'Notes for Speech on Principal's Writing Paper' (n.d.), St Hugh's Broadsheet on Going Mixed (1985/6[?]), 'Miscellaneous Papers of the Dean'.

69. The feminist label was just as likely to be a negative as it was a positive one. One article somewhat gleefully described the eventual decision to go mixed at St Hugh's as 'a dagger through the heart of feminists': Press Cutting: Femail Editorial 'The Oxford Sex War', *Daily Mail* (12 Feb. 1986), 'Principal's Papers for Steering Committee for the Admission of Men'.

70. See, for example, numerous feminist activities and debates recorded in *Hugonews* (Hilary 1982), *Ad Hoc* (Michaelmas 1984), 'Undergraduate Newssheets' (VI.26; SHCA, 1980s–90s).

71. In 1974 the JCR was 'overwhelmingly' in favour of St Hugh's admitting men. By 1976 the shift towards a more cautious approach had begun: a JCR referendum revealed that twenty-one people supported co-education in St Hugh's regardless of the policy of other colleges. Twenty-four people supported co-education if five men's colleges went mixed. Thirty-seven people approved co-education at St Hugh's if all the other colleges went mixed: 23 Nov. 1976, 'JCR Minutes and Papers'.

72. Press cutting: Stephen Glover, 'A Question of Balance', 'Principal's Papers for Steering Committee for the Admission of Men'.

73. They did not, for instance, seriously consider trying to attract students on a feminist basis, or appeal particularly to mature students, a point that was later recalled by John Robertson, Fellow and Tutor in History (1980–2010).

74. 'Notes for Speech on Principal's Writing Paper', 'Miscellaneous Papers of the Dean'.

75. *Hugonews* (1982), 'Undergraduate Newssheets'.

76. JCR Committee to Governing Body (9 Feb. 1987), 'Minutes of Governing Body' (II.1.36; SHCA, 1986–7).

77. 3 Feb. 1980, 'Minutes of Governing Body'; 'Notes for Speech on Principal's Writing Paper', 'Miscellaneous Papers of the Dean'.

78. The vote was taken at the meeting of Governing Body on 11 Oct. 1985. In February 1986 a motion was passed arranging for the college

statutes to be changed accordingly, and this was confirmed at the meeting of 12 March 1986.

79. Mary Lunn, 'Statement of Belief' (11 Oct. 1985), 'Miscellaneous Papers of the Dean'.

80. Schwartz, 'Interview with Susan Wood'.

81. Laura Schwartz, 'Interview with Marilyn and David Butler' (SHCA, 2009).

82. 21 May 1987, 'Minutes of the Steering Committee for the Admission of Men' (II.30; SHCA, 1987).

83. Press Cutting: John Clare, 'Oxford Admissions' (no. info.), 'Principal's Papers for Steering Committee for the Admission of Men'.

84. JCR to Governing Body (9 Feb. 1988), MCR Referendum (18 May 1988), 'Minutes of Governing Body' (II.1.37; SHCA, 1987–8).

85. Barbara Kennedy, 'Report on Admissions' (10 Feb. 1988), ibid.

86. JCR President to Rachel Trickett (9 Feb. 1986), 'Minutes of Governing Body' (II.1.35; SHCA, 1985–6).

87. Correspondence with Sue Adams, JCR President (1986), 'Papers Concerning Relations with JCR' (SHCA, VI.17B).

88. David Robertson to Sue Adams (n.d), ibid.; 'Report from the Steering Committee for the Admission of Men', 17 June 1987, 'Minutes of Governing Body'.

89. 'St Hugh's Women's Group: Notice of Protest' (2 June 1987), 17 June 1987, ibid.

90. Carol Dyhouse notes that it was common for the first men in the women's colleges to play up their macho credentials in order to counter the stigma of attending a predominantly female institution: Dyhouse, *Students: A Gendered History*, pp. 179–80.

91. For the reminiscences of Hume, Hollands and Dickson, see 'Men at St Hugh's', *St Hugh's Chronicle,* /72 (1998–9), pp. 61–2.

92. Rona McLeod, 'JCR', *St Hugh's Chronicle: Supplementary Issue* (1988), pp. 19–20.

4   WHO CLEANS A ROOM OF ONE'S OWN?

1. *St Hugh's Club Paper,* /2 (Jan. 1899).

2. Or so it is claimed by an undergraduate of the time: see K.M. Hobbs, m. 1924, 'Reminiscences of St Hugh's' (X8–9; SHCA, 1984).

3. Leonore Davidoff, ' "Mastered for Life": Servant and Wife in Victorian and Edwardian England', *Journal of Social History,* 7/4 (1974), pp. 406–28 (412–13).

4. Celia Fremlin, *The Seven Chars of Chelsea* (London: Methuen, 1940), pp. 1–2.

5. Judy Giles, 'Authority, Dependence and Power in Accounts of Twentieth-Century Domestic Service', in Lucy Delap, Ben Griffin and Abigail Wills (eds), *The Politics of Domestic Authority in Britain since 1800* (Basingstoke: Palgrave Macmillan, 2009), pp. 204–20 (209).

6. Alison Light, *Mrs Woolf and the Servants* (London: Penguin Books, 2008), pp. 173, 88.

7. Giles, 'Authority, Dependence and Power', p. 205.

8. Dorothy Sayers, *Gaudy Night* (London: New English Library, 1996 [first published 1935]), p. 330.

9. Selina Todd, 'Domestic Service and Class Relations in Britain 1900– 1950', *Past and Present,* 203 (2009), pp. 181–204 (202–3).

10. Sayers also portrays some of the female dons in a highly unfavourable light – Miss Hillyard, for example, is an embittered man-hater: Sayers, *Gaudy Night.*

11. Light argues that such an attitude was common in the women's movement of the 1970s as well as in the feminism of the 1930s: Alison Light, *Forever England: Femininity, Literature and Conservatism between the Wars* (London: Routledge, 1991), pp. 218–19.

12. Perry Williams, 'Pioneer Women Students at Cambridge', in Felicity Hunt (ed.), *Lessons for Life: The Schooling of Girls and Women, 1850–1950* (Oxford: Basil Blackwell, 1987), pp. 171–91 (189).

13. Giles, 'Authority, Dependence and Power', p. 208.

14. Ibid., p. 208. See, for example, 'Domestic Service', *Time and Tide,* 22 June 1923, in Dale Spender (ed.), *Time and Tide Wait for No Man* (London: Pandora Press, 1984), pp. 213–16.

15. Working-class women, of course, had always worked outside the home, though the feminist debates of this period tended to approach female waged labour as if it were a wholly new phenomenon.

16. See for example Rosalind Masson, 'Dark Stars (Unpaid) Married', *Time and Tide,* 18 Feb. 1921, in Spender (ed.), *Time and Tide Wait for No Man,* pp. 196–9. For a rare example of men being called upon to share in domestic labour, see Chrystal Eastman, 'Bedmakers and Bosses', *Time and Tide,* 12 Oct. 1923, in Spender (ed.), *Time and Tide Wait for No Man,*

pp. 119–21; Carol Dyhouse, *Feminism and the Family 1880–1939* (Oxford: Basil Blackwell, 1989), pp. 143–4.

17.   Woolf quotes Florence Nightingale: Virginia Woolf, *A Room of One's Own* (Harmondsworth: Penguin Books, 1975 [first published 1928]), p. 67.

18.   Gillian Sutherland, *Faith, Duty and the Power of the Mind: The Cloughs and Their Circle 1820–1960* (Cambridge: Cambridge University Press, 2006), p. 98.

19.   See, for example, Anon., m. 1921, 'Reminiscences of St Hugh's'; Perry Williams, 'Pioneer Women Students at Cambridge', p. 178.

20.   Woolf, *A Room of One's Own*, p. 106.

21.   Betty C. Bethenod (née Brodie), m. 1936, 'Reminiscences of St Hugh's'.

22.   14 Jan. 1915, 'Finance Committee Minutes' (II.6.1 [SHG/B/5/2/1]; SHCA, 1913–20).

23.   Wage books for 1920 record thirty-two domestic staff: 'Weekly and Monthly Wages' (IV.38–58; SHCA). The photograph (*c.*1928) depicts thirty-one staff: 'Photograph Album' (SHG/M/4/3; SHCA, 1928).

24.   Figures for Trinity Term 2010.

25.   'Weekly and Monthly Wages'.

26.   Christopher Platt, *The Most Obliging Man in Europe: Life and Times of the Oxford Scout* (London: George Allen & Unwin, 1986). The other published works on Oxford college servants are autobiographies: Albert Thomas, *Wait and See: Butler to the Principal; Brasenose College, Oxford* (London: Michael Joseph, 1944); Fred Bickerton, *Fred of Oxford: Being the Memoirs of Fred Bickerton, until recently Head Porter of University College, Oxford* (London: Evans Brothers, 1952). In 1969 Brian Harrison carried out an oral history project in which he and a number of students interviewed servants at Corpus Christi College: see Brian Harrison, 'College Servants in Corpus Forty Years Ago' (forthcoming, 2011). In 1995 Dyhouse pointed to the absence of servants in any histories of women's education and this chapter is the first to address this gap in the historiography: see Dyhouse, *No Distinction of Sex?*, p. 121.

27.   The term comes from a letter by the novelist James Hamilton Paterson, discussing St Hugh's in the 1970s: James Hamilton Paterson to Isabel Morgan (21 July 1972), Private Collection.

28. For this argument, see Lucy Delap, *Knowing Their Place: Domestic Service in Twentieth Century Britain* (Oxford: Oxford University Press, forthcoming, 2011).

29. June 1913, 'Finance Committee Minutes'.

30. Laura Schwartz, 'Interview with Two Currently Employed St Hugh's Scouts' (SHCA, 2009).

31. In the 1840s a humorous column appeared in *The New Monthly Magazine*, claiming to be written by a college scout, but which was mostly concerned with the high jinks of his undergraduate masters: see Theodore Hook, *Peter Priggins the College Scout*, 3 vols (I; London: Henry Colburn, 1841). For a nostalgic look at this 'lost' world see Platt, *Life and Times of the Oxford Scout*. For comic and/or hostile representations of college scouts in undergraduate culture, see Paul R. Deslandes, *Oxbridge Men: British Masculinity and the Undergraduate Experience, 1850–1920* (Bloomington & Indianapolis: Indiana University Press, 2005), pp. 39–41.

32. Their neighbours would typically have employed about five servants (a butler, a cook, a house or parlour maid, a between maid, a scullery maid, and a part-time morning girl or boy): see G. Gandy & B. Harrison, 'Interview with Miss C.V. Butler', Brian Harrison, 'Transcripts of Interviews with "College Servants"' (Corpus Christi College, University of Oxford [private collection], 1969), p. 6333.

33. Vera Brittain, *The Women at Oxford: A Fragment of History* (London: George G. Harrap), pp. 54, 59; F.M. Wyld, 'Letter to the Editor', *St Hugh's Chronicle, /*36 (1963–4), pp. 9–11.

34. Bursars' responsibilities included 'not only filing and account keeping, but interviews with servants and tradesmen, consultations with students on questions of health, storage of medicaments, samples etc.': 16 May 1931, 'Minutes of Accommodation Committee' (II.13.1–7 [SHG/B/8/1]; SHCA).

35. 7 June 1930, 'Minutes of Accommodation Committee'.

36. This had long been a common feature of the men's colleges: see Brian Harrison, 'Tape Recorders and the Teaching of History', *Oral History,* 1/2 (1972), pp. 3–10 (3–4).

37. Davidoff, 'Mastered for Life', p. 410.

38. C. Violet Butler, *Social Conditions in Oxford* (London: Sidgwick & Jackson, 1912), pp. 63–4, 100–3, 10.

39. Theresa McBride, *The Domestic Revolution: The Modernisation of Household Service in England and France 1820–1920* (London: Croom

Helm, 1976), p. 34. This recession lasted from about 1873 to 1896 and affected the south-east of England especially badly: see Michael John Jones, 'The Agricultural Depression, Collegiate Finances, and Provision for Education at Oxford, 1871–1913', *Economic History Review,* 50/1 (1997), pp. 57–81 (61–2).

40. Davidoff, 'Mastered for Life', p. 410. See also Pamela Horn, *The Rise and Fall of the Victorian Servant* (Dublin: Gill & Macmillan 1975).

41. *St Hugh's Club Paper* (June 1898), n.p.

42. Kate Thomas was a 'faithful servant' of St Hugh's for twenty-one years before leaving, possibly to get married, in 1910: *Minutes and Papers of Council,* 15 Nov. 1910, St Hugh's College Archive, II.1.2, p. 39. Service tended to be one part of a woman's life cycle rather than a lifelong occupation: Davidoff, 'Mastered for Life', p. 410; McBride, *The Domestic Revolution,* p. 9. Violet Butler remembered how, during her North Oxford childhood in the late 1800s, domestic servants usually married the local policemen or milkman rather than male servants: G. Gandy & B. Harrison, 'Interview with Miss C.V. Butler' (4 March 1969), Harrison, 'Transcripts of Interviews with "College Servants"', p. 6333. Yet Mrs Bob Gammond, who had worked as an under-housemaid at Mansfield College in the first decades of the twentieth century, and also at a house in St Margaret's Road, married another scout who she first met when he was carrying coal – their first 'date' took place on the roof of the college: Richard Rose & Brian Harrison, 'Interview with Mr. and Mrs Bob Gammond' (24 June 1969), Harrison, 'Transcripts of Interviews with "College Servants"', p. 6258.

43. Butler, *Social Conditions,* pp. 72–5.

44. Pamela Horn, *Life below Stairs in the Twentieth Century* (Stroud: Sutton Publishing, 2001), p. 20–25.

45. 'Most young factory or shop workers worked for less than fifty hours per week by the 1920s; servants regularly put in more than 70': Todd, 'Domestic Service', p. 184.

46. Delap, *Knowing Their Place.*

47. Nicky Gregson and Michelle Lowe, *Servicing the Middle Classes: Class, Gender and Waged Domestic Labour in Contemporary Britain* (London: Routledge, 1994), p. 4.

48. Jourdain to Ady (n.d. *c.* pre-1919), 'Ady Papers', (VIII.12a.; SHCA).

49. Platt, *Life and Times of the Oxford Scout,* pp. 79, 83.

50. Wage books for St Hugh's begin to record a much greater variation in the number of hours worked by individual staff. Most worked five

hours per day, though some worked only three, and wages thus began to be calculated at an hourly rather than monthly or weekly rate.

51. Laura Schwartz, 'Interview with Retired St Hugh's Scouts Clive Cuthbertson, Eileen Lydon & Pat Spring' (SHCA, 2010).

52. In the early twentieth century jobs might also have been found through Mrs Long's – the main agency for servants in Oxford at the time: Forbes McFall, 'Interview with Mrs Burney' (13 March 1969), Harrison, 'Transcripts of Interviews with "College Servants"'.

53. Laura Schwartz, 'Interview with St Hugh's Bursar Mary Kerr' (SHCA, 2009).

54. Schwartz, 'Interview with Currently Employed Scouts'.

55. Quoted in Platt, *Life and Times of the Oxford Scout*, p. 17.

56. The terminology used to talk about college servants at the ancient universities is confusing and highly idiosyncratic. Platt claims that in the nineteenth century the term 'scout' or 'gyp' was used to describe the male servant, while women under-servants were referred to as 'bedmakers'. At Cambridge, however, 'bedmakers' performed the main functions of the Oxford 'gyp'. Today, domestic staff (both cleaners and those who serve in Hall, male and female) are called 'scouts' at Oxford and 'bedders' at Cambridge: ibid., p. 19.

57. *The Pelican Record*, the alumni magazine for Corpus Christi College, noted in March 1958 the arrival of a 'girl-scout', asking: 'what sacred institution will be attacked next? Perhaps we shall have self-service in Hall': Harrison, 'Transcripts of Interviews with "College Servants"', p. 6370.

58. IB to Family (Oct. 1917), Brooksbank, 'Correspondence' (X.36; SHCA, 1917–20); 'Report of the Building Committee' (Oct. 1915), 'Finance Committee Minutes'.

59. The wage book for 1920 refers to five employees by their surnames, in contrast to the female staff referred to only by their first names; presumably the surnames refer to men: 'Weekly and Monthly Wages'.

60. A male porter is first recorded as having worked in the Lodge in the 1950s: Marion Basco, m. 1952, 'Reminiscences of St Hugh's'. There were still female porters at St Hugh's in the 1970s: Schwartz, 'Interview with Cuthbertson, Lydon & Spring'. The last woman porter was still in employment in 2006.

61. Sheila Margaret Ottley, m. 1940, A. E. Oakshott, m. 1945, 'Reminiscences of St Hugh's'.

62. Leonore Davidoff and Ruth Hawthorn, *A Day in the Life of a Victorian Domestic Servant* (London: George Allen, 1976), p. 78.

63. Phyllis Deards (née Cooper), m. 1921, Audrey Jean Fryer, m. 1954, 'Reminiscences of St Hugh's'.

64. Schwartz, 'Interview with Cuthbertson, Lydon & Spring'.

65. J. S. Lumsden, m. 1932, 'Reminiscences of St Hugh's'; Sayers, *Gaudy Night*, p. 127.

66. Platt, *Life and Times of the Oxford Scout*, pp. 43, 47; Bickerton, *Fred of Oxford*, p. 7. On average, domestic servants before the First World War worked a fifteen- to eighteen-hour day: McBride, *The Domestic Revolution*, p. 55.

67. Schwartz, 'Interview with Currently Employed Scouts'.

68. Schwartz, 'Interview with Cuthbertson, Lydon & Spring'.

69. 24 March 1915, 'Finance Committee Minutes'.

70. Schwartz, 'Interview with Cuthbertson, Lydon & Spring'.

71. Michaelmas 1972, 'JCR Suggestion Book' (1971–2), 'JCR Miscellaneous Papers' (VI.24; SHCA, 1970s–90s). This is also recorded as being common in the 1960s: Anon. 2, m. 1960s, 'Reminiscences of St Hugh's'.

72. Schwartz, 'Interview with Cuthbertson, Lydon & Spring'.

73. Patricia Thackwell (née Talbot), m. 1928, 'Reminiscences of St Hugh's'. Wage books recall Lydbury and Maddock as having been employed at St Hugh's consistently from 1920 to 1937: 'Weekly and Monthly Wages'.

74. Helen Robertson [?], 'Notes as to Daily Routine, Staff etc.', 'General Papers from Daily Life of College'(I.10–18; SHCA, 1919–36).

75. A. M. Carruthers (née Manger), m. 1933, 'Reminiscences of St Hugh's'. Many students suspected Thorneycroft of being a 'Red', though according to her obituary she was put off Communism after a visit to Russia in 1937 and for the rest of her life remained firmly committed to the Labour Party. Valerie Pitt, m. 1943, 'Reminiscences of St Hugh's'; Philippa Hesketh-Williams, 'Gertrude Thorneycroft', *St Hugh's Chronicle,* 1/53 (1980–1), pp. 39–41.

76. Marion Basco, m. 1952. See also M.C. Mogford, m. 1947, 'Reminiscences of St Hugh's'.

77. 'Interview by Laura Schwartz with St Hugh's graduate Isabel Morgan, m. 1971' (SCHA, 2009). By 1968 St Hugh's 'servants' were not contractually required to report breaches of regulations but were verbally asked by the college authorities to inform them if students

were absent overnight: 'Regulations Affecting Junior Members of College' (n.d. [1968]), 'Miscellaneous Papers of the Dean' (VI.28–29; SHCA, 1968–70s).

78. Patricia Thackwell (née Talbot), m. 1928, Anon. IV, 1936, 'Reminiscences of St Hugh's'. See also 'Replies to the Senior Student Questionnaire' (SHCA, 2009); Schwartz, 'Interview with Cuthbertson, Lydon & Spring'.

79. Janet Woodhead (née Middlebrooke), m. 1951, 'Replies to the Senior Student Questionnaire'.

80. See Harrison, 'Transcripts of Interviews with "College Servants"'; Platt, *Life and Times of the Oxford Scout*, p. 83. When Fred Bickerton began work as an underscout in 1897 he did not receive a salary and was expected to survive on tips: Bickerton, *Fred of Oxford*, pp. 2–5.

81. Hilary 1959, 25 Jan. 1970, 'JCR Minutes and Papers' (VI.22; SHCA, 1955–71).

82. 'Monthly Wages' (1926–7), 'Weekly and Monthly Wages'.

83. The average wage for a cook in the late 1920s was £56 per annum on top of room and board: Light, *Mrs Woolf and the Servants*, p. 176. The question of whether wages for domestic servants paid more or less than other jobs depends to a great extent on how room and board is valued. Prior to the First World War, Violet Butler believed that domestic servants in Oxford were better off than other female waged workers because of the value of their accommodation, even though 'a good domestic servant of 20' took home between £18 and £20 per annum compared with 'her sister' in the factory or dressmaking industry who earned about £31: Butler, *Social Conditions*, p. 63.

84. Account books from the 1920s to the 1960s show that the average pro rata wage of a domestic worker (with room and board factored in) was £90 in 1926, £156 in 1948, £205 in 1957, and £286 in 1963–4. The National Archive Currency Converter shows that their value remained roughly the same throughout the period – at their highest in the 1940s. See 'Weekly and Monthly Wages'.

85. 'Scout Union Meets', *The Cherwell*, 15 Oct. 1971, p. 2.

86. Figures for Trinity Term 2010.

87. Scouts at the men's colleges were paid only a very low retainer fee during the vacations, and had, as a result, to find work elsewhere, usually at hotels or holiday resorts. It was not until after the Second World War that most of the men's colleges began to cater for large conferences in the holidays: Bickerton, *Fred of Oxford*, p. 5.

88. Corpus Christi College, for example, was not wired for electricity until the 1930s: M. Brock, 'Interview with George Gandy on Domestic Servants' (6 March 1969), Harrison, 'Transcripts of Interviews with "College Servants"', p. 5522.

89. This was reported to be common practice prior to the First World War: Ina Brooksbank (m.1917), 'Reminiscences of St Hugh's'.

90. Sayers, *Gaudy Night*, pp. 49–50.

91. 24 Nov. 1928, 'Minutes and Papers of Council' (II [SHG/3/1/4]; SHCA, 1927–30), p. 99. It also arranged for a system of gratuities or special pensions to be made available for non-resident seasonal workers and servants who had to leave, through no fault of their own, before the age of sixty-five.

92. 1 Nov. 1892, 28 Jan. 1893, 'Minutes and Papers of Council'.

93. Barbara Gwyer, 'The Gaudy Dinner', *St Hugh's Chronicle, /6* (1933–4), pp. 7–12. 14 Nov. 1932, 'Minutes of Accommodation Committee', pp. 1/45b–1/47.

94. Eight staff members are listed as resident in the early 1960s, all listed as 'Miss', while retired scouts recall at least five resident scouts in the 1970s, also all unmarried: 'Weekly and Monthly Wages'; Schwartz, 'Interview with Cuthbertson, Lydon & Spring'. Information regarding Mrs Windscheffel provided by John Robertson.

95. This is recalled by M. Ker (née King), m. 1930, 'Reminiscences of St Hugh's'; Schwartz, 'Interview with Cuthbertson, Lydon & Spring'. While we do not know if this was the case at St Hugh's, it is interesting to note that in Dorothy Sayers's fictional women's college of the 1930s, it was common practice to lock the scouts in at night: Sayers, *Gaudy Night*, pp. 100–2.

96. 'Inventory of Furniture and Effects' (1922), 'Main Building' (III.20; SHCA). Sharing bedrooms was common practice; some middle-class families who could only just afford to keep servants might not provide a bedroom at all but expected servants to sleep in the corner of the kitchen or on a bed in the corridor: McBride, *The Domestic Revolution*, p. 52.

97. Jamie Cottis (née Moon), 1954, A. E. Oakshott, m. 1945, 'Reminiscences of St Hugh's'.

98. For working-class housing in Oxford before the First World War, see Butler, *Social Conditions,* chapter 5. In 1901 inspectors noted 'considerable, though not gross, overcrowding…that sanitary

accommodation and water supply were often entirely insufficient...',
p. 105.

99. McBride, *The Domestic Revolution*, p. 9.

100. Harrison, 'Tape Recorders', pp. 3–4. See also Brian Harrison,
'Interview with Alec Lynn on Domestic Service in Corpus' (8 May
1969): Harrison, 'Transcripts of Interviews with "College Servants"',
p. 5575.

101. John Betjeman is claimed to have said that scouts preferred to 'see a
young man stupefied with his first experience of mixed drinks rather
than exhilarated by his first reading of *Das Kapital*. Scouts were "all
just regular, lower-middle, upper-working class Tory, you know... just
easy-going placid types"': quoted in Platt, *Life and Times of the Oxford
Scout*, p. 12. College servants are also remembered for scabbing during
the 1926 General Strike, although according to Fred Bickerton, most
Oxford workers, including the busmen, broke the strike: Bickerton,
Fred of Oxford, p. 65. Harrison's 1969 interviews with college scouts
certainly revealed a general dislike of radical students.

102. For an overview of some of these historiographical debates, see Todd,
'Domestic Service', pp. 181–2.

103. Schwartz, 'Interview with Cuthbertson, Lydon & Spring'.

104. M. [Anon.], for example, served in Hall at Keble before coming to
St Hugh's, where she appreciated the tradition of wearing gowns
and saying a Latin grace at formal Hall: Schwartz, 'Interview with
Currently Employed Scouts'.

105. Diana Fearon (née McKenna), m. 1934, 'Reminiscences of St Hugh's'.

106. Adam Bantick, m. 1988, 'Replies to the Senior Student Questionnaire'.

107. Earlier in the century, scouts' supposed maternal role sat uncomfortably
alongside the infantilising practice of referring to them by their first
names at a time when students even called each other Miss.

108. Many senior students remembered the scouts as 'friendly and
motherly': Heather Marvin (née Sampson), m. 1971, 'Replies to the
Senior Student Questionnaire'. See also Schwartz, 'Interview with
Cuthbertson, Lydon & Spring'.

109. Lydon and Spring recall that in the 1970s and 80s almost all of their
students bought gifts for themselves or their children at Christmas and
Easter. Lydon remained in correspondence with one of her students
for many years: Schwartz, 'Interview with Cuthbertson, Lydon &
Spring'.

110. Ibid. Clive Cuthbertson's son also worked at St Hugh's.

111. 'A Trade Union for College Servants', *Oxford Journal Illustrated,* 8 Jan.
1919, p. 5. Bob Dickens, a scout at Corpus Christi, remembered this
union drive and recalled that many servants were against it. The JCR
butler at New College stood up in the meeting and said: 'Would you
class yourselves with railwaymen and bus people?': G. A. Jonge &
A. J. Purkis, 'Interview with Bob Dickens' (20 June 1969), Harrison,
'Transcripts of Interviews with "College Servants"', p. 6227.

112. This led to the formation of the 'Domestic Service Inquiry
Commission', headed by Violet Markham, which recommended the
use of more formal contracts between servants and employers.

113. 'Working Girls and Domestic Service: Oxford Conference of Club
Members', *The Times,* 31 March 1930, p. 11.

114. See, for example, Special Correspondent, 'College "Scout's" Lot
Is Not Always a Happy One', ibid. 14 Sept 1961, p. 5; University
Correspondent, 'Cranes at Oxford but No Herons in the Meadow',
The Times, 24 Oct. 1961, p. 16.

115. 'Scouts Flout Women's Lib', *The Cherwell,* 20 Jan. 1971, p. 12.

116. 'SRC Raps College on Staff Conditions', *The Cherwell,* 5 May 1971,
p. 12; 'More Pay for Scouts', *The Cherwell,* 19 May 1971, p. 1; 'Scout
Union Meets' and 'Letters', *The Cherwell,* 22 Oct. 1971, p. 2; 'Why
Won't they Join the Union?', *The Cherwell,* 29 Oct. 1971, p. 1.

117. 'Demo Forces Issue', *The Cherwell,* 23 Nov. 1972, p. 1; Haig Gordon,
'Scouts Strike at St Anne's', *The Cherwell,* 2 Nov. 1972, p. 1; Haig
Gordon, 'Stalemate at St Anne's', *The Cherwell,* 9 Nov. 1972, p. 1; Haig
Gordon, 'St Anne's Stick to their Guns', *The Cherwell,* 16 Nov. 1972,
p. 3; 'Keen to Work', *The Cherwell,* 23 Nov. 1972, p. 3; 'NUPE Forges
Ahead', *The Cherwell,* 25 Jan. 1973, p. 3. For a short account of the
strike by a Fellow at St Anne's, see Jenifer Hart, *Ask Me No More: An
Autobiography* (London: Peter Halban, 1998), pp. 144–5. It appears that
this was the first and only industrial action on the part of Oxford
domestic workers, though at Cambridge in 1982 'a comment made
by a student in *Varsity* implying that bedmakers and Fellows might
have sexual relationships nearly sparked a bedmaker strike, eventually
headed-off by a printed apology': Lucy Delap, 'Bedmakers of St
Catherine's', *St Catherine's College Magazine* (2008).

118. 9 Nov. 1972, 'JCR Minutes and Papers' (VI.23; SHCA, 1971–80).

119. For example, in 1910 Kate Thomas's twenty-first year as a housemaid
was celebrated at St Hugh's with past and present students clubbing

together to buy her a silver teapot: Leslie I. G. Bickmore, 'Senior Students' Letter', *St Hugh's Club Paper,* 1/18 (Aug. 1910), pp. 22–6.

120. Anon., 'Mrs Brown Soliloquises', *The Imp* (June 1921), pp. 12–14.

121. Shirley Smith (née Sutch), m. 1935, Ynys Johnston (née Scott), m. 1939, 'Reminiscences of St Hugh's'.

122. Jean Robinson, m. 1943, ibid.

123. 20 Oct. 1968, 25 Jan. 1970, 'JCR Minutes and Papers'.

124. 'JCR Suggestion Book' (1971–2), 'JCR Miscellaneous Papers'. The following year the JCR passed an emergency motion in which it declared itself 'disturbed' that scouts were not paid overtime for working bank holidays, 12 June 1973, 'JCR Minutes and Papers'.

125. Trish's surname has not been recorded.

126. Laura Schwartz, 'Interview with St Hugh's Graduate Isabel Morgan' (SHCA, 2010).

127. 'JCR Suggestion Book' (1971–2), 'JCR Miscellaneous Papers'.

128. Schwartz, 'Interview with Currently Employed Scouts'.

129. The phrase comes from A. E. Oakshott, m. 1945, 'Reminiscences of St Hugh's'. But even by 1972 such Formal Halls took place twice a week: West, 'Reminiscences', p. 202.

130. Gordon, 'Scouts Strike at St Anne's'.

131. 11 Oct. 1971, 'Minutes of Governing Body', p. 226.

132. Susan Thurgood, m. 1965, 'Reminiscences of St Hugh's'. The employment of women 'dailies' to replace the traditional male scouts was certainly seen as one way of reducing costs at the men's colleges: see Special Correspondent, 'College "Scout's" Lot Is Not Always a Happy One', *The Times,* 14 Sept. 1961, p. 5.

133. 12 March 1980, 'Governing Body Minutes' (II.1.29; SHCA, Michaelmas 1979–Trinity 1980), p. 151.

134. 'Review of Domestic Staff Wages', 6 Dec. 1978, 'Governing Body Minutes' (II.1.28; SHCA, Michaelmas 1978–Trinity 1979), p. 53.

135. Schwartz, 'Interview with Cuthbertson, Lydon & Spring'.

136. Schwartz, 'Interview with Kerr'.

137. Anon. 1, 'Replies to Questionnaire for Domestic and Maintenance Staff' (2009).

138. Schwartz, 'Interview with Cuthbertson, Lydon & Spring'; Schwartz, 'Interview with Currently Employed Scouts'.

139. Platt, *Life and Times of the Oxford Scout,* p. 15; Keith Thomas, 'College Life, 1945–70', in Brian Harrison (ed.), *The History of the University of*

Oxford: The Twentieth Century (VIII; Oxford: Oxford University Press, 1994), pp. 189–215 (207); Harrison, 'College Servants', p. 10.

140. Correspondent, 'College "Scout's" Lot Is Not Always a Happy One'.

141. The Franks Commission, which reported to the Government in 1966 on funding at Oxford and Cambridge, emphasised especially the need for colleges to reduce their domestic expenditure: see J. P. D. Dunbabin, 'Finance since 1914', in Brian Harrison (ed.), *The History of the University of Oxford* (VIII; Oxford: Oxford University Press, 1994), pp. 639–82 (642–3).

142. Todd, 'Domestic Service', p. 181; Gregson and Lowe, *Servicing the Middle Classes*.

143. Samuel Mullins and Gareth Griffiths, *Cap and Apron: An Oral History of Domestic Service in the Shires, 1880–1950* (Leicester: Leicestershire Museums Art Galleries and Record Service, 1986), p. 29.

5 WHOSE EDUCATION IS IT ANYWAY?

1. Quoted in Annie Rogers, 'Historical Reminiscences', *St Hugh's Chronicle* (1928–9), pp. 12–16 (10).

2. The Royal Commission of 1873 complained that too much money was spent on comfort and privileges: Brittain, *Women at Oxford*, p. 40. This continued to be a problem into the Edwardian era. Lord Curzon's *Principles and Methods of University Reform* (1909) recommended a conference of bursars to review the cost of college living as one step towards opening the University to poorer students. The Asquith Commission (1919) also commented on this: Janet Howarth, 'The Edwardian Reform Movement', in M. G. Brock and M. C. Curthoys (eds), *The History of the University of Oxford* (VII; Oxford: Oxford University Press, 2001), pp. 821–3; J. P. D. Dunbabin, 'Finance since 1914', in Brian Harrison (ed.), *The History of the University of Oxford* (VIII; Oxford: Oxford University Press, 1994), pp. 639–82.

3. Betty Kemp, 'The Early History of St Hugh's' in Penny Griffin (ed.), *St Hugh's: One Hundred Years of Women's Education in Oxford* (Basingstoke: Macmillan Press, 1986), pp. 15–47 (16).

4. Janet Howarth and M. C. Curthoys, 'Political Economy of Women's Higher Education in Late Nineteenth and Early Twentieth Century Britain', *Historical Research*, 60/142 (1987), pp. 208–31 (215–16).

5. Over 26 per cent of St Hugh's students in the 1880s and 1890s are recorded as either orphans or 'father deceased': Ann Soutter, *St Hugh's Register, 1886–1959* (forthcoming 2011). With thanks to Ann Soutter for drawing my attention to this.

6. Kemp, 'The Early History of St Hugh's', p. 16.

7. 'Principal's Copy of General Accounts' (IV.2; SHCA, 1889–1922), 1897–8; Sarah Curtis, 'Centenary Questionnaire: Key Years' (X.15; SHCA, 1984), #17.6.

8. Ethel Wallace, m. 1908, 'Reminiscences of St Hugh's' (X.8–9; SHCA, 1984).

9. None of the accounts specify the exact date when higher fees were introduced, though it appears that it was very soon after the hall was opened.

10. Howarth and Curthoys, 'Political Economy of Women's Higher Education', p. 212.

11. Janet Howarth, 'Review: Anglican Perspectives on Gender: Some Reflections on the Centenary of St Hugh's College, Oxford', *Oxford Review of Education,* 12/3 (1986), pp. 299–304.

12. Howarth, 'Edwardian Reform'; Dunbabin, 'Finance', p. 652.

13. In 1914, for example, LMH offered three scholarships of £60, £50 and £40 respectively compared with the two for £30 and two for £25 offered by St Hugh's: 18 March 1914, 'Minutes of the Scholarship Committee' (II.4 [SHG/B/1/1]; SHCA, 1912–24).

14. 25 March 1912, ibid.

15. 'Memorandum' (1918), 'Papers of the Delegacy for Women Students' (VII.12 [SHG/C/2/6]; SHCA, 1918–20), p. 1/11/f.

16. 'Regulations Printed by the Association for the Education of Women (1914)', 'Minutes of the Bertha Johnson Loan Fund Committee' (II.12 [SHG/B/5/1/1]; SHCA, 1895–1915).

17. 27 Oct. 1922, 18 Dec. 1922, 13 Feb. 1923, 5 Nov. 1917, 'Minutes of the Scholarship Committee'.

18. The debate over whether financial support at Oxford ought to be provided on the basis of merit or need stretched back to the 1850s, when poverty preferences were abolished from college statutes – a move supported by university reformers such as Benjamin Jowett and H. G. Liddell, who wanted to introduce a more competitive and meritocratic spirit. The women's colleges were part of a broader drive to reform and professionalise Oxford, perhaps explaining why St Hugh's Council was so keen to associate its few scholarships with

academic excellence rather than poor relief: M. C. Curthoys and Janet Howarth, 'Origins and Destinations: The Social Mobility of Oxford Men and Women', in M. C. Curthoys and M. G. Brock (eds), *The History of the University of Oxford* (VII; Oxford: Oxford University Press, 2001), pp. 571–95 (586).

19. 'Memorandum' (1918), 'Papers of the Delegacy for Women Students', p. 1/11/f.

20. This outline of funding in the interwar period is indebted to Chapter 1, 'Going to University in England between the Wars: Access, Finance and Social Class', in Carol Dyhouse, *Students: A Gendered History* (Abingdon: Routledge, 2006).

21. These figures were estimated in L. D. Whiteley, *The Poor Student and the University: A Report on the Scholarship System* (London: George Allen & Unwin, 1933); Dyhouse, *Students: A Gendered History*, p. 12.

22. M. Ker (née King), m. 1930, 'Reminiscences of St Hugh's'.

23. See, for example, Anon. 7, m. 1934, Dorothy Crawshaw (née Keast), m. 1933, ibid.

24. Anon. 11, m. 1923, ibid. State Scholarships were suspended entirely between 1922 and 1924: Dyhouse, *Students: A Gendered History*, p. 18.

25. Gillian Sutherland, 'The Movement for the Higher Education of Women: Its Social and Intellectual Context in England, *c.*1840–80', in P. J. Waller (ed.), *Politics and Social Change in Modern Britain: Essays Presented to A. F. Thompson* (Sussex: Harvester Press, 1987), pp. 91–116. For this argument see also Pat Thane, 'Girton Graduates: Earning and Learning, 1920s–1980s', *Women's History Review,* 13/3 (2004), pp. 347–61; Curthoys and Howarth, 'Origins and Destinations', p. 581.

26. Unless otherwise indicated, all figures for St Hugh's are based upon a survey of fathers' occupations as recorded in the College Register between 1886 and 1950, carried out by Hannah Boston in 2010. The results can only be used as a rough indicator of social background. Not only does occupation tell us very little abut income, some occupations are also difficult to categorise without contextualising information (for example, 'coal merchant' could mean owner of a large company or a door-to-door tradesman). Students from working-class families might also have been more likely to disguise their father's occupation with obscure terminology – as late as the 1970s Karen Shipp (m. 1971) was advised to describe her father's position on her UCCA form as 'bank official' rather than 'bank clerk' because her mother 'erroneously assumed that his lowly role would lower my chances of getting a

place': 'Replies to Senior Student Questionnaire' (SHCA, 2009). See also Howarth and Curthoys, 'Political Economy of Women's Higher Education', pp. 217–20; Dyhouse, *Students: A Gendered History*, p. 8.

27. Curthoys and Howarth, 'Origins and Destinations', Table 24.1.

28. Sarah Curtis, 'Origins and Outcomes', in Penny Griffin (ed.), *St Hugh's: One Hundred Years of Women's Education in Oxford* (Basingstoke: Macmillan Press, 1986), pp. 244–83 (247–8); Lisa Martineau, *Politics and Power: Barbara Castle* (London: André Deutsch, 2000) p. 17. Just before the Second World War only 2 per cent of eighteen-year-olds went to university: Carol Dyhouse, 'History and Policy Papers: Going to University: Funding, Costs, Benefits', *History and Policy* (2007).

29. For the most comprehensive typology of girls' schools, see Janet Howarth, 'Public Schools, Safety Nets and Educational Ladders: The Classification of Girls' Secondary Schools, 1880–1914', *Oxford Review of Education,* 11/1 (1985), pp. 59–71.

30. Curtis, 'Origins and Outcomes', p. 249. The category of 'public school' was distinguished in the questionnaire from 'private' and other fee-paying establishments, though this was open to interpretation by individual respondents.

31. Ibid.; Howarth and Curthoys, 'Political Economy of Women's Higher Education', pp. 227–8.

32. Howarth, 'Girls' Secondary Schools', pp. 66–7. See also Martin Daunton, *Wealth and Welfare: An Economic and Social History of Britain 1851–1951* (Oxford: Oxford University Press, 2007), p. 505.

33. There is a 'suspicious absence of tradesmen's daughters' in LMH's early admission records, though this was not true for the other women's colleges: Curthoys and Howarth, 'Origins and Destinations', p. 581.

34. See, for example, A. D. K. Peters, m. 1919, 'Interview with Mrs Lobel' (Doreen Rogers), m. 1919, Anon. 3, m. 1920s[?], 'Reminiscences of St Hugh's'.

35. 'We were brought up to be moderate in our tastes and expenditure': Beatrice Roberts (née Coleman), m. 1926. See also Anon. [?], m. 1928, Ruth Haslop, m. 1927, ibid.

36. See, for example, Anon. 3, 1920s[?], ibid.

37. Ida Moberly, m. 1924, Ruth Haslop, m. 1927 (remembering her friend), ibid. Flora Welch also describes herself as not having 'much money', though she had £21 or £22 each term to spend. Similar discrepancies can also be found during the war years. R. A. Fuller (née Andrews), m. 1940, had an allowance of £17 each term, while S. M. B. Blackhouse,

m. 1944, survived almost solely on scholarships and had only 10 shillings a week 'pocket money': 'Reminiscences of St Hugh's'.

38. Naomi Papworth, m. 1934, 'Reminiscences of St Hugh's'.
39. Barbara Castle, *Fighting All the Way* (London: Macmillan, 1993), p. 41.
40. Ina Brooksbank, m. 1917, ibid.
41. Anon. [?], m. 1928, 'Reminiscences of St Hugh's'.
42. Joan Evans, *Prelude and Fugue: An Autobiography* (London: Museum Press, 1964), pp. 68–9; Valerie Pitt (m. 1943), 'Reminiscences of St Hugh's'.
43. Nancy Salinger, m. 1930, Anon. 5, m. 1947, 'Reminiscences of St Hugh's'.
44. Pitt, ibid.
45. See Dinah Birch, *Our Victorian Education* (Oxford: Blackwell Publishing, 2008), p. 120.
46. The two somewhat differing aims were common in the women's colleges which catered to a 'dual market' – those who intended to teach and those young women from wealthier families who attended solely out of intellectual curiosity: see Howarth and Curthoys, 'Political Economy of Women's Higher Education'.
47. Curtis, 'Origins and Outcomes', pp. 266–9.
48. Mary Proudfoot (née Macdonald), 'The Gaudy', *St Hugh's Chronicle* (1955–6), pp. 8–15.
49. Salinger, 'Reminiscences of St Hugh's'. See also Helena Sanders (née Charles), m. 1930, who wrote a poem referring to Miss Gwyer as 'that old woman quite cut off from life/ sated with learning': 'Reminiscences of St Hugh's'.
50. Adam Roberts, 'Morley, Agnes Headlam (1902–1986), Historian', *Oxford Dictionary of National Biography* (online edn; Oxford: Oxford University Press, 2004). Margery Perham was another 'exception', taking advantage of the reformed university curriculum when she arrived at St Hugh's in 1924 as tutor in history, politics, philosophy and economics, to lecture on colonial administration and race relations, though she left after 1928 to pursue more active field research: Patricia M. Pugh, 'Perham, Margery Freda (1895–1982), Writer on African Affairs and University Teacher', *Oxford Dictionary of National Biography* (online edn; Oxford: Oxford University Press, 2004).
51. 'Reminiscences of St Hugh's'.
52. Naomi Papworth, m. 1934, Sylvia Levin, m. 1933, ibid.

53. Curtis, 'Origins and Outcomes', p. 267; Naomi Papworth, m. 1934, 'Reminiscences of St Hugh's'.

54. 'Reminiscences of St Hugh's'.

55. See, for example, Theo Pacey (née Hale), m. 1927, ibid.

56. 'Supplementary Correspondence', #32.11, 'Centenary Questionnaire: Papers of Sarah Curtis'.

57. #19.2, ibid.

58. Daunton, *Wealth and Welfare*, p. 509.

59. 'The University of Manchester Assessment of Student Grants' (n.d.), 'Papers of the Central Scholarship Committee' (VII.7–9 [SHG/C/3/5]; SHCA, 1953–61), p. 125g.

60. Proudfoot (née Macdonald), 'The Gaudy', pp. 14–15.

61. Between 1946 and 1958 prices at London (the most expensive of the civic universities) were only 90 per cent of the cost of studying at Oxford. In 1946 the cost of maintenance at Oxbridge was calculated at £205 per year, at London £185, and at the provincial universities £160: 'University of Manchester Assessment of Student Grants', 'The Papers of the Central Scholarship Committee', p. 125g.

62. 22 Feb. 1961, ibid.

63. Sylvia Knight (née Jones), m. 1952, 'Replies to Senior Student Questionnaire'.

64. 'Memorandum of Evidence Submitted to the Anderson Committee' (23 Jan. 1959), 'Papers of the Central Scholarship Committee', p. 1/25/e.

65. 'Views of the Colleges on the Questions Asked by the Anderson Committee', ibid., p. 1/30/d.

66. Quoted in Curtis, 'Origins and Outcomes', p. 265.

67. Supplementary Correspondence, #61.07, 'Centenary Questionnaire: Papers of Sarah Curtis'. See also Deirdre Baker (née Daniel), m. 1953, 'Replies to Senior Student Questionnaire'.

68. Angela Owen (née French), m. 1958, Anne Andrew, m. 1976, 'Replies to Senior Student Questionnaire'.

69. Elizabeth Johnstone (née Lafferty), m. 1973, ibid.

70. Prior to this, some students did take on vacation work, most commonly sorting mail for the Post Office, see Diana Townsend (née Harris), m. 1959, Angela Sell (née Crabtree), m. 1959, Hogbin (née Penney), m. 1952, ibid. Of those who participated in Sarah Curtis's study, only 15 per cent of students in the 1930s had vacation jobs, but

the figure had risen to 67 per cent in the 1960s and 77 per cent in the 1970s: Curtis, 'Origins and Outcomes', pp. 265–6.

71. The number of students at UK universities rose from an estimated 70,000 before the Second World War to 300,000 by 1965–6: Gareth Stedman Jones, 'The Meaning of the Student Revolt', in Alexander Cockburn and Robin Blackburn (eds), *Student Power/ Problems, Diagnosis, Action* (Harmondsworth: Penguin, 1969), pp. 25–56 (41). At Oxford, it was even suggested that the new radicalism was linked to the changing class background of the student population, whereby working-class students who would previously have felt both honoured and humbled to be offered a place at Oxford were now present in large enough numbers to reject such 'status anxiety' and vent their class hostility more openly: Professor Searle, 'Talk on Student Unrest' (*c.* 1970) (transcript), 'Miscellaneous Papers of the Dean' (VI.28–9; SHCA, 1968–70s). The Oxford Revolutionary Socialist Students circulated a bulletin which claimed to quote from files held by the University. One of the quotes contained a similar class-based analysis of student militancy: 'The view, the accuracy of which we cannot assess, has been expressed to us that though the membership of the movement is predominantly middle-class, some who come from working-class homes may join it out of a mixture of suspicion and guilt which Oxford excites in them; they thus mark their refusal to identify themselves with Oxford as an organ of social mobility which, by offering them tickets to relatively privileged positions in society, tempts them to forget loyalties to the unprivileged stratum from which they come': 'Bulletin' (n.d, *c.* 1970), 'Miscellaneous Papers of the Dean'.

72. In a talk attended by St Hugh's SCR members in 1970, Professor Searle suggested that the lower levels of conflict at Oxford could be attributed to the collegiate system, which tended to nurture personal relationships between students and tutors: Searle, 'Student Unrest', 'Miscellaneous Papers of the Dean'.

73. Sub-Rector, Exeter College, to Mary Lunt (1968), ibid.

74. Beverly Mather, 'The JCR, 1975', *St Hugh's Chronicle,* /48 (1975–6), pp. 16–17.

75. K. M. Hobbs (m. 1924), 'Reminiscences of St Hugh's'.

76. Ann Elizabeth Smith (née Pearson), m. 1947, Una Mary Ponsonby (née Kenny), m. 1949, Jocelyn O'Neilly (née Roffey), m. 1948, Ann Watson, m. 1957, 'Replies to Senior Student Questionnaire'.

77. Judith Pitchon (née Stevenson), m. 1962, 'Reminiscences of St Hugh's'. For complaints about this system, see also 'JCR Minutes and Papers', Michaelmas 1964.
78. For a (largely unsympathetic) report of Oxford's May 1968, see *Isis*, 12 June 1968.
79. Michaelmas 1964, 'JCR Minutes and Papers'. In 1966 fifty-six undergraduates were told, with very little warning, that there was no room for them to live in college the next academic year, but despite JCR outrage, no action was taken: 'JCR Minutes and Papers', 27 May 1966.
80. Helen Everett's Manifesto for JCR President (n.d. 1970[?]), 'Miscellaneous Papers of the Dean'.
81. Catherine Dooley to Kathleen Kenyon (11 Oct. 1971), 'Minutes of Governing Body', p. 227.
82. 11 Oct. 1971, 27 Oct. 1971, ibid.
83. In Michaelmas 1973, for example, forty-two students withheld the full payment: 'Joint Committee Report' (7 Nov. 1973), ibid.; 'College Fees 1973/4: 'Confidential Report to Finance Committee from A. P. Wells, Treasurer' (7 May 1973), 'Miscellaneous Papers of the Dean'.
84. Commenting on such activities across the Oxford colleges, Keith Thomas has concluded that 'junior members are no ineffective bargainers': Thomas, 'College Life', p. 674.
85. Although extremely generous by subsequent standards, even by the late 1960s some students were complaining that the government was not willing to keep funding in line with student expansion; see for example Stedman Jones, 'The Meaning of the Student Revolt', p. 41.
86. Press cutting: 'Student Grants', letter to the Editor of *The Times* from the Wardens of University Halls, Reading (n.d. [1971]), 11 Oct. 1971, 'Minutes of Governing Body', p. 228; 'College Fees: Confidential Report to Finance Committee from A. P. Wells, Treasurer' (7 May 1973), 'Miscellaneous Papers of the Dean'. The DES recommended maximum charge for university accommodation in 1973 was calculated at £92 per term, St Hugh's charged £101: see 'College Prices and National Grants' (11 May 1973), 'Miscellaneous Papers of the Dean'.
87. Bronwen Hoare, 'JCR Report', *St Hugh's Chronicle*, /41 (1968–9), pp. 20–1.
88. 24 May 1970, 17/13[?] June 1970, 'JCR Minutes and Papers'.
89. Dooley to Kenyon (11 Oct. 1971), 'Minutes of Governing Body', p. 225.

90. 27 Oct. 1971, 3 Nov. 1971, ibid.

91. 3 May 1971, 'JCR Minutes and Papers'.

92. Catherine Dooley, 'JCR, 1971', *St Hugh's Chronicle*, /44 (1971–2), pp. 17–18. Student unions (at Oxford the JCRs) were funded through individual subscriptions, which, in the case of students on a grant, were paid for by the Local Authorities as part of approved fees. Thatcher's 'Consultative Document' proposed to end the LA's payment of subscriptions and for SU funds to come instead via the University (in Oxford via the colleges), who would be able to decide the amount of money they granted and measure it against other claims on their resources: see 'How the Government's Proposals Will Affect Your JCR' (n.d.[1971]), 'Miscellaneous Papers of the Dean'. In the face of united opposition from student unions and trade unions, the proposals were 'postponed': Matthew Salusbury, *Thatcherism Goes to College: The Conservative Assault on Higher Education* (London: Canary Press, 1989), p. 9. St Hugh's Governing Body also unanimously opposed these proposals: 'Student Union Finances: Replies of Colleges', 'Miscellaneous Papers of the Dean'.

93. Dooley to Kenyon (11 Oct. 1971), 'Minutes of Governing Body', p. 226.

94. 'JCR Representation Discussion Paper', Karin V. Bote (JCR President), 13 May 1970, 'Minutes of Governing Body' (II.1 [SHG/B/1/22]; SHCA, 1969–70).

95. Higher education funding had already begun to slow down by the beginning of the 1970s, and the first cuts in spending were introduced by the Labour government in 1973–4. 1979 was nonetheless a turning point, marking the beginning of the Conservative Party's ideologically-driven programme to permanently reduce state support for higher education. Margaret Thatcher became well known for her dislike of academia, not to mention the left-wing thinkers and student militants who lurked within the campus walls. Instead of boosting the economy, as the Robbins Report had predicted, Thatcher viewed an expanding system of higher education as a drain on government money, one that could only worsen unless drastic action were taken: R. D. Anderson, 'British Universities Past and Present' (London: Hambledon Continuum, 2006), pp. 163–9.

96. Differential fees for overseas students had already been introduced in 1966: see J. M. Lee, 'Overseas Students in Britain: How Their Presence Was Politicised in 1966–67', *Minerva*, 36/4 (1998), pp. 305–21.

97. From then on, universities had increasingly to compete with each other for funding based upon objectively determined criteria such as the Research Assessment Exercise. In 1988 the Education Reform Act created the University Funding Committee, responsible for distributing funds while policy remained in the hands of central government. The 1992 Further and Higher Education Act ended the binary system of universities and polytechnics, but entrenched an informal hierarchy through competition for funds: Anderson, 'British Universities', pp. 171–4.

98. Priscilla West, 'Reminiscences of Seven Decades' in Penny Griffin (ed.), *St Hugh's: One Hundred Years of Women's Education* (Basingstoke: Macmillan, 1986), pp. 62–243 (233–4).

99. In 1984, 60 per cent of students were overdrawn: Salusbury, *Thatcherism Goes to College: The Conservative Assault on Higher Education*, p. 43.

100. Heidi Kaye, 'MCR', *St Hugh's Chronicle*, /62 (1988–9), pp. 36–7; Daisy Pomeroy, 'JCR', *St Hugh's Chronicle*, /67 (1993–4), p. 44; Ian Williams, 'JCR', *St Hugh's Chronicle*, /69 (1994–5), pp. 42–3; Derek Wood, 'Principal's Report', *St Hugh's Chronicle*, /67 (1993–4), pp. 11–17.

101. Derek Wood, 'Principal's Report', *St Hugh's Chronicle*, /70 (1996–7), pp. 7–12; Derek Wood, 'Principal's Report', *St Hugh's College Archive*, /72 (1998–9), pp. 7–10.

102. Laura Schwartz, 'Interview with Former St Hugh's Principal Derek Wood' (SHCA, 2010).

103. For the problems of measuring the value of higher education solely in terms of future earning power, see R. D. Anderson, *Universities and Elites in Britain Since 1800* (Basingstoke: Macmillan, 1992), pp. 177, 91; Dyhouse, 'History and Policy Papers: Going to University: Funding, Costs, Benefits'.

104. Laura Schwartz, 'Interview with Campaign for Free Education Activist' (SHCA, 2010).

105. Beth Hodson, 'Mourning Call', *Oxford Student*, 26 Feb. 1998, p. 1; Daljit Bhurji, 'Students Hit the Streets', *Oxford Student*, 5 March 1998, p. 1.

106. Yue Man Lee, 'Can't Pay, Won't Pay', *Oxford Student*, 28 May 1998, p. 1; Schwartz, 'Interview with CFE Activist'.

107. Jonathan Tseng, 'Hugh's Fresher Fury', *Oxford Student*, 15 Oct. 1998, p. 3; 'Hugh's Fee Success', *Oxford Student*, 29 Oct. 1998, p. 3; 4 Nov. 1998, 'Minutes of Governing Body' (SHG/B/3/1/55; SHCA, 1997–2001).

108. 2 Dec. 1998, 'Minutes of Governing Body'.

109. Six undergraduates at other colleges held out until the beginning of Hilary Term 1999: 'Rebels Face Exclusion', *Oxford Student,* 14 Jan. 1999, p. 1. Occupations of the Bodleian Library and the Exam Schools followed: Barney Jones and Jonathan Worth, 'Occupied Territory', *Oxford Student,* 21 Jan. 1999, p. 1; Laura Barton, 'We Fight Back', *Oxford Student,* 28 Jan. 1999, p. 1.

110. 29 Nov. 2000, 'Minutes of Governing Body'; Vinothan Sangarapillai, 'Non-Payment at St Hugh's' (SHCA, 2009). In 1999 St Hugh's students were strongly encouraged to sign pledge cards promising not to pay their tuition fees, but there is no record in the minutes of Governing Body that they resisted payment for any length of time.

111. Mark Stevenson, 'Meritocracy?', *Oxford Student,* 29 Oct. 1998, p. 7. It was calculated that over the course of the 1990s state schools accommodated 93 per cent of the nation's children, yet constituted only 43 per cent of Oxford's undergraduate places; Independent schools served only 7 per cent but made up 50 per cent of Oxford's junior members: A. H. Halsey and N. G. McCrum, 'A Fair Target', *Oxford Magazine,* Hilary Term/Eighth Week (1998), pp. 1–3 (p. 2).

112. Samantha O'Brien, 'Don Discrimination?', *Oxford Student,* 29 Oct. 1998, p. 5; Halsey and McCrum, 'A Fair Target', p. 2.

113. Siobhan Garrigan, 'JCR', *St Hugh's Chronicle,* /62 (1988–9), pp. 35–6.

114. Schwartz, 'Interview with Derek Wood'.

115. Ike Nwafor, 'Oh Yes, Oxford Has More Class', *Oxford Student,* 25 Nov. 1999, p. 6; Katy Hodgins, 'Student Body Slams Oxford's Private Links', *Oxford Student,* 15 June 2000, p. 5; 'Revealed: Oxbridge Public School Links', *The Independent,* 12 June 2000.

116. 'Oxford's Full of Posh Kids Who Laugh at Poor People', *Oxford Student,* 2000, p. 1.

117. Derek Wood, 'Principal's Report', *St Hugh's Chronicle,* /73 (1999–2000), pp. 8–9.

118. Halsey and McCrum, 'A Fair Target', p. 2. Even at the national level it is hard to provide a definitive answer to this question. Studies by the National Union of Students indicate that changes in funding have noticeably deterred students from 'less privileged and non-traditional backgrounds' from applying to university and restricted the choices of those who do so: see 'Equal Access or Elitist Entry? The Impact of Student Funding on Access to Higher Education: Four International Case Studies' (National Union of Students, 2000); Judith Watson and Andrew Church, 'Funding the Future: The Attitudes of Year 10 Pupils

in England and Wales to Higher Education' (National Union of Students, 2008). Universities UK, on the other hand, despite noting a 4.3 per cent decline in applications between 2005/6 and 2006/7 (the year when variable fees were introduced), found that there was 'no significant change in the ethnic, social class, or age profile of accepted applicants' between 2004 and 2008: Nigel Brown, 'Variable Tuition Fees in England: Assessing Their Impact on Students and Higher Education Institutions: A Third Report' (Universities UK, 2010).

119. In 2009, Oxford admitted 53.9 per cent from the state 'maintained' sector (which includes grammar schools, Sixth Form colleges and FE institutions as well as comprehensives) and 46.1 from independent schools – only 22.7 per cent of successful candidates, however, had studied at a comprehensive: 'Undergraduate Admission Statistics 2009 Entry', http://www.ox.ac.uk/about_the_university/facts_and_figures/undergraduate_admissions_statistics/index.html, accessed 28 June 2010. In 1988 46.1 per cent of successful candidates came from the maintained sector, 46.2 per cent from fee-paying schools; in 1988 44.6 per cent and 47.4 per cent respectively. Nationally, only 8.7 per cent in 2008 and 8.5 per cent in 2009 of successful university applicants came from independent schools: 'UCAS National Figures', http://www.ucas.ac.uk/about_us/stat_services/stats_online/data_tab, accessed March 2010.

120. This figure has remained relatively stable since 1998, when 66 students came from independent schools compared with 62 from state schools. These figures are for UK-domiciled students and exclude overseas students who usually make up about 10 per cent of accepted applicants. Figures for 2002–2009 made available by St Hugh's Senior Tutor; for 1998 figures, see 'Report on Admission, 1998–9', 22 April 1999, 'Governing Body Agenda' ([SHG/B/3/1/57] SHCA, 1998–99).

121. The hardship fund was started in 1993–4 by the JCR. Governing Body began supporting it from 1995, administering a fund of £6,000: Wood, 'Principal's Report, 1993–4'. 'Access Agreement between the University of Oxford and the Office for Fair Access' (2006).

122. Jessica Vasagar, Jessica Shepherd and Allegra Stratton, 'Elite Universities Welcome Flexibility to Triple Students' Fees', *The Guardian*, 3 Nov. 2010.

123. Schwartz, 'Interview with Derek Wood'.

124. Barbara Castle, 'Keynote Address', in Mary Clapinson (ed.), *St Hugh's College in the Twentieth Century: A Record of the Colloquium Held at the*

College on 18th September 1999 (Oxford, 1999), pp. 9–13, 40; Castle, *Fighting All the Way.*

125. In 2005–6 the JCR President 'looked back through the archives' to find out information on previous rent strikes before organising against further rent rises: Martin McCluskey, 'JCR', *St Hugh's Chronicle,* /79 (2005–6), pp. 23–4.

AMONGST WOMEN AND BETWEEN MEN

1. Laura Schwartz, 'Report of Conversation with Former St Hugh's Fellow and Tutor in Geography John Wilkinson' (SHCA, 2010).
2. Schwartz, 'Interview with Derek Wood'.
3. Rachel Trickett, 'Principal's Report', *St Hugh's Chronicle,* /58 (1985–6), pp. 11–14.
4. Rachel Trickett, 'Principal's Centenary Speech', *St Hugh's Chronicle,* /58 (1985–6), pp. 14–17.
5. Liz Webster, 'JCR Report', ibid./60 (1987–8), p. 28.
6. Figures for students beginning their academic course in October 2010. The preceding year, St Hugh's admitted 51.5 per cent men and 48.5 per cent women.
7. Oxford University accepted 3,202 applicants for entry in October 2009, of which 53.4 per cent were women. The success rate for male applicants in December 2008 was 22 per cent, for women 19.9 per cent: see 'Undergraduate Admission Statistics 2009 Entry',
8. These figures are for 2008–9. The overall percentage has been calculated by factoring-in junior academic staff on fixed-term posts (Junior Research Fellows and Career Development Fellows), of which there are eight women and five men. The percentage of female Fellows and Tutors at St Hugh's fell from 89 per cent in 1978–9, to 37.5 per cent in 1988–9, to 28 per cent in 1998–9. National figures are from the 'Labour Force Survey: Employment Status by Occupation and Sex, April–June' (Office of National Statistics, 2009). 63,000 men and 42,000 women were listed as working full-time in the category of higher education teaching profession.
9. Quoted in Sophia Parker, 'Kings of the Castle', *Oxford Student,* 13 January 2000, p. 19. Marilyn Butler, 'Women at Oxford in the 1990s', in Mary Clapinson (ed.), *St Hugh's College in the Twentieth Century: A Record of the Colloquium Held at the College on 18th September 1999*

(Oxford, 1999), pp. 37–40. Figures from the Hansard Society's report 'Women at the Top'.

10.   Celia Coleman, 'Women in Politics: The Suffragettes and Beyond', *St Hugh's Chronicle,* /68 (1994–5), pp. 72–3; 'ASM Colloquium: The Glass Ceiling', *St Hugh's Chronicle,* /78 (2004–5), pp. 40–6; Valerie Pitt, 'Gaudy Address St Cross Church', *St Hugh's Chronicle,* /63 (1988–9), p. 66; Derek Wood, '68', *St. Hugh's Chronicle,* /68 (1994–5), pp. 10–14.

11.   The phrase is from Valerie Pitt, 'The Gaudy 1988', *St Hugh's Chronicle: Supplementary Issue* (1988), pp. 30–3.

12.   In 1999 22 per cent of men and only 17 per cent of women gained a First in final examinations. For discussion of the 'Finals Gap', see Nicky Henderson, 'Report Shows Oxford Is Still a Man's World', *Cherwell,* 2009; Judith Judd, 'Secret of Men's Success at Oxford Is Bluffing Their Way through Exams', *The Independent,* 14 Aug. 2000; Jane Mellanby, M. Martin, and J. O'Doherty, 'The "Gender Gap" in Final Examinations at Oxford University', *British Journal of Psychology,* 91/3 (2000), pp. 377–90; 'Gender Equality Scheme, 2007–2010', http://www.admin.ox.ac.uk/eop/gender/ges.shtml, accessed 1 July 2010.

13.   In 2004, for example, Gillian Sutherland spoke at St Hugh's about the overly exam-orientated Oxbridge history curriculum, which favoured male students better socialised to be able to make a forceful point in a limited time period: 'ASM Colloquium: The Glass Ceiling'.

INDEX